THE PERILS OF PROSPERITY, 1914–1932

THE CHICAGO HISTORY OF AMERICAN CIVILIZATION
Daniel J. Boorstin, EDITOR

THE
PERILS
OF
PROSPERITY
1914–1932

SECOND EDITION

William E. Leuchtenburg

THE UNIVERSITY OF CHICAGO PRESS

Chicago and London

WILLIAM E. LEUCHTENBURG is
William Rand Kenan, Jr. Professor at the
University of North Carolina, Chapel Hill
and a recent past President of the
American Historical Association.

The University of Chicago Press, Chicago 60637
The University of Chicago Press, Ltd., London
© 1958, 1993 by The University of Chicago
All rights reserved. Published 1993
Printed in the United States of America
02 01 00 99 98 97 96 95 94 93   1 2 3 4 5
ISBN: 0-226-47370-8 (cloth)
0-226-47371-6 (paper)

Leuchtenburg, William Edward, 1922–
    The perils of prosperity, 1914–1932 / by William E. Leuchtenburg.
—2nd ed.
        p.   cm.
    Includes bibliographical references and index.
    1. United States—Economic conditions—1918–1945.   2. World War,
1914–1918—Economic aspects—United States.   I. Title.
HC106.3.L3957   1993
330.973′0913—dc20   92-44912
                                                            CIP

Contents

Editor's Foreword to the
Second Edition

Mr. Leuchtenburg's lively interpretation of one of the most widely debated eras of our recent past has had wide appeal. For he has avoided the temptation to be defensive or moralistic and has placed the story in the long movements of American and Western history. In this new edition he has further widened the context of the story in the light of forces that have become more conspicuous in the three decades since the first edition appeared. He has broadened and deepened his view of World War I, of the role of the United States in that war, and of its consequences. And he has put these years in the perspective of the increasing concern for civil rights and the opportunities of women and minorities. He has added new insights, too, into literature, the arts, and the transformed technology of daily life. In this edition, Mr. Leuchtenburg has further justified his reputation as an elegant stylist by making countless verbal revisions to sharpen and enliven his choice of words. This book gives us a rare opportunity to enjoy the matured interpretation of an American historian who has returned to the story and seen how recent decades have added meaning and vividness to this epoch of our history.

Daniel J. Boorstin

Editor's Foreword to the
First Edition

The years between America's entrance into World War I and the end of postwar prosperity, which Mr. Leuchtenburg covers in this volume, have been peculiarly attractive to historical moralists and to critics of American civilization. The idealism of Woodrow Wilson and our failure to follow his lead into the League of Nations have become symbols for the continuing weaknesses of American diplomacy and for our refusal to accept responsibilities as a world power. Especially for European observers, the prosperity of our "Jazz Age" has seemed to illustrate "American materialism" at its worst. Most Americans, although finding it hard not to envy an age which held its liquor so well and had so much fun, shake their heads and defensively try to explain the period away. Glad to put its excesses outside the main stream of our history, we have called those years a national jag—a time when the American people took a vacation from sober traditional virtues. We have liked to think that the era proved next to nothing about our true national character. We have readily believed that its only legacies were a hangover and an instructive catalogue of the Deadly Sins.

In this volume, Mr. Leuchtenburg has placed the era in the full context of American history. He is neither defensive nor moralistic. With the advantage of being too young to lose objectivity through his own recollections, he reconstructs the story and the spirit of the age from its documents. He rediscovers people we mistakenly thought we knew, and he shows us that what we remember of Harding, Coolidge, and Hoover is not their character but their reputation. He stirs our sympathy for opinionated and bewildered men by letting them speak for themselves and by giving us a sense of the turmoil in which they lived.

The age itself, Mr. Leuchtenburg reminds us, cannot be taken in isolation from its past and future. He finds movements in the period which reach back to the nineteenth century: the rise of the city, the change from handicraft to assembly lines, the ascent to the world stage. He sees the beginnings of institutions which would produce the New Deal and with it the changed attitude toward government that has stayed with us ever since. For him the age was not a frolic, in which a people stepped out of character, but a climax of passions long brewing. He reminds us of the gulf which separates horse-and-buggy America from the new age of Franklin Roosevelt, but he also shows us how the crossing of that gulf was itself a major event in American history.

Daniel J. Boorstin

Prologue

In 1914, the United States was not so far from the early years of the republic. There were men still living whose fathers had known Jefferson and John Adams and had been acquainted with Longfellow. In prairie towns, women remembered the day Ralph Waldo Emerson had alighted from the train to talk to the local Chautauqua. There were thousands of men still alive who had fought under Stonewall Jackson at Chancellorsville or had stood with George Thomas at Chickamauga, even a few veterans who had marched with Winfield Scott on the Halls of Montezuma. A small company of loyal Democrats who voted for Woodrow Wilson in 1912 had cast their first ballots for Martin Van Buren or James K. Polk. Blacks walked the streets of Savannah and Charleston who had been born in slavery.

In railroad towns strung along the Burlington or the Great Northern, men sat in the sun who had fought the Nez Percés or the Sioux, who had scouted with Kit Carson and traded with Jim Bridger. In the Nevada hills, miners with picks and burros still prospected for gold and silver; the last great strike had been made just eleven years before. Much of the land west of the Missouri was yet to be homesteaded. Arizona and New Mexico had been states for only two years. On the edge of modern, prosperous western towns, tribes of Indians still pitched their tents.

Only eighteen years later, when 1932 rolled around, it seemed an aeon since the days of the nineteenth century. The task of industrialization had been essentially completed. Machines had replaced the old artisans; there were few coopers, blacksmiths, or cobblers left. The livery stable had been torn down to make way for the filling station. Technology had revolutionized the farm. In 1918, there were 80,000 tractors; in 1929, 850,000. The Old West had disappeared; ranchers were even concerned for a time lest they lose their cowhands to movie westerns. The empire builders like James J. Hill were gone.

Life seemed to have lost a good deal of its earlier intimacy and pungency. It was proverbial that the apartment-house dweller did not know his neighbor. The Horace Greeley tradition of the crusading journalist was all but ended; readers had no idea who edited their magazines or newspapers. The aspiring attorney no longer read law in the office. The social worker ministered to the town drunkard. No one listened to the village atheist. The schoolmaster held a diploma from Teachers College.

The depression destroyed the Chautauqua, but it could scarcely have survived the competition of the radio and the movies in any event. "Now the players do not come to the towns," wrote Sherwood Anderson in 1932. "They are in Los Angeles. We see but the shadows of players. We listen to the shadows of voices. Even the politicians do not come to us now. They stay in the city and talk to us on the radio."

In 1914, the Progressive movement was at its height. Americans believed that by adopting institutional changes—the direct primary, the short ballot, the recall—political life might be made over. There was no scourge that would not eventually yield to reason and goodness, they thought. When the reformers crusaded—against the city machine, the sweatshop employer, the traction magnate—they could identify the enemies they were fighting. In 1932, Americans no longer had the same sense of confidence either in themselves or in the efficacy of reform. Nor did they believe evil would be so easily routed.

So, too, social authority became diffused. Each American town of 1914 had its old families and church elders who fixed the social standards. Parents were confident enforcers of the moral code. By 1932, much of this sense of authority was gone. Save in rural outposts and in ethnic enclaves, the church had lost some of its hold. "We haven't enough religion among us," one man grumbled, "to get up a good church fight." Parents were no longer certain they knew how to raise their children. The old arbiters—the Newport aristocracy, the town gentry—were ignored. Although boxing bouts had once been staged on offshore barges to avoid the police, by 1932 it had become a mark of social acceptance to hold a ringside seat at a championship match. The old family restaurants like Shanley's and Rector's vanished, and night spots such as Texas Guinan's took their place.

In retrospect, the years before World War I seemed like a lost Arcadia. Men and women remembered county fairs and church socials, spelling bees and sleigh rides, the excitement of the circus train or the wild dash of firehorses from the station house, the cool smell of an ice cream parlor and the warm fragrance of roasted chestnuts. They recalled the sound of peanut whistles and the hurdy-gurdy, the clang of the trolley, the cry of the carnival pitchman, the oompah of the military band on a summer evening, the clatter of victorias and sulkies, the shouts of children playing blindman's bluff and run-sheep-run. They remembered people: the paper boy with his off-key whistle, the brawny iceman sauntering up the walk with his five-cent cake of ice, the black stable boys, the printers and devils in newspaper offices, Mark Twain on the streets of Hartford in a creamwhite suit. They recollected general stores: the bolts of calico and muslin, the jars of cinnamon and gunpowder tea, bins of dried peaches and cornmeal, kegs of mackerel, canisters of striped candy. From the vantage point of 1932, it seemed as though they had danced endlessly at tango teas and strummed mandolins every evening.

Each age seems to the next an era of matchless innocence and simplicity. By 1932, the prewar years had taken on a luminescence that they did not wholly have at the time. Perhaps this was because the reminiscences were written mostly by the sons of the secure and relatively prosperous middle class. Actually, in the great cities before the war lived people who knew nothing of elm-lined streets, midsummer lawn parties, or gay cotillions. When the Children's Bureau, founded in 1912, began to examine American society, it discovered that a quarter of a million babies were dying each year. The United States had the highest maternal death rate of any "civilized" country in the world. Even in the times of plenty, millions lived in brutal poverty. Though America venerated the Declaration of Independence, it denied equality to blacks, to Native Americans, to Hispanic Americans, to recent arrivals from southern and eastern Europe, and to women.

In 1914, the United States was far from being a bucolic premachine culture. For more than a century, textile mills had drawn young people from Merrimack farms to the looms. Well before the Civil War, iron forges and foundries had dotted the countryside. Since the war, especially since the 1880s, America had been industrializing at a rapid pace, and with industrialization had come a raft of problems—noisome slums, unassimilated immigrants, and class animosity. From the time of the great railway strikes of 1877, America had known considerable industrial violence. In 1914, in Ludlow, Colorado, the militia and mine guards machine-gunned a tent colony of strikers, burning to death a number of women and children. Although America was still, in many ways, remarkably provincial, the tradition of isolation from foreign affairs had been eroded by the imperialist surge of the 1890s and the Spanish-American War.

Yet America had still not been made over by the machine in 1914. Technology had not invaded the home. Only a small percentage of families even owned telephones. Technology was not awesome—it suggested Josephine and the flying machine, the Wrights' frail crate, the Singer sewing machine, and the Victrola. The scientific heroes of the age, Thomas Edison and Luther Burbank, could be likened to early inventors like Benjamin Franklin. Robert Fulton had been honored at a gigantic celebration five years before. Automobiles were still mired in rural roads, and RFD mail carriers even had to ford streams. Just a few years before, Teddy Roosevelt, after taking a short automobile jaunt, had been commended for his "characteristic courage."

Though the country had experienced severe dislocation, many Americans, especially the old-stock gentry of the small towns, felt secure and serene. The world they experienced was comprehensible. The people they saw were people they knew. Men spoke without embarrassment of their love of the flag; celebrated Memorial Day and the "old-time Fourth"; and could still declaim Webster's reply to Hayne. With the Atlantic secured by British friendship and British power, it seemed in 1914 that the United States could have all the advantages of prosperity and power and none of the disadvantages.

But it was impossible for Americans to keep their Arcady. By 1914, the course of industrialization and urbanization had gone too far. In 1909, Taft rode to the inauguration on Capitol Hill in a horse and carriage; in 1913, Wilson traveled in an automobile. The assault on the decorum of nineteenth-century America was already far advanced before the 1920s. In 1907, girls had sung, "I'd rather two-step than waltz, Bill," but by 1914, ragtime had replaced the two-step. Hollywood was well along the road "from the long chase to the chaise longue." As early as the 1890s, Stephen Crane, Frank Norris, and Theodore Dreiser had been writing in a naturalistic vein. Beneath the complacency of the age lay a grave disquiet. "We are unsettled to the very roots of our being," wrote Walter Lippmann in 1914. "There isn't a human relation, whether of parent and child, husband and wife, worker and employer, that doesn't move in a strange situation."

In the years from 1914 to 1932, intellectuals led an assault on the groups which had traditionally exercised moral authority, and not without reason. Even for the middle class, 1914 scarcely represented Paradise Lost. Lives were much more sharply circumscribed than they were to be in 1932, and the rigid morality of the time produced a great deal of cant and not a little cruelty. Over the life of all classes, especially in the areas of rural Protestantism, hung the pall of Puritanism, "the haunting fear," as H. L. Mencken wrote, "that someone, somewhere, may be happy." By 1932, the nation no longer had the same reverence for the old folkways, and it was determined to free itself from the harsh imperatives of religious asceticism.

During these same years, the city contested the supremacy of rural, small-town America. The city represented a challenge for economic power: the determination of finance capitalism to regain the political preeminence that had been pared away in the Progressive era. The city threatened to disrupt class stability through the drive by unskilled labor to form industrial unions. The city imperilled the hierarchy of social status through the clamor of new immigrant groups for acceptance. Most of all, the older America was alarmed by the mores of the metropolis. The city represented everything—Europe, Wall Street, religious skepticism, political radicalism, sophistication, intellectual arrogance—that prewar America most feared.

The assault on the authority of the older America would have created severe problems in the best of times; the experience of World War I made matters worse. It would have been better, observed Oswald Garrison Villard, if the lives of the soldiers had been taken "in cold blood on Broadway." The war and its aftermath killed much of the humanistic, cosmopolitan spirit of 1914. It reinforced the conviction that evil came from outside America and from alien sources within, and evil became identified with the groups demanding change. The war destroyed much of the traditional confidence in the ability of American society to assimilate all manner of men. By the time the country had gone through the bruising experience of the war, the League fight, and the Red Scare, it had lost much of the equipoise of the prewar Age of Confidence.

At the very moment when the country was confronting attacks on traditional standards, the United States was plunged into the responsibilities of becoming the world's greatest power. Never did a nation accept authority more reluctantly. Unlike Elizabethan England after the Armada, the United States experienced no thrill in new-found might. The country did not want to abandon its isolation, and the disruption of Europe by the war did not make involvement in Continental politics any more inviting. "If I had influence at the United States Treasury," wrote the British economist John Maynard Keynes, "I would not lend a penny to a single one of the present governments of Europe." Even more important, a century of tranquillity had taught the country that it was safe from the threat of foreign invasion and that it need have no concern with the disorders of Europe or Asia.

By the end of the Harding era, some of the wounds of wartime had healed, and the country could turn to the more exciting spectacle of the boom economy. Prosperity held the promise not merely of personal gain but of eliminating poverty, spreading knowledge, making American society more urbane, and resolving class bitterness. The country was infused with a benevolent materialism.

But prosperity held perils of its own. It served to justify investing enormous political and social power in a business class with little tradition of leadership. It placed economic primacy in the hands of a country unprepared to guide world trade. It made money the measure of man. High above New York's Columbus Circle, a huge electric sign blinked: "You should have $10,000 at the age of 30; $25,000 at the age of 40; $50,000 at 50." Prosperity fostered a shallow view of the universe, a desiccated religion typified by the vulgar Aimee Semple McPherson, billed as "the world's most pulchritudinous evangelist." It undermined facets of the American character that had developed under an economy of scarcity; in particular, it encouraged an anxious concern for social approbation. Certain that prosperity would endure forever, the architects of the New Era assumed that they had achieved a far more equable division of wealth, a sounder economy, and greater prescience than, in fact, they had. They ignored the rotten beams in the economic structure. In 1929, everything toppled.

The failures of the period are easier to see than its achievements, but the achievements also deserve attention. The economy, for all its shortcomings, did improve the lot of millions of people. The creativity in literature and in the arts was extraordinary. Writers of marriage manuals in the 1920s took for granted that women, too, enjoyed sex and that sexual pleasure was one of the chief components of wedded bliss. Furthermore, women, thanks to the suffrage amendment, were able to participate in politics more freely than ever before. And on university campuses and in settlement houses, reformers were nurturing the ideas that were to see fruition in the New Deal.

It was an age of shameful persecution of minorities when white-hooded men rode into the night to impose their will on victims of a different race or religion, but it was a time of gain too. Many people became more outspoken in their commitment to democracy and individual rights. The American Civil Liberties Union was formed; John Collier and others halted an attempt to grab land from the Pueblos; and the Supreme Court, at long last, began to incorporate the Bill of Rights in the Fourteenth Amendment. When Al Smith was assailed as a Catholic in the 1928 campaign, non-Catholics answered the canards. When Henry Ford's *Dearborn Independent* launched a campaign of anti-Semitism in 1920—among other inanities, it alleged that Benedict Arnold had committed treason as an agent of a "Jewish front"—121 distinguished non-Jews, including President Wilson, former President Taft, Archbishop Hayes, and William Jennings Bryan, signed a letter of protest to Ford.

Through the decade, the United States moved quietly away from the rigid isolationism of 1920. By 1930, the United States had participated in more than forty League conferences, and by the following year, there were five permanent American officials in Geneva. Senator Borah charged, with some truth, that the country was entering the League by the back door. The Wilsonian crusade produced a small corps of men—Wilson's Secretary of War, Newton D. Baker, for example—who had a sense of reli-

gious consecration to the cause of internationalism. "The acceptance of a strange and perverse fate called upon me who loved the
life of youth to come to your houses and ask you to give me your
sons that I might send them into those deadly places," Baker said.
"I swore an obligation to the dead that in season and out, by day
and by night, in church, in political meeting, in the market-
place, I intended to lift up my voice always and ever until their
sacrifices were really perfected." Some of Wilson's chief Republican critics—notably Elihu Root and Nicholas Murray Butler—
swung around to defend Geneva and The Hague in Wilsonian
terms. Although the internationalists achieved little tangible in
the 1920s, they opened the way toward the expanded world role
of a later era.

The period brought a great deal that had been festering in the
prewar years into the open. Much of it was ugly, but it had been
no less ugly when it was concealed. For the first time, the United
States came face to face with the swift pace of technological innovation and was confronted with the need to fashion instruments
and attitudes appropriate to an economy of abundance. It was
forced to do so at a time of terribly rapid change (Stieglitz remarked that there was a new generation every five years). It had
to bridge the enormous gap between the boyhood of Booth Tar-
kington's *Penrod* (1914) and James T. Farrell's *Young Lonigan*
(1932). The generation of 1914–32 did not invent the problems
with which it had to deal—it would have preferred to ignore
them. Its success was less than complete, but this was the first
serious attempt of Americans to make their peace with the twentieth century.

1

Armageddon

In the autumn of 1815 the *Northumberland,* bearing the captive emperor Napoleon Bonaparte, dropped anchor before Saint Helena Island and opened a century of peace in western Europe. Localized wars there were—bloody enough in the American Civil War and the Franco-Prussian struggle—yet war itself appeared more and more to be an anachronism, a dying institution. In 1913 David Starr Jordan, director of the World Peace Foundation, observed: "What shall we say of the Great War of Europe, ever threatening, ever impending, and which never comes? We shall say that it will never come. Humanly speaking, it is impossible."

Even the assassination of Archduke Franz Ferdinand, heir to the Austro-Hungarian throne, by a young Bosnian terrorist in June, 1914, did not seem to mean war. "Never since Christ was born in the Manger," wrote a Maine newspaperman as late as July 30, "was the outlook for the universal brotherhood of man brighter than it is today." Through the summer of 1914, Americans watched the growing crisis almost with indifference. When, after weeks of gestures and countergestures, war came, it seemed like a bomb dropped from the sky into a pleasant country picnic. In *Harper's Weekly,* Norman Hapgood wrote, "For Germans and French, with a whole complex and delicate civilization in common to be using death engines to mow down men and cities is so unthinkable that we go about in a daze." People, commented Jane Addams afterwards, "went about day after day with an oppressive sense of the horrible disaster which had befallen the world and woke up many times during the night," and in the first year of the European conflict, Henry James told a friend, "It's vain to speak as if one weren't living in a nightmare of the deepest dye."

The only reasonable explanation was that Europe had gone berserk. The European powers, declared the *New York Times,* "have reverted to the condition of savage tribes roaming the forests and falling upon each other in a fury of blood and carnage to achieve the ambitious designs of chieftains clad in skins and drunk with mead." If the war had any rational basis, Americans thought, it could be found in the imperialist lust for markets. "Do you want to know the cause of the war?" asked Henry Ford. "It is capitalism, greed, the dirty hunger for dollars." "Take away the capitalist," Ford asserted, "and you will sweep war from the earth." Americans rejoiced in their isolation from Old World lunacy. "We never appreciated so keenly as now," wrote an Indiana editor, "the foresight exercised by our forefathers in emigrating from Europe."

President Woodrow Wilson urged a course of complete neutrality: he even asked movie audiences not to cheer or hiss either side. The war, he said, was one "with which we have nothing to do, whose causes cannot touch us." Wilson cautioned the American people to be "impartial in thought as well as in action," but this proved impossible. German-Americans and Irish-American Anglo-phobes sided with the Kaiser. So did some of the progressives, for Britain suggested monarchy, privileged classes, and their ancient enemy Lombard Street (seat of international financiers), whereas Germany (the Wisconsin reformers' model for a generation) connoted social insurance, the university scientist, and municipal reform. Sympathy for the Central Powers, however, was a minority theme. Overwhelmingly, American sentiment went out to the Allies. Men who as schoolboys had read Gray and Tennyson, who knew Wordsworth's lake country as though they had tramped it themselves, who had been stirred by stories of Sir Francis Drake and Lord Nelson, could not be indifferent to the English cause. Nor did any nation evoke a greater attachment than France, the country of Lafayette, the land that had come to the aid of the Colonists in their struggle for independence.

Moreover, the United States had eyed German militarism nervously ever since the accession of Kaiser Wilhelm II in 1888. When Germany invaded Belgium in the early days of the war, Americans were outraged not only by the violation of the borders of a neutral nation but by Chancellor Bethmann-Hollweg's indiscreet remark that the treaty with Belgium was "just a scrap of paper." The execution of Nurse Edith Cavell, the destruction of the Cathedral of Rheims, and the mass deportation of French and Belgian civilians to forced labor completed the picture of a Prussian militarism which in its deliberate *Schrecklichkeit* menaced Western civilization. Nevertheless, despite the indignation over Belgium, the United States had no thought of intervening. Even the bellicose Theodore Roosevelt, who would soon be the leader of the war hawks, wrote: "Of course it would be folly to jump into the gulf ourselves to no good purpose; and very probably nothing that we could have done would have helped Belgium."

As the struggle in Europe settled down to a war of attrition between great land armies, it quickly became clear that victory would go to the alliance that could maintain control of the seas. Britain, the preeminent naval power of the world, lost no time in taking advantage of its strategic position. Starting in November,

1914, it mined shipping channels in the North Sea, forced all merchant vessels to thread a narrow channel under their control, arbitrarily curbed the right of neutrals to trade with other neutrals, defined even foodstuffs as contraband, and boarded and searched American ships as they had done in the War of 1812.

President Wilson could have taken a strong line with Britain, which did not dare provoke a serious quarrel with her chief source of supply, but he thought it would be unneutral behavior, at a time when the Germans had overrun Belgium, to deprive Britain of her naval superiority. Moreover, Wilson could not help but be influenced by his own sympathies, however much he tried to control them. He had modeled himself on English statesmen, he was an extravagant admirer of British government, and he even courted his second wife by reading passages from Bagehot and Burke.

Many of Wilson's closest advisers, too, were firmly committed to the Allies. Robert Lansing, first Counselor and then Secretary of State, deliberately delayed the resolution of disputes in order to avoid a showdown with Whitehall. Lansing was convinced that American democracy could not survive in a world dominated by German power. Wilson's alter ego, Colonel Edward House, was scarcely less pro-Ally, and, whenever notes of protest were sent to London, the strongly pro-British ambassador, Walter Hines Page, watered them down. On one occasion, Page took an American protest to Sir Edward Grey and said: "I have now read the despatch, but I do not agree with it; let us consider how it should be answered!" The result was the same as if the United States itself had embargoed all trade with the Central Powers. Commerce with Germany and Austria fell from $169 million in 1914 to $1 million in 1916.

Conversely, trade between the United States and the Allies

flourished to such an extent that it jeopardized American neutrality. The outbreak of war at first produced a serious recession in this country, but by the spring of 1915 Allied war orders were stoking American industry and opening up new markets for farm products. Boom times came to the United States as trade with the Allies jumped from $825 million in 1914 to $3,214 million in 1916. Before the war was many months old, the Allied cause and American prosperity became inextricably intertwined. When Allied funds were quickly exhausted, the United States confronted the alternatives of permitting the Allies to borrow from American bankers or of allowing purchases to fall off sharply, with the probable consequence of a serious depression. At the outset of the war, Secretary of State William Jennings Bryan had warned that money was "the worst of all contrabands because it commands everything else," and Wilson, anxious about the country's gold reserve, had banned American loans and let it appear that he shared Bryan's concern. In March, 1915, however, the government relented and permitted the House of Morgan to float a half-billion-dollar loan. By spring of 1917, the Allies had borrowed over $2 billion, much to the discomfort of the Germans.

In February, 1915, Germany struck back at the Allied blockade by declaring a war zone around the British Isles and announcing that its submarines would destroy all enemy vessels in the area, "although it may not always be possible to save crews and passengers." Neutral ships in the war zone would be in danger, the Germans warned, since the British often flew neutral flags. Wilson responded that the Kaiser's government would be held strictly accountable for loss of American life or property. Under this pressure, Berlin eventually backed down. Not until 1917 would German-American relations be troubled by a threat to U.S. lives and property on *American* vessels.

Instead, diplomats faced a new problem: the determination of Americans to sail on the ships of belligerent nations. Americans persisted in booking passage on British liners, which carried munitions into the war zone, and Wilson brushed off attempts to ban such travel. On May 7, 1915, came the inevitable tragedy. The queen of the Cunard fleet, the *Lusitania,* unarmed but carrying a cargo of hundreds of cases of munitions, was torpedoed by a U-boat off the Irish coast; eighteen minutes later it sank with a loss of 1,198 lives, 128 of them American.

The United States was horrified. Yet few Americans wanted war, and, with the country divided, Wilson resolved to avoid a rupture with Germany. "There is such a thing as a man being too proud to fight," the President said, to the disgust of Theodore Roosevelt and the bellicose nationalists. "There is such a thing as a nation being so right that it does not need to convince others by force that it is right." Nonetheless, Wilson sent three vigorous notes. In June, Germany, fearing war with the United States, ordered submarine commanders to spare all large passenger liners, including those of the enemy, but in August a U-boat commander violated orders and sank a British White Star Liner, the *Arabic,* with the loss of two American lives. When Wilson sent an even stronger protest, Germany gave assurances that the *Arabic* incident would not be repeated, that no unresisting passenger ship would be sunk without warning or without care for the safety of passengers and crew.

The submarine wrought havoc with Wilson's neutrality policy and ultimately brought the United States into the war. It was an accepted principle of international law that no naval vessel would destroy an enemy merchantman without first giving warning and providing for the safety of those aboard. This was reasonable enough when merchant ships were defenseless, but in the late summer of 1915 the British started arming its merchants and ordering them to attack; a single shot, or even ramming, could destroy a fragile submarine. A U-boat commander could not distinguish an armed from an unarmed vessel, and Britain and Italy were arming even their passenger liners. Wilson himself recognized the difficulty for a time. "It is hardly fair," he wrote Colonel House in October, 1915, "to ask submarine commanders to give warning by summons if, when they approach as near as they must for that purpose, they are to be fired upon."

When on February 10, 1916, however, the Germans, not unreasonably, announced they would sink all armed merchantmen, Wilson took a stern line. Asked by House Democratic leaders what would happen if a U-boat sank an armed vessel on which Americans were traveling, the President said he would break relations with Germany and that this might well mean war. Wilson's course was inconsistent, unrealistic, and, in view of his acquiescence in Allied transgressions, unneutral. Yet the Allied and the German maritime policies were not strictly comparable. If Britain seized American ships, the United States always had recourse to law and might obtain an indemnity; nothing would restore the loss of life from the ships Germany sank. Wilson felt justified in protesting mildly against seizure but issuing ultimatums about sinkings. Moreover, granting that passenger liners sometimes carried munitions and that after a time they were armed, the German policy of sinking them was unconscionable. The U-boat commander who deliberately fired on the *Lusitania* did not fear attack, for the *Lusitania* was unarmed. The Germans were using terror as a weapon. They ruthlessly took the lives of noncombatants and they exulted over their acts.

Yet many American leaders still sought to avoid war over this issue. Bryan, who had resigned as Secretary of State because he thought Wilson's second *"Lusitania* note" too provocative, headed a movement to prohibit Americans from sailing on belligerent vessels. "Germany has a right to prevent contraband going to the Allies," Bryan had written Wilson, "and a ship carrying contraband should not rely upon passengers to protect her from attack—it would be like putting women and children in front of an army." When Germany announced it would sink all armed merchant ships, strong support developed in Congress behind resolutions introduced by Senator Gore of Oklahoma and Representative McLemore of Texas to warn Americans not to travel on belligerent vessels destined for war zones. In the House, sentiment ran 2–1 for the resolutions, but Wilson brought such enormous pressure to bear against them that they were sidetracked in March, 1916. "Once accept a single abatement of right," he wrote, "and many other humiliations would certainly follow."

In that same month, a U-boat torpedoed an unarmed French channel steamer, *Sussex,* with heavy loss of life; no Americans were killed, but several were injured. This blatant violation of the German promises made after the *Arabic* incident created a diplomatic crisis. Wilson appeared before Congress on April 19 to read an ultimatum to Germany that unless it abandoned unrestricted submarine warfare against all vessels, even armed belligerents, the United States would sever diplomatic relations. The Kaiser, convinced he did not yet have enough U-boats to risk war, decided to appease the President. Germany replied on May 4, 1916, that its submarines would no longer sink merchantmen without warning and without humanitarian precautions, so long as they did not resist. But, the Germans added, this so-called *"Sussex* pledge" was conditioned on America's persuading the Allies to give up their blockade, which was intended to starve Germany into submission. If the United States did not, Germany would retain freedom of action.

Wilson chose to ignore the German conditions and to accept the pledge. He thereby achieved a great (however temporary) diplomatic triumph. The main threat of war—the U-boat—was removed. Yet Wilson had adopted such a strong line that if Germany resumed submarine warfare, which, given the continuation of the British blockade, it was likely to do, America would almost certainly be plunged into war. The decision for peace or war was taken from Washington and given to Berlin.

For nine months after the "*Sussex* pledge" not only did relations with Germany greatly improve but troubles with the British mounted. American opinion, incensed by the ruthless suppression of the Irish rebellion of April 24, 1916, particularly the execution of Sir Roger Casement, was angered still further by Britain's intensification of economic warfare. The British opened American mail, dealt cavalierly with U.S. diplomatic protests, and blacklisted American firms suspected of trading with Germany. By July, 1916, Wilson was confiding to Colonel House: "I am, I must admit, about at the end of my patience with Great Britain and the Allies." By the autumn of 1916 it appeared that the United States might be drifting toward an open break with Britain.

As the 1916 Presidential election approached, Wilson's Republican critics made a strong bid to defeat him by arguing that in his attempt to preserve peace he had sacrificed national honor. In their effort to dislodge Wilson, the Republicans had the support of the head of the Progressive party, Theodore Roosevelt, who viewed Wilson as a "demagogue, adroit, tricky, false, without one spark of loftiness in him, without a touch of the heroic in his cold, selfish and timid soul." When the Republicans nominated Charles Evans Hughes for the presidency (Hughes had distinguished himself first as a reform governor of New York and then as Supreme Court Justice), Roosevelt secured the Progressive nomination for him as well.

One of the ironies of the 1916 campaign is that the Republicans attacked the President for a lack of concern with the need to build up the armed forces at the very time when Wilson was under fire from radicals precisely because they thought he had become so chauvinistic. When Martin Glynn, former governor of New York, prepared his keynote address for the Democratic convention in June, Wilson instructed him to emphasize Americanism and the flag, and Glynn dutifully did so. The delegates, however, sat unresponsively as he went through his spread-eagle remarks. Glynn also felt called on to give some defense for Wilson's series of diplomatic notes, which the Republicans had scored as un-American timidity, and he cited a number of precedents for Wilson's actions. Fearing he would tire his audience with further examples, Glynn started to pass on to another subject, but delegates rose from their seats and shouted, "No! No! Go on!" An old campaign war horse, Glynn rose to the occasion. Each time he offered an example from the past when, provoked to the point of war, a President sent a diplomatic note instead, the crowd would yell, "What did we do? What did we do?" And Glynn would shout back, "We didn't go to war! We didn't go to war!"

The developments at the Democratic convention caught Wilson by surprise. On the very day of Glynn's speech, Wilson had led a preparedness parade in Washington with a flag draped over his shoulder. He felt exceedingly uneasy about the new Democratic slogan, "He Kept Us Out of War." ("I can't keep the country out of war," Wilson protested to Secretary of the Navy Daniels.

"They talk of me as though I were a god. Any little German lieutenant can put us into the war at any time by some calculated outrage.") Despite his doubts, Wilson made good use of the peace theme by charging Republicans with being the war party. On the combined appeals of peace, prosperity, and progressivism, Wilson won a narrow victory. The passion for peace proved so strong that Hughes was frequently forced to softpedal his attacks on Wilson's foreign policy and Roosevelt's belligerent nationalism was a handicap. The Republicans, noted the *Saturday Evening Post* after the election, "woefully misread the public mind. They thought it was truculently heroic, and writhing under a sense of national disgrace, when, in fact, it was merely sensible."

As peace sentiment in America reached a high pitch, Wilson stepped up his efforts to bring the war to an end. All through the war, Colonel House had crisscrossed Europe in search of a formula for peace. Early in 1916, House and Sir Edward Grey, the British Foreign Secretary, drafted a memorandum providing that Wilson, on hearing from the Allies when the time was opportune, would call a peace conference. If the Germans refused to attend such a parley or if they would not agree to reasonable terms, the United States would "probably" enter the war on the side of the Allies. Wilson's adamant stand against Germany in regard to armed merchantmen early in 1916 stemmed chiefly from a desire to maintain his usefulness as a mediator by not antagonizing the Allies. But in May, 1916, all the President's careful plans were blown sky high when the Allies decided not to pursue further the program outlined in the House-Grey agreement. Wilson's ultimatum of April, 1916, had given Britain and France reason to believe that a break between Germany and the United States was imminent. Furthermore, the Allies were unwilling to risk a peace conference at a time when Germany held Belgium, northern France, and much of eastern Europe without a firm pledge from the United States to fight unless Germany evacuated these areas.

Irked by the Allied rebuff, Wilson now decided on mediation without prior consultation with the Allies. To make clear his independence from the chancelleries of London and Paris, Wilson adopted a severe attitude toward the Allies. He won legislation from Congress in September, 1916, to permit him to deny clearance and harbor facilities to nations that discriminated against American commerce and to use force to carry out these powers. He also got the Federal Reserve Board to caution American bankers to use care in financing the Allied war trade. When Germany was derelict in upholding the *"Sussex* pledge"—in two cases, which Berlin held were "mistakes," American lives were lost— the President disregarded the provocations.

Wilson had decided on a bold change of policy to free himself from the tangle of maritime rights. He wanted greater maneuverability than a foreign policy geared to German submarine attacks offered. In the last eight months of 1916, Wilson said almost nothing about freedom of the seas, his chief concern since 1914, and stressed instead the impact of the war on democratic ideals and the future of Western civilization. The only way to avoid involvement in the war, the President concluded, was direct American mediation, even at the cost of surrendering the tradition of U.S. isolation from Europe's disputes. In a speech in October, 1916, Wilson counseled: "When you are asked, 'Aren't you willing to fight?' reply, yes, you are waiting for something worth fighting for; you are not looking around for petty quarrels, but you are looking about for that sort of quarrel within whose intricacies are written all the texts of the rights of man; you are looking for some cause . . . in which it seems a glory to shed human blood, if it be necessary, so that all the common compacts of liberty may be sealed with the blood of free men."

On December 18, 1916, Wilson sent identical diplomatic notes to the belligerent capitals asking them to state their war aims and to indicate upon what terms they would be willing to end hostilities. Since Germany, for reasons of its own, had made a peace feeler six days before, Wilson's message was received with dismay in Allied circles. Sir Henry Wilson fulminated about "that ass President Wilson," and Lord Northcliffe told Page, "Everybody is mad as hell." If Berlin desired a reasonable peace, Wilson had provided the opportunity. But the Germans were interested in a peace conference only as a device to split the Allies. At the very least, Germany was determined to control Belgium. "Albert shall keep his Belgium, since he too is King by Divine Right," the Kaiser advised Prince von Bülow in the autumn of 1916. "Though, of course, I imagine our future relationship as rather that of the Egyptian Khedive to the King of England." The Germans, whose dreams of glory included acquisition of the Belgian Congo, a large indemnity from France and England, and the end of British naval supremacy, aimed at nothing less than the destruction of Allied power. To achieve that end, they were even willing to invite war with America.

On January 31, 1917, the German ambassador informed the State Department that on the following day his country would resume unrestricted submarine warfare. U-boats would sink all ships, passenger and merchant, neutral and belligerent, armed or unarmed, in the war zone. With the British blockade squeezing off supplies and with the war deadlocked, Berlin was staking everything on one great exertion. The German government knew that the result would almost certainly be war with the United

States, but it reasoned that the submarine campaign would end the war before the United States could give any more aid than it was already supplying as a neutral. "England will lie on the ground in six months," the German Navy assured the Kaiser, "before a single American has set foot on the continent." Wilson promptly broke off diplomatic relations with Germany.

American ships, fearing submarine attack, clung to port; they refused to sail unless they were armed. As wheat and cotton piled up on Atlantic piers, railroads were forced to embargo shipments to the seacoast. Wilson faced the grim prospect that, with ships rusting at their docks, factories, in the absence of markets, would throw men out of work and farmers would suddenly be plunged into a devastating depression. The United States had permitted the Allies to cut off its trade with Germany; could it afford to permit Germany to cut off trade with the Allies as well? Yet Wilson refused to ask Congress for authority to arm ships. When on February 23 cabinet officers urged him to do so, he attacked them for attempting to revive the *code duello*. Two days later, however, Wilson changed his mind; from Ambassador Page he had received a dispatch that made him angry clear through.

Page's dispatch enclosed a message, which the British Secret Service had intercepted and decoded, from the Under Secretary of the German Ministry of Foreign Affairs, Alfred Zimmermann, to the German minister to Mexico. The Zimmermann telegram read: "We intend to begin on the first of February unrestricted submarine warfare. We shall endeavor in spite of this to keep the United States of America neutral. In the event of this not succeeding, we make Mexico a proposal of alliance on the following basis: make war together, make peace together, generous financial support and an understanding on our part that Mexico is to reconquer her lost territory in Texas, New Mexico, and Arizona." Japan was also to be invited by Mexico to join in the scheme.

On February 26, 1917, Wilson asked Congress for authority to arm merchant ships and to carry on an undeclared naval war. When a group of eleven senators led by Robert La Follette of Wisconsin filibustered the bill to death, the President, after attacking his opponents as a "little group of wilful men" who "had rendered the great government of the United States helpless and contemptible," went ahead and armed the vessels on the authority of an ancient statue of 1797. In March the first American merchantmen left port with orders to shoot on sight.

Still there was no war. Wilson had the clearest grasp of what war would mean. (Page had written him of the "acres of bloated human bodies, careless of sun or rain, giving off stench.") The terrible campaign of the Somme in 1916 had cost more than a million men and the president shrank from throwing American lives into the same inferno. Moreover, he wished to avoid war because, he told Secretary Lansing, it was necessary that the United States keep itself intact so as to maintain the dominance of "white" civilization. At a cabinet meeting in February, Wilson declared, according to Secretary Houston, that if "in order to keep the white race or part of it strong to meet the yellow race—Japan, for instance, in alliance with Russia, dominating China—it was wise to do nothing, he would do nothing and would submit to . . . any imputation of weakness or cowardice." Late in February, when U-boat marauders had been roving the seas for days, the President was still opposed to war. He could not sleep. His face was ashen. He was racked with doubt.

Yet he had reached a point of no return. A few hours before Wilson asked Congress to arm merchantmen, a German submarine had torpedoed a Cunard liner with the loss of twelve lives, including those of two American women. On March 12 an unarmed American merchant vessel was sunk without warning; on March 18 U-boats sank three more unarmed merchantmen with heavy loss of life. When this news came, the last member of Wilson's cabinet to hold out for peace capitulated. Wilson himself, incensed by the Zimmermann note and angered by the sinkings, was given a new reason for war by the downfall of the Czar, which, by removing the last despot among the Allies, made the war at last seem a clear-cut fight between democracy and autocracy.

On April 2, 1917, on a black, wet, Washington evening, Wilson went before Congress to declare that a state of war already existed with Germany. It would be a struggle of democracy against autocracy, for only autocrats would sanction such fiendish acts as the U-boat commanders had committed. "The world must be made safe for democracy," Wilson proclaimed. "Its peace must be planted upon the tested foundations of political liberty." Congress burst into applause, and men rushed forward to congratulate him. "My message today was a message of death for our young men," the white-faced Wilson remarked afterward to his secretary. "How strange it seems to applaud that."

In both houses of Congress a small band of Progressives spoke out against war. "We are going into war," declared Senator George Norris of Nebraska, "upon the command of gold." But they were overwhelmed. Two days after Wilson's message, the Senate voted war 82–6, and early on Good Friday morning the House adopted the war resolution 373–50. On April 7 the New York *Tribune* headlined the end of the long months of fretful neutrality: "AMERICA IN ARMAGEDDON."

Why did the United States intervene? In later years millions became convinced that America was led into war by a conspiracy of bankers and munitions makers or was hoodwinked by British propaganda, but neither Wall Street nor Reuters (the British news service) played a decisive role. Nor is it true, as a number of historians have contended, that the United States intervened out of a realistic recognition of the need to maintain the balance of power in Europe, an equilibrium from which America benefited. Although a few men articulated the potential menace of German domination of the Continent to U.S. interests, they were in a decided minority.

One can readily discern the precipitating cause of America's decision for war: the resumption of submarine warfare. Wilson never fully escaped the trap he set for himself when he insisted that an American citizen had the right to travel on a belligerent ship, even one carrying munitions, and that the American government must uphold that right as a matter of national honor. In fact, a citizen had no such right under international law, and the determination to assert such a right not only defied common sense but also warped perceptions of the dimensions of the peril constituted by underseas operations. Few seemed aware that in the entire period of neutrality, only three U.S. citizens died on American ships, while 175 lost their lives travelling on belligerent (Allied) vessels. Submarine assaults, though terrifying, did not inevitably draw neutrals into war. The Scandinavian nations absorbed more substantial relative losses from U-boats than did the United States, yet remained at peace. Although by 1916 Wilson sought to chart a new course, his efforts to liberate himself from the fateful struggle over maritime rights were too little and too late.

The United States did not go to war, however, primarily to uphold the freedom to travel. Once the U-boats started sending to the bottom every ship that came within their periscope sights,

they threatened to drive all American cargo vessels from the Atlantic, thereby precipitating a serious depression. Not only "merchants of death" but also millions of American workers and farmers had a stake in not letting that happen. Furthermore, the
sinking of U.S. ships came in the same season as the revelation of
the Zimmermann note. From the beginning of the war, Germany
had been both arrogant and reckless in displaying its hostility to
America. When a German consul carelessly left his briefcase on a
Third Avenue Elevated train in Manhattan, it was found to be
laden with incontrovertible evidence of espionage. Still worse,
German agents were linked to the Black Tom explosion on the
Erie Railroad docks in New Jersey and were detected plotting to
blow up the Bethlehem Steel plant in Pittsburgh. In the context
of these episodes and of the merciless undersea attacks, the Zimmermann message was the last straw.

Wilson had one final set of motivations for war. In order both
to fashion a new world order and to foster America's commercial
interests, he wanted a seat at the peace table, and he knew that if
the United States did not become a belligerent, that opportunity
would be denied him. If his country remained neutral, the most
he would be able to manage, he said, would be to "shout through
a crack in the door." Wilson, informed of secret treaties in which
the Allies had already divided up the anticipated spoils of war and
conscious of their desire to seize markets, distrusted what they
would do after the war almost as much as he feared German ambitions. The President's expectation that by going to war he could
shape the peace rested on quicksand, though. Behind his back,
Allied leaders sneered at his aspirations, while Senators, whose
votes Wilson would need to ratify any postwar treaty, expressed
skepticism about his ideals. In the debate on intervening in the
European conflict, Republican Senator William E. Borah an-

nounced: "I join no crusade; I seek or accept no alliances; I obligate this Government to no other power. I make war alone for my countrymen and their rights, for my country and its honor."

The decision to fight, and the assumptions on which America entered the war, did not represent the President's will alone but the attitude of a generation with a strong sense of mission and a new consciousness of national power. The literary critic Alfred Kazin later wrote, "In one sense the war was even the last great skirmish in the battle for People's Rights. As the direct primary had been won, the wickedness of the great trusts exposed, so were the bosses in the Wilhelmstrasse to be removed, and all governments everywhere to be restored to the people." Admiral Mahan had compared the duty of the United States to repress evil abroad to that of the obligation of the rich to wipe out slums, an assumption that had the ironic effect of requiring "peace-loving" Americans to resort to killing to impose virtue abroad.

The declaration of war brought to a climax, too, an era of political discourse in which Bryan could at an 1896 convention liken the currency situation to the crucifixion and Teddy Roosevelt could at a 1912 convention speak of standing at Armageddon. When in 1917 Congress voted for war, the pacifist Emily Balch wrote, "So, nearly 1900 years after the death on the cross this is to be the celebration of Good Friday," and a month later, the mayor of New York greeted a French commission by saying, "We hail you as allies to whom we owe an obligation . . . that will not be discharged by loans, by munitions, by food supplies, by ships, or by ought else save the devoted service and blood sacrifice of American manhood, side by side, upon the battlefields of France." The culmination of a long tradition of emphasis on decisive moral combat, the war was embraced by not a few as that final struggle where the righteous would do battle for the Lord.

2

Innocents Abroad

Today World War I has a kind of musical comedy flavor: it suggests George M. Cohan and lines of jaunty Empire soldiers singing, "It's a long way to Tipperary"; it brings to mind men dressed in American Legion uniforms and selling red poppies or reminiscing about the "Mademoiselle from Armentières"—almost anything but the bloody, pointless warfare of the trenches and what it did to bring centuries of Western civilization to an abrupt stopping place. "Events," wrote Winston Churchill in 1929, "passed very largely outside the scope of conscious choice. Governments and individuals conformed to the rhythm of the tragedy, and swayed and staggered forward in helpless violence, slaughtering and squandering on ever-increasing scales, till injuries were wrought to the structure of human society which a century will not efface, and which may conceivably prove fatal to the present civilization."

The United States entered the war at a critical time for the military fortunes of the Allies. In the spring of 1917, a French offensive on the Aisne had failed, certain French politicians and bankers were talking of peace, and ten French divisions had mutinied. In the autumn of 1917, Italy almost collapsed after the Austrian victory at Caporetto, and the Russian front vanished when the Bolshevik Revolution in November led to the negotiation of a separate peace that freed forty German divisions on the Eastern Front for an assault on the west. Token American forces were landed in Europe as early as the summer of 1917, but no major unit moved to the front until October, 1917. By March, 1918, there were 300,000 Yanks in France; by November, more than two million, 1,400,000 of whom saw action.

In March, 1918, before the American Expeditionary Force could have any important effect, Germany launched an offensive that drove the British back in the Somme valley; in late May, they turned against the French, captured 40,000 prisoners in a week, and reached the Marne fifty miles from Paris. In June, green but reckless American units helped hurl German troops back across the Marne at Chateau-Thierry and cleared Belleau Wood. Militarily unimportant, the appearance of fresh American troops, who had not been unnerved by years of battle, gave a great lift to Allied morale. On July 15, the Germans began their last great drive for Paris, the Second Battle of the Marne, which engaged 85,000 American soldiers. Three days later, the Germans were finished. "On the 18th," wrote the German Chancellor, "even the most optimistic among us knew that all was lost. The history of the world was played out in three days." The German Seventh Army, wrote its chief of staff, "achieved brilliant initial successes, with the exception of the one division on our right wing. This encountered American units! Here only did the Seventh Army . . . confront serious difficulties."

On July 18, permitting neither his own soldiers nor the enemy's to rest, Marshal Foch ordered American and French colonial troops to counterattack. In July and August, the British and French played the major role in the Allied offensive, supported by hundreds of thousands of American doughboys in the destruction of the Aisne-Marne flank. In September, in the brief struggle at St. Mihiel, where more than half a million U.S. troops wiped out the weak German salient and captured 16,000 prisoners, and in the bitter 47 days of the Meuse-Argonne, the assaults were primarily the work of American forces. Under General John J. Pershing, the Americans, now fighting as independent units, drove the Germans out of the Argonne Forest. The bloody Meuse-Argonne battle engaged 1,200,000 U.S. troops at a cost of 120,000 casualties; more Americans lost their lives in the Argonne than in all the rest of the battles combined. Together with British and French victories on the northern and central fronts, the A.E.F. successes in the southern sector broke the Hindenburg Line and brought a triumphant end to the war.

Forty-eight thousand Americans were killed in action, 2,900 were listed as missing, and 56,000 died of disease—a considerable loss of life, yet less than the major European powers suffered in a single battle like Verdun. Germany lost 1,800,000 men in the war, Russia 1,700,000, France 1,385,000, Austria-Hungary 1,200,000, and Britain 947,000. The United States "won the war" only in the sense that, after four years of combat in which Britain and France had given infinitely more in blood and treasure, American troops afforded the Allies a preponderance of power. General Ludendorff, who commanded the Western Front for Germany, greatly underestimated the capacity of Allied troops to hold their lines until the United States was able to achieve the miracle of training and equipping two million troops and landing them in France.

Without naval support, the military success would have been impossible. The Germans calculated that if they could sink 600,000 tons of shipping each month, they could force Britain to ask for terms in six months. In February they sank 540,000 tons;

in April, as the days grew longer, 881,000. On May 4 the first American destroyers, six of them, reached Ireland. At the urging of Admiral William S. Sims and Secretary of the Navy Josephus Daniels, the British relented in their opposition to the convoy system, and by July U.S. destroyers were convoying merchantmen. By December losses to submarines had been cut in half, and by the spring of 1918 the U-boat was no longer a major menace, in part because the British accepted an American proposal to lay a mine barrage in the North Sea. Freed of this danger, British and American transports were able to achieve the miracle of moving two million U.S. troops to Europe; and only two transports, both British, were sunk during the eastern voyage.

On the home front the war altered drastically the familiar patterns. Men who would once have balked at spending thousands soon learned to talk casually of disbursing millions. Secretary of the Treasury William McAdoo propped himself up in bed at night with a yellow writing pad on his knees to work out the financing of the war. "The noughts attached to the many millions were so boisterous and prolific," he recalled, "that, at times, they would run clear over the edge of the paper." "Sure we paid," replied Charles G. Dawes when his fellow Republicans were unfairly censuring Democratic officials after the war. "We would have paid horse prices for sheep if sheep could have pulled artillery to the front. . . . Damn it all, the business of an army is to win the war, not to quibble around with a lot of cheap buying. Hell and Maria, we weren't trying to keep a set of books, we were trying to win the war!" Despite the abandon with which money was spent, the war was conducted without major scandal, and, in the closing months, with increasing efficiency.

In the first year of the war inexperienced officials badly bungled the job of administering the economy, and important areas never did get straightened out. Production of heavy guns got into high gear only after the war had ended. American plants produced almost no tanks. American aviators flew British and French planes, and most of the artillery pieces the Americans fired in Europe were supplied by the French. Most serious was the failure of shipbuilding. In the early weeks of the war General Goethals pointed out that "birds were still nesting in the trees from which the great wooden fleet was to be made." At the end of the war many of the birds were still nesting there. The first vessel from the largest government shipyard (at Hog Island, near Philadelphia) was not delivered until the war was over; the total output from all yards was negligible. Only by buying and seizing German and Dutch ships and American ships built in private yards did the Shipping Board meet the desperate need for merchantmen and transports. By early 1918, with railroad transportation close to breaking down and soldiers at camp lacking adequate clothing and shelter, the country approached a crisis.

Stung by congressional criticism, Wilson, on March 4, 1918, summoned Bernard Baruch, a Wall Street speculator, to head a reinvigorated War Industries Board, which exercised sweeping authority over priorities and allocations. The board could determine what materials manufacturers could use and what they could or could not make. It issued the most minute regulations: elevator operators were told how often they could stop, and traveling salesmen were limited to two trunks. Operating as economic dictator, Baruch did a superb job of unsnarling red tape and bringing the mobilization to high efficiency.

The war marked the first large-scale experience with government control in America with federal agencies directing every important economic sector. The Fuel Administration doled out coal and oil, imposed "heatless Thursdays," introduced the European innovation of daylight saving time, and closed down unessential factories one day a week; the Emergency Fleet Corporation oversaw shipbuilding; the War Trade Board licensed foreign commerce; the War Finance Corporation, with a billion dollar treasury, provided capital to firms converting to war production; and the Railroad Administration, under Treasury Secretary McAdoo, operated the nation's railways as a single system.

On April 27, 1917, Ambassador Page warned Wilson that Britain did not have enough food for more than six to eight weeks. Under the adroit leadership of Food Administrator Herbert Hoover, the entire nation was alerted to the need to conserve food. Restaurants served shark steak and whale meat, and bakers devised coarse breads to save wheat. ("Do not permit your child," wrote *Life,* "to take a bite or two from an apple and throw the rest away; nowadays even children must be taught to be patriotic to the core.") Hoover entered the grain market to purchase and distribute wheat, and he pegged hog prices so high that farmers doubled production. He bought the entire Cuban and American sugar crops and ordered grocers to limit each individual to two pounds a month. The Hoover program was an outstanding success; under it, the United States was able to ship three times as much food to the Allied countries as it had before the war.

The war opened new opportunities in government for professors, social workers, and other university-trained men and women. The Felix Frankfurters and Isador Lubins who in the 1930s would be an important aspect of the New Deal got their first taste of national power in 1917. Many of this corps of administrators rejected the Victorian competitive ideal for the goal of a planned economy. They were exhilarated by what the philosopher John Dewey called "the social possibilities of war," the direction of the economy for public ends rather than private profit. There was, the critic Randolph Bourne observed acidly, a "peculiar congeniality between the war and these men. It is as if the war and they had been waiting for each other."

To the reformer, Brand Whitlock, it seemed that more was achieved for radicalism in the war than the radicals themselves could have accomplished in three hundred years. "Every single contention that we have ever made as to the precedence of public right over private right, of public property over private property, has all been conceded by the very ones who used to oppose them." In the course of the war, the federal government took over telephone and telegraph companies, warehouses, terminals, express companies, and sleeping-car companies. The kind of pressure Washington could exert on businessmen was revealed inadvertently by the priorities commissioner of the War Industries Board who said: "We never used any compulsion. Of course, if a man . . . didn't want to play with us, he found he couldn't get any fuel or railroad cars or any labor or anything; but we never used any compulsion." Furthermore, the War Revenue Act of 1917 imposed an excess profits levy as high as 60 percent; stepped up both personal and corporate income tax rates; jacked up the estate tax; and increased taxes on luxuries. "Laissez-faire is dead," exulted one progressive. "Long live social control."

During the war, to the delight of the advanced progressives, the federal government compelled businessmen to deal with unions and threw its weight behind minimum wages and other benefits for labor. A National War Labor Board guaranteed collective bargaining, mediated labor disputes, and, to gain compliance with its edicts, even commandeered an arms plant. By 1920 the American Federation of Labor claimed a membership of 3.26 million, most of it represented by a wartime increase of 2.3 million. With immigration virtually closed off, and with the armed forces drawing millions out of the work force, wages rose in response to the increased demand, while from 1915 to 1918 the real income of farmers grew 30 percent. The national government also broke new ground by involving itself for the first time in public housing and social insurance.

The war changed, too, the situation of African-Americans. In many ways, blacks suffered grievously during the war years—a dreadful race riot in East St. Louis in the summer of 1917 took many lives, and blacks endured humiliating treatment in the armed forces. But there was one very consequential development of the war period—the Great Migration to Northern cities of hundreds of thousands of Southern blacks who found unprecedented job opportunities. In Chicago, their rate of population growth was seven times that for whites. In the North, they often were wretchedly housed, but they found a degree of freedom they had never experienced before. Since coming to Philadelphia, one migrant reported: "Don't have to mister every little white boy comes along. . . . I can ride in the electric street and steam cars any where I can get a seat . . . and if you are first in a place here [shopping] you don't have to wait until the white folks get thro tradeing." "I should have a been here 20 years ago," a Chicago newcomer wrote back home. "It's a great deal of pleasure in knowing that you have got some privilege. My children are going to the same school with whites and I dont have to umble to no one. I have registered—Will vote the next election and there isnt any 'yes sir' and 'no sir'—its all yes and no and Sam and Bill."

That sense of exhilaration, though, proved short-lived. In the first year after the war, 74 blacks were lynched, and race riots shook more than two dozen cities. In Longview, Texas, whites burned down shops and homes in the black quarter, and in Chicago, race war claimed 38 lives. The bitter resentment aroused by such experiences were subsequently captured in the writings of black poets like Countee Cullen and Claude McKay, notably in "To the White Fiend" in McKay's *Harlem Shadows* (1922). It took a different form in the Universal Negro Improvement Association founded by Marcus Garvey, who was, like McKay, an immigrant from Jamaica. Garvey glorified blackness; he claimed that both God and Jesus were black, and, despairing of white America, sponsored a steamship company, the Black Star Line, to transport American blacks to Africa. Though his critics, black as well as white, viewed Garvey, with his plumed hat, braided uniform, showy limousine, and Emperor Jones manner, as a charlatan, hundreds of thousands of blacks flocked to him. His steamship line foundered, other plans went awry, and in 1925 he entered a penitentiary to serve a five-year term for fraud; in 1927, his sentence was commuted, but he was deported to Jamaica. NAACP and other African American leaders welcomed the dismissal of a man they viewed as a dangerous hustler, but his message of black power was not forgotten, and a black newspaper said of his influence: "In a world where black is despised, he taught them that black is beautiful."

World War I had yet another important consequence: the victory of the movement for women's suffrage. In 1914 both political parties had opposed the suffrage amendment, and so did Woodrow Wilson. But sentiment shifted markedly during the war, for it seemed inconsistent to take part in a struggle for democracy and forbid more than half the population to vote. On September 30, 1918, the President surprised the Senate by coming personally before it to urge passage of the Susan Anthony Amendment. "I tell you plainly that this measure which I urge upon you is vital to winning the war," he declared. The Senate vote fell short of the required two-thirds, because Southern Democrats saw the amendment as a step toward enfranchising blacks, but the elections of November, 1918, sent to Congress enough additional advocates of women's suffrage to insure its adoption. In June, 1919, the Senate provided the necessary two-thirds approval, and by the following summer, the thirty-sixth state, Tennessee, had ratified the amendment, just in time to permit women to vote in the presidential election of 1920. The Nineteenth Amendment was the fulfillment of her greatest dream, Carrie Chapman Catt informed a victory celebration in New York. "We are no longer petitioners, we are not wards of the nation, but free and equal citizens."

Afterwards, though, many of the progressives who had seen the war as the dawn of a new era of social justice were disappointed. If it opened up horizons for reformers, it also visited power on an army of businessmen who came to Washington to work in hot cubicles in temporary buildings and made the most of their authority. Despite the steep increase in taxes, the war created some 42,000 new millionaires. Moreover, many of the departures that loomed so large during the war proved ephemeral. Most of the women who flocked to the factories in wartime returned to their homes, and blacks met discrimination in the North as in the South. To be sure, some things did endure. Women did now have the ballot; the blacks who had migrated did remain in the Northern cities. But in the long run, World War I was less important for the changes it wrought than for the precedents it set. It gave the nation its first glimpse of the twentieth-century state, with an aggrandized presidency, the capacity to mobilize the economy, the ability both to bring new benefits to people and to inflict new kinds of duress—in short, with all of its potential for good and evil.

The progressives learned, ultimately to their sorrow, that the national state that could curb businessmen could also coerce other Americans. The war ended the casual voluntarism of the nineteenth century in the passage, over bitter protests, of the Selective Service Act. (Champ Clark, Speaker of the House, said that "in the estimation of Missourians, there is precious little difference between a conscript and a convict.") Although there had been a draft in the Civil War, it was undertaken in the middle of the war as an emergency measure, provided for the alternative of purchasing a substitute, and was enforced with great difficulty. The World War I draft proved to be the main source for the American Expeditionary Force. In the spring of 1917, the regular army and the National Guard together added up to less than 379,000. At the end of the conflict, only a year and a half later, the total had reached 4.8 million, and three million of these were draftees. Under General Hugh Johnson, who would later head the New Deal's National Industrial Recovery Act mobilization, the draft was administered in the methodical manner that a powerful twentieth-century state goes about its business of turning lives to public ends.

The wartime draft was only one of a number of measures that indicated for the first time that an efficient state had been developing in the years of the Progressive era, changing the romantic, individualistic world of the Spanish-American War to the systematic routine of World War I. In 1916 America still adhered to nineteenth-century values of decentralization, competition, equality, agrarian supremacy, and the primacy of the small town. By 1920 the triumph of the twentieth century—centralized, industrialized, secularized, urbanized—while by no means complete, could clearly be foreseen. Although a conflict between old and new values would rage throughout the 1920s, a significant change in the temper of American society had occurred.

The coercive nature of government in wartime also found expression in the attitude toward the sex lives of American men in uniform. At the outset, Secretary of the Navy Daniels, a prominent North Carolina progressive, insisted that the only answer to the problem of venereal disease was total abstinence, but as disease rates soared, he yielded to the social worker Raymond Fosdick's insistence on coercion. By the end of 1918, the U.S. government had closed down every important red-light district in the country, including Storyville with its intimate associations with New Orleans jazz.

The welfare of the soldier overseas proved a knottier problem. After a tour of inspection in France, Secretary of War Baker reported to a women's group that he had not seen a doughboy who was not "living a life which he would not be willing to have his mother see him live." But Baker knew better. The French premier, Georges Clemenceau, in a gesture of unparalleled generosity, offered to share his nation's prostitutes with his American brethren. When Fosdick forwarded this offer to Baker, the Secretary of War cried, "For God's sake, Raymond, don't show this to the President or he'll stop the war."

World War I crowned yet another coercive movement with success when in December, 1917, Congress adopted and sent to the states the Eighteenth Amendment, prohibiting the manufacture, sale, or transportation of alcoholic beverages. Repeated efforts by the drys had failed in the past, but the war gave them a new arsenal of arguments. They pointed out that alcohol dimmed the wits of both doughboys and war workers, that outlawing beer would further the aims of grain conservation by saving barley, and that brewers bore names from the country of the enemy, Germany. In January, 1919, the thirty-sixth state ratified the amendment, and that October, Congress, over Wilson's veto, enacted the Volstead law which defined "alcoholic" rigidly as one-half of 1 percent by volume. The Prohibition Commissioner promised that no liquor would be manufactured, "nor sold, nor given away, nor hauled in anything on the surface of the earth or under the earth or in the air."

The coercive mood manifested itself at its most vicious in the suppression of dissenters. Many Americans viewed the war with a discernible lack of enthusiasm. The War Department put the total of draft dodgers at 171,000, and in two Oklahoma counties, a "Green Corn Rebellion" of tenant farmers, Indians, and blacks defied draft authorities and resorted to violence. Areas where German-Americans or Anglophobic Irish-Americans or peace-minded Scandinavians were dominant greeted the war with sullen hostility. The Socialists, unlike their counterparts abroad, were bolder. On April 9, 1917, they adopted a resolution, later approved in a party referendum by a vote of 21,000 to 350, which proclaimed: "We brand the declaration of war by our government as a crime against the people of the United States." In the 1917 municipal elections, Socialist candidates received 22 per cent of the vote in New York City, 34 per cent in Chicago (where they had polled less than 4 percent a year before), and 44 percent in Dayton.

To combat popular opposition to the war, the government moved in a number of ways. Under the Espionage Act of 1917 and the Sedition law of 1918, it arrested more than 1,500 persons. The infamous Alien and Sedition Acts of John Adams brought ten convictions, the World War I prosecutions a thousand. Attorney General Thomas Gregory warned opponents of the war to ask mercy from God "for they need expect none from an outraged people and an avenging government," and he was good to his word. A producer who turned out a film on the American

Revolution, *Spirit of '76,* drew a ten-year jail term for generating suspicion of our British ally. The government was especially zealous about hounding radicals. "If you stopped to collect your thoughts," said the Socialist Max Eastman, "you could be arrested for illegal assembly." The Socialist leader, Eugene V. Debs, and Milwaukee's Socialist Congressman, Victor Berger, both received twenty-year jail terms for criticizing the war, and the conviction of one hundred leaders of the Industrial Workers of the World, including Big Bill Haywood, at a trial in Chicago before Judge Kenesaw Mountain Landis all but destroyed that organization.

In 1919, the Supreme Court validated the Espionage and Sedition Acts in two significant cases. In *Schenck v. United States,* a unanimous court sustained the conviction of a Socialist who had mailed anti-draft leaflets to men eligible for the draft. "Free speech," said Justice Oliver Wendell Holmes, Jr., "would not protect a man in falsely shouting fire in a theater, and causing a panic," and, in this instance, Schenck's activity created "a clear and present danger." In *Abrams v. United States,* the Court upheld the conviction of a man who dropped circulars out of a window opposing American intervention against the Bolsheviks in Russia, but this time Holmes as well as Justice Louis Brandeis dissented, since the "surreptious publishing of a silly leaflet by an unknown man" constituted no menace.

Wilson also set up a Committee on Public Information, under George Creel, which whipped up hatred of all things German, and in many communities the response went far beyond what the Creel Committee had intended. The war, as Ludwig Lewisohn observed, was fought with a "peculiarly unmotivated ferocity." Aroused to fury at an enemy 3,000 miles distant who they could not strike directly, civilians sought enemies within. Vigilantes, including even the Boy Spies of America, ferreted out any indication of lack of fervor for the war. Flying squads invaded farm-houses to force farmers to buy a quota of bonds, and if a farmer refused, they nailed a yellow placard to his house or splashed it with yellow paint. Men suspected of disloyalty were forced to kneel to kiss the flag. Supposedly responsible Red Cross leaders warned that German-Americans had infiltrated their organization to put ground glass in bandages; while in humorless patriotic zeal sauerkraut was renamed "liberty cabbage," dachshunds became "liberty pups," and Fritz Kreisler was driven from the concert stage.

There appears in wartime, observed Walter Lippmann, a Gresham's law of the emotions whereby leadership passes from statesmanship to virulent jingoism. At first directed at German-Americans and alleged spies, the crusade for conformity quickly focused on any criticism of the war from any source. "Woe be to the man," warned Wilson, "that seeks to stand in our way in this day of high resolution when every principle we hold dearest is to be vindicated and made secure." "He who is not with us, abso-lutely and without reserve of any kind, is against us, and should be treated as an alien enemy," declared Theodore Roosevelt. "Our bitter experience should teach us for a generation . . . to crush under our heel every movement that smacks in the smallest degree of playing the German game." In a similar expression of elite sen-timent, the *New York Times* editorialized on the conscientious ob-jector: "We should not ask about the sincerity of such a man. If he puts his belief into practice, we should either put him to death or shut up in an asylum as a madman."

With such instruction from the nation's leaders, fanatics who, in Santayana's phrase, redoubled their effort when they had for-gotten their aim, soon lost all sense of discretion. In Chicago when Burton Rascoe printed selections from *Areopagitica* under the by-line "John Milton," he was deluged with letters denouncing Milton as an agent of Prussian *kultur*. A federal judge in Texas declared that La Follette and five other senators should be stood up against an adobe wall and shot. President Nicholas Murray Butler of Columbia University, speaking of La Follette, told the American Bankers Association that "you might just as well put poison in the food of every American boy that goes to his transport as to permit that man to talk as he does." Inevitably, on some occasions words gave way to action; in Butte the crippled IWW leader Frank Little was dragged from bed by a band of masked men and hanged from a railway trestle.

The war offered an outlet for the messianic zeal of the Progressive era without jeopardizing the structure of American society. A sense of national unity, partly real, partly imposed, quieted the concerns about rifts of class and party and race that haunted the last years of the era. It was this psychic release from baffling internal problems that L. P. Jacks had in mind when he wrote of "the peacefulness of being at war." "The mass of the worried middle classes," observed Randolph Bourne, the keenest critic of the war, "riddled by the campaign against American failings, which at times extended almost to a skepticism of the American State itself, were only too glad to sink back to a glorification of the State ideal, to feel about them in war the old protecting arms, to return to the old primitive sense of the omnipotence of the State, its matchless virtue, honor, and beauty, driving away all the foul old doubts and dismays."

Wilson and his circle transmuted the war into a crusade, in which were invoked the old theme of the church militant and the more modern one of the secular religion of democracy. Secretary Baker wrote of America's "high and holy mission"; Secretary Lane spoke of "the world of Christ" coming face to face with the world of force; while a government pamphleteer noted the conviction of the American people that the "war across the sea was no mere conflict between dynasties, but a stupendous civil war of all the world." The war, declared the Creel Committee, was "a Crusade not merely to re-win the tomb of Christ, but to bring back to earth the rule of right, the peace, goodwill to men and gentleness he taught."

The president and his intellectual supporters, such as John Dewey, believed that this "most terrible and disastrous of all wars" could be countenanced only by perceiving of it as the harbinger of eternal peace. This presumption was fantastic given what was actually happening in Europe in 1917: the breakdown of the whole nineteenth-century order that had made possible a longer peace than Europe had ever known and a wider spread of democracy than the world had ever seen. Such extravagant expectations only intensified the disillusionment that would come with peace.

The utopian spirit of the war took concrete form in Wilson's proposal of a postwar federation of nations, in itself not a utopian scheme but one which, from the first, was freighted with utopian aspirations. "It is the hour and the day," Max Eastman had written as early as February, 1915, "for President Wilson to take the first step towards international federation. He has it in his hands to make his administration a momentous event in planetary history—a thing not for historians, indeed, but for biologists to tell of." The idea of a parliament of man, of a world organization to abolish the scourge of war, had excited the imagination of poets and statesmen for centuries; it had elicited considerable interest in Europe, particularly in England, before and during the war; but it was not until Woodrow Wilson formulated his belief in a postwar league of nations that the idea began to become a reality.

In May, 1916, the President publicly espoused American membership in a postwar association, and on January 22, 1917, in an address to the Senate, he not only reaffirmed this notion, but also for the first time sketched his conception of the peace. It was to be a "peace without victory," a "peace among equals," not a peace of indemnities and annexations. A year later, on January 8, 1918, to counteract Bolshevik arguments that the war was merely an imperialist struggle, Wilson went before Congress to explain to the world the kind of peace for which the United States and its allies were fighting. He called for abolition of secret diplomacy, for freedom of the seas, self-determination of nations, removal of economic barriers among nations, reduction of armaments, and adjustment of colonial claims in the interest of the inhabitants of the colonies as well as the powers concerned. Most important was Point 14: "a general association of nations . . . affording mutual guarantees of political independence and territorial integrity to great and small states alike."

At first contemptuous of the Fourteen Points, Germany had been driven by October, 1918, to begin negotiations with Wilson for peace on the basis of them. Thinking the president would be an easy mark, General Ludendorff planned to use him to give Germany a breathing spell before resuming fighting, but Wilson proved a tough negotiator. He demanded that the Germans evacuate Belgium and France and guarantee they would not continue hostilities. To the true representatives of the German people, Wilson added, the terms of the Fourteen Points were available, but to the "military masters of the monarchical autocrats of Germany," they were not. Partly in response to Wilson's suggestion that a republic would win better terms than an imperial monarchy, the German people rebelled, forcing the Kaiser to abdicate and flee to Holland on November 9, 1918. Although Ludendorff's maneuver had been foiled, the negotiations had one disastrous consequence. By insisting on dealing only with democratic representatives, Wilson rescued the German military caste from the obloquy of surrender, and he provided the basis for the myth, which Hitler was to exploit, that Germany lost the war not through military defeat but as the result of a "stab in the back" by democratic politicians.

Before Wilson could conclude the terms of peace, he had to meet Allied objections to negotiating with Germany on the basis of the Fourteen Points. The Allies, who had concluded a number of secret treaties carving up the choicer portions of the German Empire, were determined to wring from Germany as much as they could to compensate for a bloody, costly war. When Colonel House suggested that, if the Allies persisted in a vindictive policy, America might make a separate peace, the Allies yielded, but on two conditions: that Germany would pay reparations for damages to civilians, and that the Allies would individually reserve sovereignty of action on the principle of freedom of the seas. "War would not be war if there were freedom of the seas," Clemenceau explained. On this basis, the armistice was signed on November 11, 1918 in a railroad car in Compiègne Forest.

The war for democracy had ended, it appeared, in total triumph. "Every ancient right of princes or castes or classes to dispose of the wills of other men is on the table for liquidation," wrote the editors of the *New Republic* in November, 1918. "At this instant of history, democracy is supreme." The way was now cleared for the fulfillment of Wilson's dream: the creation of a great postwar federation of nations.

3

The Fourteenth Point

Woodrow Wilson was the Victorian statesman incarnate. At sixteen he hung a portrait of Gladstone over his desk—he called him "the greatest statesman that ever lived"—and he spent a lifetime trying to emulate the Englishman. The Fourteen Points were essentially the credo of British liberalism, and Wilson approached the Paris conference with a program—political democracy, self-determination, free trade—which spoke the language of Cobden and Bright. The Peace Conference would test the ability of nineteenth-century liberalism to survive in a twentieth-century world.

Like a British Prime Minister, Wilson viewed his own party as an alliance of men of the same ideological persuasion, with himself as head of a party government. Fearing that his position at the conference would be seriously jeopardized if his party was repudiated in the November, 1918, congressional elections, Wilson on October 25 issued an appeal to the voters: "If you have approved of my leadership and wish me to continue to be your unembarrassed spokesman in affairs at home and abroad, I earnestly beg that you will express yourselves unmistakably to that effect by returning a Democratic majority to both the Senate and the House of Representatives." Despite Wilson's appeal (his critics said because of it), the Republicans captured both houses of Congress. Although the election turned less on Wilson's message than on domestic issues like the price of wheat and wool, it was taken as a rejection of Wilson, and it damaged his bargaining position in Paris. It appeared to European statesmen that Wilson, on the eve of the conference, had sought and lost a vote of confidence.

The leaders of the Republican party shared Wilson's conviction that foreign policy was a partisan matter, and Wilson was bitterly hated by two of the most influential Republicans, Theodore Roosevelt and Senator Henry Cabot Lodge of Massachusetts. Both had shown considerable interest in the idea of a League at one time, but essentially they believed in balance-of-power politics and sneered at Wilson's idealism. Moreover, however favorably they might have been disposed to the idea of a League in the abstract, they would have nothing to do with a Wilson League. Nor did they intend to permit the Democratic party to go to the polls in 1920 claiming credit both for having waged a victorious war and for having created a League of Nations. In their distrust of the proposal of the League, in their hatred of Wilson, in their concern for the fortunes of the Republican party, they would stop at nothing, even if they completely undermined the president's position and played into the hands of European nationalists.

On November 27, 1918, Theodore Roosevelt issued a statement which was duly noted in the capitals of Europe: "Our allies and our enemies and Mr. Wilson himself should all understand that Mr. Wilson has no authority whatever to speak for the American people at this time. His leadership has just been emphatically repudiated by them. The newly elected Congress comes far nearer than Mr. Wilson to having a right to speak the purposes of the American people at this moment. Mr. Wilson and his Fourteen Points and his four supplementary points and his five complementary points and all his utterances every which way have ceased to have any shadow of right to be accepted as expressive of the will of the American people."

Two weeks after the election, Wilson made the surprising announcement that he would head the American peace delegation to Paris. Never before had a president left U.S. territory while in office. Wilson's immediate predecessor, William Howard Taft, had refused even to visit his summer vacation home across the border in Canada because he thought it would be unconstitutional. Going abroad, Wilson's critics have pointed out, not only broke precedent, but also had the further disadvantage of removing the President from the problems that were mounting for him at home. Yet Wilson's decision was not as unreasonable as it has been portrayed. Every other delegation was headed by the leader of the government, and Wilson, by appearing in person, could use his immense moral prestige to fend off a Carthaginian peace.

The President's critics stood on firmer ground in criticizing his choice of American delegates. To accompany him to Paris, Wilson named Secretary of State Lansing, Colonel House, a general, and an able career diplomat. Of the group, not one was from the Senate, and the only Republican, Henry White, was not a major figure in the party. Wilson was buying trouble by these appointments, since he would one day have to get the treaty through a Republican-controlled Senate. (McKinley, in contrast, had named no fewer than three senators to the peace conference following the Spanish-American War.) But Wilson saw no alternative. He felt he could not pick Lodge, the obvious choice, since Lodge had long been a bitter foe, and to appoint any other Senate Republican would be an affront to Lodge. It is no less true that Wilson's decision revealed a fatal flaw of character; he could not work with men of his own stature, and he detested day-by-day jockeying for position. Wilson preferred the enunciation of high principles to the intimate, personal associations of political maneuvering.

Wilson believed that he had to go to Paris because "the leaders of the allies did not really represent their peoples," and that he alone spoke for the masses who yearned for eternal peace. When he arrived in Europe, he was hailed as the leader of a country that had brought an apparently endless war to a triumphant end, and as the prophet who declared that never again would men have to wage war. Wherever he went, he was greeted with wild acclaim, beyond that ever before accorded a democratic political figure. In France, a crowd of two million cheering Parisians showered violets and rose petals on him, and Italians grew hoarse shouting "Viva Wilson!" The ecstatic mobs reinforced the President's conviction that he alone spoke for the people of Europe, indeed of the world, and that with their support he could compel their leaders to accept a "peace without victory." This was a fundamental error. The masses who adored Wilson also hated the Germans and were determined to gain both revenge and recompense for the war. On the very day the president reached Paris, British voters gave David Lloyd George a vote of approval in an election notable for the government's promise to squeeze Germany "until the pips squeak." Wilson's real problem lay less with the leaders, many of whom (like Lloyd George) had considerable sympathy with his aims, than with the people, who forced the leaders into extreme positions.

The Peace Conference at Paris opened on January 12, 1919 in an atmosphere of seething unrest. "I am doubtful," Lloyd George later told Parliament, "whether any body of men with a difficult task have worked under greater difficulties—stones crackling on the roof and crashing through windows, and sometimes wild men screaming through the keyholes." Since no effective treaty could be drafted by delegates from twenty-seven nations meeting at one time, the conference turned the chief task over to a Council of Ten which quickly gave way to a Council of Four: Wilson, Lloyd George, Clemenceau, and, although he was often absent, Vittorio Orlando of Italy. The eloquent Orlando was concerned only with problems affecting Italy; the energetic Lloyd George, though anxious to preserve British power, had a larger view.

Most of the debates in Paris revolved around the aspirations of one of the Four: Woodrow Wilson. His strength stemmed from his understanding that the world could ill afford another global conflict and that balance-of-power politics would almost certainly prove inadequate to prevent one. He also recognized that a vindictive peace would never last. His great weaknesses were that he had little comprehension of power and that he thought in abstractions. Wilson's attitude, wrote Walter Weyl, "is part of a curiously a priori metaphysical idealism. His world stands firmly on its head. Ideas do not rest upon facts but facts on ideas. . . . To him railroad cars are not railroad cars but a gray general thing called Transportation; people are not men and women, corporeal, gross, very human beings, but Humanity—Humanity very much in the abstract."

Wilson's chief foe, Clemenceau, a fierce partisan who had won the sobriquet of "The Tiger," was now seventy-eight. He sat at the conference table, a black skull cap on his wrinkled head, with burning memories of the past—of the Franco-Prussian War, of the humiliation at Sedan, of the siege of Paris, during which people had been forced to eat cats to stay alive, of that second invasion of 1914, of the bodies piled high at Verdun, of the ruthlessness of the Germans as they retreated. He had one interest, France, and one concern, that Germany must never march again. If Wilson could assure him of that, they could agree. He wanted either the promise of American armed power or the destruction of the sources of German strength. For the rest, he cared nothing. "God gave us the Ten Commandments, and we broke them," Clemenceau allegedly declared. "Wilson gives us the Fourteen Points. We shall see."

Often depicted as a fool trapped by the wily diplomats of Europe (John Maynard Keynes called him a "blind and deaf Don Quixote"), Wilson was in fact an adroit negotiator. He succeeded in preventing a distribution of colonial spoils on crude imperialist lines and instead obtained adoption of the mandate system (primarily the contribution of Jan Smuts of South Africa). He held to the principle of self-determination in blocking Italy's claim to the Yugoslav port of Fiume and in opposing Clemenceau's proposals for a buffer state west of the Rhine or permanent French occupation of the territory. When the conference deadlocked, the president threatened to return home, and the French were forced to compromise on occupation of the Rhineland for a maximum of fifteen years and of the Saar for the same period, with a plebiscite at the end of that time to determine whether the Saarlanders wanted to belong to France or Germany. In return, Wilson agreed to a treaty promising armed aid if France were the victim of an "unprovoked" attack by Germany, although both he and Clemenceau should have known that the Senate would never agree to such a pact. Even though the Versailles treaty did not conform wholly to the principle of self-determination, never in the history of Europe were so few people left under foreign domination. Winston Churchill estimated that after the new boundary lines of 1919 were drawn, less than 3 per cent of the people of Europe would have preferred to live in another country.

Wilson's most spectacular triumph came when the Conference on January 25, 1919, voted to incorporate the League of Nations as an integral part of the treaty. The most important feature of the League Covenant was Article X, which committed member nations to respect and preserve the territorial integrity and political independence of one another and, in case of an act of aggression, consult on the options of invoking economic or military sanctions. In contrast to Clemenceau, who favored an international police force, Wilson put his main hope for peace in moral suasion. He thought that with most of the countries of the world in agreement on the principle of collective security, and with the forum offered by the League, sanctions would be needed only as a last resort. On February 15 Wilson, flushed with victory as the last important details of the structure of the League of Nations were put in place, sailed for home for a month-long stay.

At home, he encountered dismayingly strong opposition on Capitol Hill. He told the Democratic National Committee that his critics were "blind and little, provincial people. . . . They have not even good working imitations of minds." But he was brought up short when Henry Cabot Lodge introduced a Republican round robin, signed by 39 senators or senators-elect, more than enough to defeat the treaty, which required two-thirds approval. It declared that "the constitution of the League of Nations in the form now proposed to the peace conference should not be accepted by the United States." Furthermore, the round robin stated, no League proposal should be considered until the peace had been concluded. That night, Wilson, who had returned for a brief visit to America, struck back at his critics at an enthusiastic rally in New York. "When that treaty comes back," he announced, "gentlemen on this side will find the covenant not only in it, but so many threads of the treaty tied to the covenant that you cannot dissect the covenant from the treaty without destroying the whole vital structure."

Lodge made his point, though. When Wilson went back to Paris, he was forced to renegotiate in order to place some of the Republican demands in the League Covenant. He gained specific recognition for the Monroe Doctrine and inserted a two-year "escape" clause providing for the withdrawal of member nations from the League. In return for these concessions, the other members of the Big Four required concessions also, and Wilson's hand was weakened. "You come over here," one delegate shouted, "and dictate what we should do and what we should not do, and yet you do not let us have our say as to what you propose doing over there!"

Attacked by partisan nationalists at home, confronted by an alliance of European nationalists at Paris, Wilson had to abandon, wholly or in part, many of his cherished principles. Although he believed in open covenants openly arrived at, the treaty was drafted behind closed doors. Although he espoused the self-determination of nations, he consented to turn over the Austrian Tyrol to Italy, to put Germans under Polish rule in Silesia and the Corridor, and to allow Japan to take over the German sphere of influence in Shantung. Although he advocated a peace among equals, he agreed that Germany must pay an immediate indemnity of $5 billion, sign a blank check for future reparations (including the full cost of pensions to Allied soldiers), surrender vast amounts of coal- and iron-rich territory, lose much of her merchant marine, and be stripped of her entire overseas empire. Although he had expressed doubt about the causes of the war, the treaty pinned the "war guilt" on Germany. The document made no mention of freedom of the seas and did nothing to break down economic barriers, in part because, as Wilson confessed on one occasion, he was "not much interested in the economic subjects." Nonetheless, when Wilson sailed home from Europe, he brought with him a treaty that included provision for the league that was his heart's desire.

The League of Nations met a warm response in the United States, but also summoned up determined resistance. In the summer of 1919, the majority of the American people appear to have favored entrance into the League; the proposal received the indorsement of thirty-three governors of both parties. If the League were not approved, wrote an Ohio editor, "God pity us all, for there will be war from now to kingdom come." The chief opposition came from a group of about fourteen Republican and two Democratic irreconcilables led by Senator William Borah of Idaho, who vowed war to the death on the "unholy thing with the holy name." "If the Savior of man," asserted the intractable Borah, "would revisit the earth and declare for a League of Nations, I would be opposed to it." Morbidly fearful of the emasculation of American nationality, former Senator Albert Beveridge denounced the League as the work of "amiable old male grannies who, over their afternoon tea, are planning to denationalize America and denationalize the Nation's manhood." German-Americans execrated the treaty as a merciless *Diktat,* Italian-Americans were infuriated by Wilson's resistance to seizure of Fiume by Italy, and Irish-Americans insisted that the League was a British conspiracy. Progressives were horrified by the severity of the treaty; the terms of the pact, wrote La Follette, were "enough to chill the heart of the world."

Powerful as the irreconcilables were, they alone did not have enough votes to kill the treaty. More important was the band of "strong reservationists" led by Senator Lodge who wanted, at the very least, major stipulations before approving the treaty. Some of the strong reservationists would have been content with that; others merely used the demands to conceal their outright hostility to the League. Among the strong reservationists, the Roosevelt-Lodge group played a critical role. In July, 1918, Beveridge wrote Roosevelt, "Wilson has hoisted the motley flag of international-ism. . . . That makes the issue, does it not? Straight American-ism for us." Roosevelt answered, "You understand exactly how we feel." When Alice Roosevelt Longworth, Teddy's daughter, saw Wilson enter the White House on his return from Paris, she made the sign of the evil eye and cried: "A murrain on him, a murrain on him, a murrain on him!"

As chairman of the Senate Foreign Relations Committee, Lodge held a strategic redoubt. Although he professed to favor the Versailles treaty with reservations, Lodge packed the commit-tee with senators who opposed it in any form. With public opin-ion against him, Lodge resorted to delaying tactics until opposi-tion to the League could build. He was not an isolationist; he was, if anything, more willing than Wilson to engage in European power politics. But he was a fierce Republican partisan with his eye on the 1920 election. Furthermore, he fancied himself a "scholar in politics," and he resented Wilson's assumption of the same role. "I never expected to hate anyone in politics with the hatred I feel towards Wilson," Lodge had written Roosevelt in 1915. As the historian John Garraty concluded, "In the last analysis, Lodge preferred a dead league to the one proposed by Wilson."

Faced by such formidable adversaries, Wilson could hope to prevail only by adding to the votes of faithful Democrats those of the "mild reservationists," and by courting the latter group among the Republicans. Unfortunately, he could not bring him-self to conciliate the doubters in the Senate; many of them, he felt, were men with "bungalow minds." When the Democratic floor leader, Senator Martin of Virginia, told Wilson that he was not sure the treaty could win the required two-thirds vote, the President was furious. "Martin!" he rasped, "Anyone who opposes me in that I'll crush! *The Senate must take its medicine.*" He hated controversy, of which he had had his fill in Paris, and he rebelled against further compromise where he felt a matter of principle was involved. "Better a thousand times to go down fighting," Wilson told his wife, "than to dip your colours to dishonourable compromise."

Through the summer of 1919, while Lodge held intentionally fruitless hearings, opposition to the League mounted, as the spotlight focused on professional haters of England like Senator James Reed, still nursing grievances over the Stamp Act, and on ridiculous warnings that the League would be dominated by the Vatican or by the colored races of the world. While Wilson was in Paris, twenty-six Democratic members of the Massachusetts legislature cabled him to return home to reduce the high cost of living, "which we consider far more important than the League of Nations." Passenger ships docked with their cargoes of war-weary soldiers, released from the nightmare of shell barrages and lice-ridden trenches, who returned with tales of being fleeced by French storekeepers and condescended to by the British.

Exasperated by Lodge's delaying tactics, Wilson, like a British Prime Minister, decided to go to the country. In early September he left Washington on an eight-thousand-mile journey. Warned by his doctor that he was in no physical condition to undertake such a strenuous tour, Wilson, perhaps unconsciously seeking martyrdom, determined to go ahead anyway. As he crossed the Middle West, he met with indifferent success—in some places high enthusiasm, in others moderate interest—but when he reached the Far West, he was greeted with ovations, and his tour of California was nothing short of a triumphal procession, with large crowds voicing their approval of the League. As he swung back east toward Washington, he stopped at Pueblo, Colorado, where he delivered one of the great speeches of his career. People wept openly as he talked of the graves of doughboys in France and said that Americans should never again have to die in foreign fields. That night, exhausted by the grueling schedule, Wilson was stricken with severe pain. Determined to go on nonetheless, he was only with great difficulty persuaded to cancel the remainder of his tour. Four days after returning to the White House, the President was found by Mrs. Wilson lying unconscious on the floor. He had suffered a stroke that paralyzed the left side of his body. He would never again rise from his sickbed.

The speaking tour proved to be a disaster. Despite his warm reception in the West, Wilson did not change a single Senate vote. More important, his illness deprived the League cause of its leader. For seven and a half months the president did not meet his cabinet. For the next year and a half, from October, 1919 to March, 1921, the country had no president; it was ruled by a regency headed by his wife. Although the stroke did not becloud his mind, it changed Wilson's personality. He became more irritable; he lost his judgment; at times, he broke down in tears. Compromise became less possible than ever.

On November 6, 1919, Lodge finally reported the treaty out of committee, but appended to it fourteen reservations, giving the competitive senator the same number as Wilson's fourteen points. The most important of these declared that the United States, in accepting Article X, assumed no obligation to fulfill its requirements unless Congress so provided in each case. If this was

Lodge's price, the Senate Democrats were willing to pay it. Wilson was not. He denounced the Lodge reservation as a "knife thrust at the heart of the treaty," because it removed any *moral* obligation on the part of the United States.

On November 19, a Senate motion to approve the treaty with the Lodge reservations failed by a vote of 39 for to 55 against. Under orders from Wilson, Democrats voted to reject the motion, and they were joined in opposition by the irreconcilables, who did not want the treaty in any form. An attempt to ratify the treaty without reservations lost 38–53, with only a single Republican voting in favor. The treaty, it should be noted, was not defeated because of the two-thirds requisite; neither side could get even a majority.

When Congress reconvened in December, 1919, a groundswell of public opinion demanded a compromise to save the treaty. Neither Wilson nor Lodge would budge. When Lodge met with Democrats to talk over terms, Senator Borah threatened to remove him as majority leader, and Lodge broke off negotiations. Even without Borah's intervention, it is unlikely that Lodge would have yielded enough to create a document acceptable to Wilson. And Wilson was more adamant than ever. He warned that he would simply put the treaty in his pocket if the Senate ratified it with the Lodge reservations.

Exasperated by Wilson's obstinacy, his party split. The most important Democratic newspapers announced they would now go along with the Lodge reservations if that was the only way America could enter the League, and a number of Democratic senators broke ranks. On March 19, 1920, the Senate voted for the second and last time on the Versailles treaty. Twenty-one Democrats defied Wilson and voted for the treaty with the Lodge reservations, enough to yield a 49–35 majority. But it fell seven votes short of the necessary two-thirds. Twenty-three Democrats, at Wilson's request, had joined the Republican bitter-enders to defeat the motion. "We can always depend on Mr. Wilson," Senator Brandegee observed cynically to Lodge. "He never has failed us."

Who killed American membership in the League? Thomas A. Bailey has written: "In the final analysis the treaty was slain in the house of its friends rather than in the house of its enemies. In the final analysis it was not the two-thirds rule, or the 'irreconcilables,' or Lodge, or the 'strong' and 'mild reservationists,' but Wilson and his docile following who delivered the fatal stab. . . . This was the supreme act of infanticide. With his own sickly hands Wilson slew his own brain child."

If one accepts this judgment, one must think Wilson mistaken on at least one of two crucial points. Wilson believed that if he had accepted the reservations, one or more of the other nations would have refused to ratify the treaty. No one can say with finality whether this was so. Britain might have balked at the reservation stating that the U.S. would not be bound by decisions where the British Empire cast six votes, as well as the reservation placing the Senate on record in favor of Irish independence. Latin-American nations might have taken exception to the reservation on the Monroe Doctrine, Japan to Senate refusal to sanction the Shantung arrangement. It seems more probable, however, that the other powers would have preferred American ratification, even with such egregious reservations, to absence of the United States from the League. In any event, that assumption was worth a try.

More important was Wilson's objection to Lodge's reservation on Article X. Since, under any circumstances, the United States could not send troops without action by Congress, Wilson's strong protest appears tenuous at first glance. (So, it should be added, does Lodge's persistence.) Yet there was much sense in Wilson's refusal to accept a world organization which gave the illusion of security but did not actually gain it. Although most Americans favored the League, few understood the implications of collective security. The League fight became polarized as one between internationalists and isolationists, but the real issue was much more complex. Wilson himself understood that the League involved a sharp break with the tradition of isolation. Many of the "internationalists," on the other hand, supported the League not as an assumption of new responsibilities but as a magical formula that would free the United States from the obligation of foreign wars.

In the end Wilson failed largely because the country had never really abandoned its isolationist predilections, particularly the assumption that the United States unaided could maintain its national security. During the war, these convictions were driven underground. It is astonishing that despite the tradition of isolation, despite Wilson's collapse, despite partisan bitterness and the animosity of ethnic groups, 85 per cent of the senators voting on November 19 were willing to accept the League in some form. Yet even if the country had entered the League, it is doubtful that Americans would have been willing to assume their full obligations. The United States had not been prepared by a threat to its own security for the kind of enterprise it was later to undertake in Korea. It had insufficient incentive for abandoning either isolation or absolute national sovereignty. It would take the chastening experience of World War II, Hiroshima, and the Cold War to provide that incentive.

This is not to say that Wilson did not make serious blunders, although his responsibility for the failure to accept the League scarcely matched that of Lodge. As early as the spring of 1917, Wilson knew of the secret treaties; yet he did nothing to force the Allies to rescind them. At the time he held all the aces; he could even have fought a wholly maritime war until he got the terms of peace he wanted. Yet out of a deepseated inability to face unpleasantness and a Calvinist sense of destiny, Wilson ignored the fact of the treaties, and he proclaimed idealistic war aims as though the treaties did not exist. His messianic zeal and his cold self-righteousness earned him enemies, and in the fight for the peace treaty in the Senate, he was unable to bring himself to seek an effective compromise.

Wilson's defeat is a sad chapter in American history, even if one rejects the more romanticized versions of it. A generation later, it became commonplace to say that the refusal of the United States to enter the League was responsible for Hitler's conquests and a needless second world war, but, in fact, it would have required more than Wilson's moral force and a greater commitment to collective security than the West ever made to have stopped Hitler and averted war. Furthermore, the League, far from being a concert of altruistic nations, was an instrumentality of the victors, and, though Wilson anticipated that the League would in the future redress any injustices in the peace settlement, it was not at all clear how change was to come. In 1917 Wilson claimed that "the United States was the only nation which was absolutely disinterested," but in fact American commercial interests would have flourished in the kind of world order he championed, and there were decided limits to Wilson's idealism, as the Japanese learned when he killed off their proposal to recognize the equality of the races. Nonetheless, for all his shortcomings, Wilson understood and articulated, better than any man of his time, the need to begin to create a structure to facilitate international agreements. He won eternal fame by achieving more than any other man ever had to bring the nations of the world into a parliament of man. For that very reason, his own failings were deeply tragic for himself and for the world.

4

Red Scare

In the year 1919, Senator McKellar of Tennessee advocated sending native-born American citizens with radical beliefs to a penal colony in Guam. South Carolina's James F. Byrnes asked for the intervention of the federal government to balk an uprising of Negroes that he declared Reds were planning in the South. Some New York schoolteachers were dismissed after a campaign to determine "Who's Red and Who's True Blue." General Leonard Wood, the Army Chief of Staff, noted his approval of a minister's call for the deportation of Bolshevists "in ships of stone with sails of lead, with the wrath of God for a breeze and with hell for their first port." "If I had my way with these ornery wild-eyed Socialists and I.W.W.'s," shouted the evangelist Billy Sunday, "I would stand them up before a firing squad and save space on our ships." In Indiana a jury deliberated two minutes before acquitting Frank Petroni, who had shot and killed a man for yelling, "To hell with the United States!" The great Red Scare of 1919 was underway.

Although there had been concern about radicalism, particularly anarchism, before the war, and although radicals had been censured during the war as pro-German, the Red Scare did not really begin until the creation of the Communists' Third International in March, 1919. The Bolshevik Revolution of November, 1917, had awakened fears, but it was less the revolution itself than the spread of revolutionary principles to other countries that excited alarm. In March, 1919, Communist uprisings in Bavaria and Hungary aroused anxiety that bolshevism might engulf the Western world. Few doubted that a revolution in the United States had a high place on the Communists' agenda. Karl Radek, the executive secretary of the Third International, boasted that money sent to Germany for the Spartacist uprising "was as nothing compared to the funds transmitted to New York for the purpose of spreading bolshevism in the United States."

If the zealots of the Red Scare erred in failing to distinguish between genuine revolutionaries and radicals of a peaceful persuasion, the Socialists themselves contributed to the confusion. For a time, Socialists of the most varied persuasions were pro-Bolshevik. The anti-war and uncompromisingly anticapitalist position of the Bolsheviks had an electrifying appeal to American radicals. Debs, who, as Daniel Bell has remarked, had "an almost compulsive desire to be 'left' of orthodox labor opinion," gave outright support to the Russian Revolution, although he was to sour on it in the last years of his life.

Even before the Russian Revolution, Bolshevik leaders had come to the United States, and in a stunningly short time Russian and other foreign elements would utterly transform the American left. At the end of 1916, Nikolai Bukharin arrived in New York, where he edited the journal of the Russian Socialist Federation; early in 1917, Leon Trotsky joined the staff of the same paper, in the back of a rank cellar at 77 St. Mark's Place. Foreign-language federations had always been a minority within the American Socialist party, but the Bolshevik Revolution brought a flood of new members into the Slavic groups. Soon the foreign-language federations—enthusiastically pro-Bolshevik—outnumbered the

English-speaking groups in the Socialist party. In September, 1919, at a Russian Federation hall in Chicago which they renamed "Smolny" after a school for daughters of the nobility that became the first Soviet headquarters in Petrograd, the foreign-language federations organized the American Communist party. Only 7 per cent of the new party spoke or understood English.

At the same time, a left-wing faction within the Socialist party, led by native-born radicals, attempted to convert the party to the Bolshevik pattern of an immediate revolution guided by a small cadre of party workers. The most prominent member of the native-born left-wing faction was John Reed, an Oregonian who had been a cheerleader at Harvard. This romantic, who had followed war, strikes, and revolution from New Jersey to Mexico, ardently admired the Russian coup. He declared approvingly: "The Bolsheviki believe in democracy of the working class, and no democracy for anybody else." Reed, however, was unwilling to permit the radical movement in America to fall into the hands of foreign-language groups. In September, 1919, meeting at the same time as the foreign-language Communists, the Reed faction organized the Communist Labor party. This party was also overwhelmingly composed of members who did not know English, but its leaders—men like Reed and Ben Gitlow—were English-speaking. No question of ideology divided them; both parties, which ultimately, under orders of the Comintern, were to merge as the Communist Party of America, sent envoys to Moscow to plead for recognition. Henceforth, the fate of American Communism would be determined not in the United States but in the Kremlin.

The Russian Revolution came at a critical moment for American radicals. American Socialists were demoralized; after a generation of agitation, they were weaker than they had been many years before. The Bolshevik coup not only promised a reversal of fortunes but suggested that radicals need not go through the painful process of educating a majority to their point of view. In May, 1917, there had been only 11,000 members of the Bolshevik party in all of Russia. Five months later, the Bolsheviks held power. Captivated by this pattern of success, many American radicals, knowing they outnumbered the May, 1917 Bolsheviks, believed that a revolution in the United States was imminent, and some thought it would come in a matter of months. John Reed wrote Roger Baldwin, who had been sent to jail as a conscientious objector, that he would be freed from prison by the workers long before his sentence ended.

The belief in imminent revolution that stirred the Communists was only one aspect of a spirit of millenarianism that swept the United States and Europe immediately after the war. John Dos Passos recalled of the spring of 1919: "Any spring is a time of overturn, but then Lenin was alive, the Seattle general strike had seemed the beginning of the flood instead of the beginning of the ebb, Americans in Paris were groggy with theatre and painting and music; Picasso was to rebuild the eye, Stravinski was cramming the Russian steppes into our ears, currents of energy seemed breaking out everywhere as young guys climbed out of their uniforms, imperial America was all shiny with the new idea of the Ritz, in every direction the countries of the world stretched out starving and angry, ready for anything turbulent and new, whenever you went to the movies you saw Charlie Chaplin."

Organized labor had long been the despair of the radicals—Lenin dismissed Samuel Gompers, head of the AF of L, as merely an "agent of the bourgeoisie"—but in 1919 the millennial spirit caught up many of the old-line union leaders, some of whom had tasted national power for the first time during the war. It was less the Russian Revolution, however, than the Nottingham program of the British Labour party, with its demand for nationalization of basic industries, that piqued their imagination. Most important of the postwar proposals was the Plumb Plan: the railway brotherhoods, which had flourished under government operation of the lines during the war, advocated nationalization of the railroads. Despite the opposition of Gompers, the AF of L endorsed the Plan, which congressional critics denounced as "a bold, bald, naked attempt to sovietize the railroads of the country."

If the Socialist support of bolshevism served to wipe out distinctions between various shades of radicalism, the growing militancy of organized labor in 1919 appeared to align labor unions with world-wide radicalism. The postwar inflation, which saw the cost of living climb in 1920 to 105 per cent above the prewar level, not only created a public sense of irritation on which the Red Scare could feed but also touched off a wave of strikes by workers attempting to keep up with rising prices. In 1919 no fewer than four million workers walked out on their jobs. Accustomed to orthodox union techniques, the country was deeply shaken by the dramatic strikes of 1919.

When, on January 21, 1919, 35,000 Seattle shipyard workers struck for higher wages and shorter workdays, the Seattle Central Labor Council, representing all organized labor in the region, voted to conduct a general strike to support their brothers, a decision taken under the influence of an admirer of the Russian Revolution. For five days the city of Seattle was paralyzed; streetcars ceased to run, schools closed their doors, business came to a standstill. In the end, the general strike was crushed, but not before it had alienated middle-class opinion and persuaded the country that a genuine threat of revolution might be in prospect.

Many Americans had always associated radicalism with terrorism, and in the spring of 1919 the popular stereotype began to take on substance. On April 28 a small brown parcel arrived in the office of the anti-labor mayor in Seattle; when opened, it was found to contain a homemade bomb. On the following day a similar package came to the home of former Senator Thomas W. Hardwick of Georgia; when his maid opened it, it blew off her hands. The next day a New York postal clerk, reading a newspaper account of the Hardwick episode on the subway, remembered having set aside sixteen similar parcels, bearing "Gimbel's" stickers, for insufficient postage. He raced back to the post office and located them before any damage was done; postal authorities around the country, warned by New York, intercepted eighteen more. The packages had been sent (timed for May Day) to John D. Rockefeller, Postmaster General Burleson, Judge Kenesaw Mountain Landis, and a group of other foes of organized labor and advocates of immigration restriction. In addition, parcels had been mailed to men who were apparently thought to be enemies of labor or of radicalism but who actually had liberal records: Senator Hardwick, Justice Holmes, Secretary of Labor William B. Wilson, and Frederic C. Howe, commissioner of immigration at Ellis Island and a warm friend of the foreign-born.

On the evening of June 2, a new series of bombs exploded in eight different cities at the same hour. Once more, there was little logic to the attacks, which struck indiscriminately at minor officials and major figures. Most important was the bombing of Attorney General A. Mitchell Palmer's home in Washington, D.C., which shattered the front of his house. (Palmer's neighbors across the street, Franklin and Eleanor Roosevelt, narrowly escaped the blast.) The bomb-thrower himself was blown to pieces by the blast, but enough evidence was found to indicate that he was an Italian alien from Philadelphia and an anarchist.

The detonations of June 2 were obviously the result of a coordinated effort and had the semblance of a revolutionary plot, but it is extremely unlikely that Communists had anything to do with them. The first set appears to have been the work of one or more deranged individuals, the second set the activity of anarchists who were probably psychotic. In no way did the bombings fit into Communist strategy, and the manner in which they were carried out suggested the actions not of professional revolutionaries but of ignorant and deluded men. At the same time, it is understandable that many Americans, already edgy over bolshevism and increased labor militancy, viewed the explosions as an organized conspiracy to capture control of the government by violence.

At this critical juncture, with the middle class uncertain whether workers in America were pledged to their own government or to some alien creed, the Boston police went on strike. Underpaid, imposed on, with miserable working conditions, they had voted in the summer of 1919 to affiliate with the AF of L. Policemen in many American cities had taken such action without arousing public concern, but the decision of the Boston police was seen, in the hothouse atmosphere of 1919, as proof of radical inclinations, although the police were not at all involved in radical activity. Boston's police commissioner, a tactless, overbearing man with a long record of hostility to labor, brought the issue to a head on September 8, 1919, by firing nineteen policemen for union membership. In response, the angry police walked off their jobs. Although the police had serious grievances and although they had been provoked by the commissioner, the strike was a serious blunder, for it left the city without protection and arrayed the middle class solidly against them.

Within twenty-four hours, violence broke out on the streets of Boston. Two men were killed in South Boston and another in

Scollay Square. Shop windows were smashed on Summer Street and Washington Street, and passers-by helped themselves to shoes and neckties. The actual amount of damage done in the rioting and looting was small, but the country fastened on the image of thugs brazenly rolling dice on Boston Common in the shadow of the State House while the city was left defenseless against criminals until prominent businessmen and Harvard students organized a vigilante force. Public opinion strongly condemned the strike, President Wilson calling it "a crime against civilization."

Samuel Gompers urged the men to return to their jobs and let the issues be arbitrated, and the police unanimously agreed. But the commissioner, supported by the nation's press, was determined to punish the strikers; he declared that no policemen would be reinstated and that he would recruit an entirely new force. The next day, Governor Calvin Coolidge, who had done almost nothing during the walkout, wired Gompers his refusal to arbitrate: "There is no right to strike against the public safety by anybody, anywhere, anytime." Overnight, Coolidge became a national hero.

Two days after the Boston police struck, steel workers issued a strike call for September 22, 1919. Of all areas of industry, steel had put up the stiffest resistance to organized labor; since the bloody Homestead strike of 1892, the AF of L had virtually abandoned efforts to unionize the mills. With the confidence gained from its stronger position during the war, the federation decided on a new attempt. A different kind of leadership was required, and it was supplied by William Z. Foster, reared in a foul Philadelphia slum, who had, after a stint with the radical IWW in the mining and lumber camps of the West, left the Wobblies to organize industrial unions within the AF of L.

The grievances of the steelworkers were acute. Nearly half the men worked twelve hours a day, seven days a week, for an average wage of $28 a week; many of the workers lived in drab shacks of the most primitive sort. The industry was run by autocrats like Judge Elbert Gary, the head of U.S. Steel and a fierce defender of the open shop. The strike began when Gary refused to recognize the union or even to meet such elementary demands as one day's rest in every seven; by the end of the week, 365,000 men were out. Although the country initially had considerable sympathy for the workers' demands, the steel companies, aided by Attorney General Palmer, aroused the public against the strike by depicting it as another radical outbreak. Since radicals did in fact play some part, particularly in Gary, the attempt to discredit the strike as a Red uprising gained credence. With public opinion against them, the workers had little hope. After two months, they returned without a single gain; the strike had cost twenty lives and over $100 million in wages.

While the steel strike was sputtering to an end, a new stoppage—the third major strike that fall—was called in the bituminous coal industry. The United Mine Workers had negotiated a no-strike compact with the Fuel Administration in 1917, to expire in March, 1920; when the war ended, the union contended that the agreement expired too. Although anthracite miners had gotten raises, the soft-coal miners had received none. By the summer of 1919, as food prices zoomed upward, the miners were in almost open rebellion against their leaders, who were forced to yield to demands for a strike.

The great coal strike of 1919 drew workingmen, unions, industry and government into a fierce contest of wills, set in the matrix of the Red Scare. Despite the conservatism of the strike leader, John L. Lewis, and the opposition of the UMW to radical unionists, the mine owners, following the example of the steel operators, pinned the label of radicalism on the walkout. The chief spokesman for the operators even charged that the strike was being financed by Moscow gold on direct orders from Lenin and Trotsky. Woodrow Wilson, partially recovered from his stroke but still seriously ill, denounced the proposed strike as "a grave moral and legal wrong." Cut off from the more liberal members of his cabinet, the president was persuaded by Attorney-General Palmer to take drastic action. Palmer, using powers under the wartime Lever Act, obtained a temporary injunction from a federal judge to halt the strike, although union leaders had supported the Lever Act only after a promise from Wilson that it would not be used against them. Moreover, since the Fuel Administration had stopped controlling coal prices, the workers concluded that Wilson was arguing that the war was over for the operators but not for them. With 394,000 men out of the mines, Lewis calmly perused Homer's *Iliad* while he waited for the owners to surrender. But when the judge issued a second, and permanent, injunction, Lewis declared, "We cannot fight the government," and ordered the men back to work. Defying both Lewis and the court, the miners refused to return; the coal strike went on as though nothing had happened. It finally required a personal appeal from the President, accompanied by an offer of a substantial wage increase, to end the walkout.

By the autumn of 1919 millions of old-stock Americans had come to believe that the country was faced by the menace of alien revolutionaries. Up to a point, that alarm was understandable. Millions of immigrants had entered the country in the past decade, and in the recent war they had shown that they continued to hold fierce attachments to their homelands. In World War I, sabotage by aliens had not been a figment of the imagination. Communists had actually overturned governments in other lands, and their foreign-speaking alien counterparts in America had every intention of using the same revolutionary methods to seize power.

But during the Red Scare political careerists, reactionary employer groups, and assorted fanatics did not merely address the legitimate concerns about public safety, but also stirred up new alarms and exploited the sense of panic, in part out of ignorance, in part to serve their own ends. An Anti-Saloon League official asserted that the bombing of Palmer's home "was inspired by Germans with wet tendencies," while the head of New York's Lusk Committee declared, in all seriousness, that radicalism "was started here and elsewhere by paid agents of the Junker class in Germany as a part of their programme of industrial and military world conquest." On May Day, 1919, some four hundred World War I veterans invaded the offices of New York's Socialist paper, *The Call,* and brutally mauled the staff. Industrialists took full advantage of the Red Scare mentality to characterize the closed shop as "sovietism in disguise," and when rail workers struck for such modest demands as overtime pay on Sundays and holidays and a twenty-minute lunch break, they were denounced as Bolsheviki.

As the wave of strikes followed the bombings, the government was urged to take action against alien radicals, with the spotlight focusing on Attorney General A. Mitchell Palmer. Regarded by many as the father of women's suffrage and the child labor law, a strong advocate of the League of Nations, Palmer was the prototype of the advanced Wilsonian liberal. The Democratic party's contact man with labor in the 1916 campaign, he was appointed Attorney General partly because of his popularity with labor and the foreign-born. Yet no sooner had he been sworn into office in March, 1919, than he started a campaign against enemy aliens. After the June 2 bombings, he hired a reputed expert on anarchism, and asked for and received a $500,000 increase in his budget in order to combat radicalism. In August he set up an antiradical division in the Department of Justice under young J. Edgar Hoover.

On November 7, 1919, the first of the Palmer raids began, with the arrest of 250 members of the Union of Russian Workers in a dozen cities. Many were roughly handled, particularly in New York City, where they were beaten by the police, and released with "blackened eyes and lacerated scalps." On December 21, 249 aliens, most of whom had committed no criminal offense, were deported to Russia on an army transport. Despite the alarm about a Bolshevik conspiracy, few of the people deported were Communists; most were anarchists, including Emma Goldman and Alexander Berkman, and many of them were philosophical anarchists who had no intention of ever using violence.

Palmer turned next to the Communists. Working with an agent in the Labor Department, which had authority over deportations, the Attorney General secured warrants for the arrest of over 3,000 aliens who were members either of the Communist party or the Communist Labor party. On a single night in January, 1920, more than 4,000 alleged Communists were arrested in coast-to-coast raids in 33 cities. If the persons arrested were citizens, they were turned over to state authorities for prosecution under antisyndicalist laws; if they were aliens, they were held for deportation.

Palmer's agents carried out his orders with abandon. They invaded union headquarters and meeting halls, even homes. People were held incommunicado, denied counsel, and subjected to kangaroo trials. In one city, prisoners were handcuffed, chained together, and marched through the streets. In New England, hundreds of people were arrested who had no connection with radicalism of any kind. In Detroit, 300 people were arrested on false charges, held for a week in jail, forced to sleep on the bare floor of a vile corridor, and denied food for 24 hours, only to be found innocent of any involvement in revolutionary activity. Not for at least half a century, perhaps at no time in our history, had there been such a wholesale violation of civil liberties. The raids yielded almost nothing in the way of arms and small results in the capture of dangerous revolutionaries, but they did reduce the membership of the Communist parties by at least 80 percent. Although a few individuals (the steel baron Charles M. Schwab was one) protested against the raids, Palmer emerged from the episode a national hero. "There is only one way to deal with anarchy, and *that is to crush it,*" commented one law journal, which expressed the hope that punishment would be *"not a slap on the wrist, but a broad-axe on the neck."*

Yet the Red Scare ended almost as quickly as it began. The beginning of the end came in New York State. Directed by the irresponsible Lusk Committee, the antiradical campaign there reached its climax when the state legislature expelled five Socialist members of the Assembly, although the Socialist party was legally recognized and the members were innocent of any offense. Throughout the country, newspapers and public figures, including the *Chicago Tribune* and Senator Warren G. Harding of Ohio, denounced the action. Most effective was Charles Evans Hughes, who not only reproached the legislature but offered the Socialists legal counsel. Legislators condemned Hughes as "disloyal" and "pro-German," but the campaign against the radicals had been dealt a heavy blow. Not only had a firm stand been taken on democratic principle, but the idea that the New York legislature felt threatened by five mild Socialists made the Red Scare appear more than a little ridiculous.

Early in 1920 an insurrection against Palmer in the Labor Department, led by Secretary of Labor Wilson and Assistant Secretary Louis Post, turned deportation proceedings in a saner direction. Aided by court decisions which held that men could not be deported on evidence illegally obtained, Post insisted on giving aliens proper counsel and the right to fair hearings. Convinced that Palmer had been violating civil liberties, Post cancelled action against dozens of aliens and by spring released nearly half of the men arrested in Palmer's January raids. Palmer demanded that Post be fired for his "tender solicitude for social revolution," but when Post was hauled before a congressional committee, he made such an excellent presentation that his critics were forced to back down. In the end, although 5,000 arrest warrants had been sworn out in late 1919, only a few more than 600 aliens were actually deported.

Finally, Palmer, seeking the 1920 presidential nomination, let his attempts to capitalize on the Red Scare get out of hand. In April he issued a series of warnings of a revolutionary plot that would be launched on May 1, 1920, as a step toward overthrowing the U.S. government. Buildings were placed under guard, public leaders were given police protection, state militias were called to the colors, and in New York City the entire police force of 11,000 men was put on 24-hour duty. May Day passed without a single outbreak of any kind. Not a shot was fired. Not a bomb exploded. As a result, the country, vexed at Palmer, concluded he had cried wolf once too often. Congress now turned to an investigation not of the radicals but of Palmer.

On September 16, 1920, at the lunch hour, a wagonload of bombs exploded in New York on the corner of Broad and Wall Streets, the financial center of the nation, killing 33 people, injuring over 200 more, and wrecking the building of the House of

Morgan. None of the people killed was a financier; all were work-ers—clerks, stenographers, runners. Palmer blamed the event on Bolsheviks conspiring to overthrow the government; a year be-fore, he would have had the nation behind him. This time, de-spite horror at the awful deed, judgment was suspended, and the country took the episode in stride, assuming, with logic, that it was probably the result of a group of demented anarchists, not a Communist plot.

By the end of 1920 the Red Scare in its most virulent form was over. It was pushed to the rear pages of the newspapers as the country turned to more absorbing topics like the Chicago Black Sox scandal, which involved bribery of big-league baseball players by gamblers. By 1920 the Communist wave had been turned back in Europe, and the nation, as it felt secure from external threats, came to realize that the internal danger had been vastly exagger-ated too. The ensuing decade, despite its chauvinism and conserv-atism, proved unreceptive to the spirit of the Red Scare; interest in politics receded to its lowest ebb in half a century as the coun-try sought release from the kind of political intensity epitomized by Palmer. When New York's insouciant mayor, Jimmy Walker, was asked to comment on a proposed censorship bill, he re-marked, "I have never yet heard of a girl being ruined by a book." In 1925 an American Legion committee deplored the fact that "Americans have become apathetic to the monotonous appeal of the patriotic exhorter," and by 1928, the Communist party, once a virtual outlaw, could be found on ballots in thirty-four states. In 1925, in *Gitlow v. New York,* the U.S. Supreme Court, though validating a law under which the Communist Ben Gitlow was convicted, acknowledged for the first time that the First Amend-ment was among the liberties protected by the Fourteenth

Amendment and hence binding on the states, and in 1931, in *Stromberg v. California,* the Court, in the case of the "girl Red," Yetta Stromberg, struck down California's red flag law as a violation of the Fourteenth Amendment right to free speech. (Two weeks later, in a landmark ruling in *Near v. Minnesota,* it extended this principle by safeguarding freedom of the press from actions by the state.) Nonetheless, the Red Scare produced a bitter heritage of suspicion of aliens, distrust of organized labor, hostility to reformers, and insistence on political conformity that served to smother reform efforts in the 1920s.

One legacy of the Red Scare left a running sore. In May, 1920, Nicola Sacco and Bartolomeo Vanzetti were arrested for a shoe-company robbery and the murder of a paymaster and his guard in South Braintree, Massachusetts. In July, 1921, Judge Webster Thayer sentenced them to death after a trial in which, critics argued, the court was swayed less by the evidence than by the anarchist beliefs and Italian origins of the accused. Thayer himself was heard to refer to them as "those anarchist bastards." For the next six years, they remained in prison while legal experts such as Felix Frankfurter punched holes in the case, judges and state officials heard and rejected appeals, and the fate of Sacco and Vanzetti became a matter of international concern. As the day of execution approached, riots in Paris took twenty lives, Londoners marched on the U.S. embassy, an American flag was burned in Casablanca, and in Uruguay workers declared a general strike, American products were boycotted, and the Chamber of Deputies formally requested President Coolidge to intervene. On August 23, 1927, their last appeal having been denied, Sacco and Vanzetti died in the electric chair.

Since all the forces of upper-class respectability—Judge

Thayer, the governor of Massachusetts, the president of Harvard, the best old families of the cradle of democracy—had a part in the affair, the execution of Sacco and Vanzetti appeared to be an act of class reprisal and made words like democracy and freedom seem merely cloaks for class interest. Scholars who re-examined the evidence in later years found it hard to believe that both of the men were innocent (though they did not deny that the judicial process was biased), but at the time intellectuals harbored no such doubts. The novelist John Dos Passos, who had stood watch in the shadows of Charlestown Prison, expressed the belief of many others that the case had wiped out all middle ground and split the nation into two warring camps.

> they have clubbed us off the streets   they are stronger they are rich   they hire and fire the politicians the news-papereditors the old judges the small men with reputations the collegepresidents the wardheelers (listen businessmen college-presidents judges   America will not forget her betray-ers). . . .
>   all right you have won   you will kill the brave men our friends tonight
>   America our nation has been beaten by strangers who have turned our language inside out who have taken the clean words our fathers spoke and made them slimy and foul. . . .
>   all right we are two nations

No single act did more to turn liberal intellectuals to radical-ism. "Don't you see the glory of this case," remarked a character in Upton Sinclair's *Boston* (1928). "It kills off the liberals." In the 1920s, most intellectuals were too non-political for radicalism to make much impact. "It was characteristic of the Jazz Age," re-corded Scott Fitzgerald, "that it had no interest in politics at all."

"Politics and voting," pontificated Gertrude Stein, "do not make any difference." But in the 1930s, after the crash of 1929 had split American society asunder, intellectuals outraged by the execution of Sacco and Vanzetti would join the radical cause. The Red Scare of 1919, apparently ended by the fall of 1920, would cast a long shadow over the politics of 1930s.

5

The Politics of Normalcy

By 1920 the nerves of the country had been rubbed raw by acrimony over the war, the debate on the League, the Red Scare, and postwar inflation. In a word, the nation had had enough of Wilsonism. The Wilson years climaxed a long era of muckraking, of harping upon the evils of society. A good number of Americans yearned for release from the preaching of the reformers and the demands they made for altruism and self-sacrifice. "The moralist unquestionably secures wide popular support; but he also wearies his audience," pointed out the historian Charles Seymour, "and many a voter has turned from Wilson in the spirit that led the Athenian to vote for the ostracism of Aristides, because he was tired of hearing him called 'The Just.'" Wilson had become, in Mark Sullivan's words, "the symbol of the exaltation that had turned sour, personification of the rapture that had now become gall, sacrificial whipping boy for the present bitterness."

Although Republican conservatives took full advantage of the rejection of Wilson, they were not alone in viewing him as a pariah. In 1920 one Democrat wrote another from South Dakota: "The bitterness toward Wilson is evident everywhere and deeply rooted. He hasn't a friend." Much of this bad feeling came from progressives who believed that Wilson had betrayed the cause.

The era of business supremacy is traditionally associated with the Republican reign in the 1920s, but it actually began in Wilson's final months when the government abruptly ended all of the wartime regulation. As it cut back severely on spending, unemployment soared to 20 percent, while between 1914 and 1920 prices more than doubled. When, in these bleak circumstances, workers went out on strike, they were shocked by the naked hostility of the Wilson administration. Yet if anti-Wilson sentiment was not confined to the well-to-do, they knew how to exploit it. At the Republican convention, Henry Cabot Lodge said of his longtime nemesis: "Mr. Wilson and his dynasty, his heirs and assigns, or anybody that is his, anybody who with bent knee has served his purposes, must be driven from all control, from all influence upon the Government of the United States."

The reaction against Wilson and the Democrats threw the nominating process out of balance. The Republican Old Guard, confident of victory in 1920, did not have to name men of stature; they could pick a weak party regular who they could control. They could afford to bypass the three strong candidates for the GOP nomination—the former Army Chief of Staff General Leonard Wood, Governor Frank Lowden of Illinois, and isolationist Senator Hiram Johnson of California. Although little public attention was paid to Ohio's Senator Warren Harding, as early as February his manager, Harry Daugherty, had predicted that the three front-runners would kill one another off and that Harding would get the nod from the Old Guard leaders who would dominate the convention. After the convention deadlocked, Daugherty forecast, the winner would be chosen by a gathering of "fifteen or twenty men, somewhat weary" at "about eleven minutes after two o'clock on Friday morning."

The Republican convention in Chicago did not quite follow

Daugherty's script but it came close. On Thursday, when the balloting began, the three leading candidates quickly established a stalemate, and Lodge recessed the meeting until the next day. At a suite in the Blackstone Hotel that night, a group of party leaders, mostly senators, debated what to do; although not all agreed, the majority decided on Harding. "This man Harding is no world beater," they told reporters, "but we think he is the best of the bunch." At a little after two o'clock on Friday morning, Harding entered the "smoke-filled room" in the Blackstone and was asked for and gave assurances that nothing in his background would embarrass the party. On the next day, after several ballots, he won the nomination. "Well," Harding allegedly said, "we drew to a pair of deuces and filled."

Although the story of the "smoke-filled room" quickly became a legend, Harding's nomination derived less from a cabal of senators who conspired to foist their candidate on the convention than from the fact that the senator embodied perfectly the conservatism of the delegates. President Nicholas Murray Butler of Columbia University later said that he had never witnessed such a shocking attempt to buy the presidency, and William Allen White of the Emporia, Kansas, *Gazette* wrote: "I have never seen a convention—and I have watched most of them since McKinley's first nomination—so completely dominated by sinister predatory economic forces as was this." But the lobbyists for industrial and financial interests did not have to force Harding on the delegates. A party reliable, he was the man the convention wanted. The times, said Connecticut's Senator Brandegee with a shrug, did not require "first-raters."

The Democrats showed little more aptitude for finding a man of first rank. Like the Republicans after Theodore Roosevelt's death in 1919, they had been deprived, by Wilson's incapacity, of their strongest leader. The President made matters still worse by indicating that, despite his illness and the no-third-term tradition, he wanted to be renominated. By his enigmatic role, Wilson destroyed the political hopes of the party's one attractive candidate, his son-in-law William Gibbs McAdoo. (There were also some prominent Democrats, including Franklin D. Roosevelt, who wanted to give the Democratic nomination to Herbert Hoover.) Badly divided among several candidates, the Democratic convention took forty-four ballots to settle on another Ohio politician, Governor James Cox, as their presidential nominee; Franklin Roosevelt, who had been a popular Assistant Secretary of the Navy, was chosen as his running mate.

Wilson wanted the 1920 election to be a "solemn referendum" on the issue of the League, but it was a good deal less than that. The Democratic platform was a compromise with the isolationist wing of the party, while Cox, after making a forthright statement in favor of the League, later waffled. Harding made full use of his exceptional talent for taking a clear issue and rendering it obscure, and Republican internationalists who supported him confused matters still further. In part, they rationalized their action by arguing that once in office Harding would be an internationalist even if he had not been in the past. As one commentator dryly remarked, Harding was the first president to be elected "in the belief that he [would] not keep his promises."

Before the campaign even began, it was a foregone conclusion that Harding would win. If it were a prize fight, said Hiram Johnson in October, "the police would interfere on the grounds of brutality." By mid-October, odds on the election were 7–1 in favor of Harding, the highest electoral odds ever recorded. All the Republican party had to do was play it safe. (From his deathbed, Boies Penrose, the Pennsylvania machine politician, advised: "Keep Warren at home. Don't let him make any speeches. If he goes out on a tour somebody's sure to ask him questions, and Warren's just the sort of damned fool that will try to answer them.") By Election Day the odds had jumped to 10–1, but, obvious as it was that Harding would win by a handsome margin, no one anticipated the magnitude of his victory. With 61 per cent of the popular vote, Harding won the greatest majority in the history of party competition, and restored the Republican predominance of the party system of the 1890s. Harding captured every borough in New York City and every county on the Pacific Coast. He even cracked the Solid South by taking Tennessee, the first time in forty years that any state of the former Confederacy voted for the party of Lincoln. As Joseph Tumulty said, "It wasn't a landslide, it was an earthquake."

The 1920 election represented a national disavowal of the ideas for which Wilson had stood, and Cox was lost in the process. Harding won through a combination of opposites, people who thought the peace too harsh and people who thought it too lenient, those who believed Wilson had betrayed internationalism at Versailles and those who believed he had forfeited national integrity, workers who held him responsible for the high cost of living and businessmen who damned him for coddling workers. Many Americans were convinced that Wilson and the Democrats had broken a promise to keep the country out of war; even closer to the mark is the historian Preston Slosson's observation that the average citizen felt that "while his government could perhaps not have avoided the war, the war ought somehow to have avoided America." The outcome pleased no one more than Henry Cabot Lodge. "We have torn up Wilsonism by the roots," he said. "I am not slow to take my own share of vindication which I find in majorities."

The Republicans capitalized on an immense feeling of nostalgia for the years before the war, when life was simpler. In a speech in May, 1920, Harding caught the spirit of the country in urging a return to "not heroism, but healing, not nostrums but normalcy," thereby coining a word and defining a mood. The country, bemused by Wilsonian rhetoric, wanted to return to a reality that was concrete, that had the hardness and durability of matter. The election of 1920, declared the Republican vice-presidential candidate Calvin Coolidge, in one of his rare turns of phrase, was "the end of a period which has seemed to substitute words for things."

Harding had no qualification for being president except that he looked like one—which is, given the ceremonial role of the president in American culture, not an unimportant consideration. He was handsome, silver-haired, with a splendid figure, but as the head of a nation rising to pre-eminence as a world power, Harding was hopelessly miscast. On one occasion he dismayed a Washington correspondent by saying, "I don't know anything about this European stuff." He found the mastery of domestic policy no less elusive. "I can't make a damn thing out of this tax problem," he confessed to his speech-writer. "I listen to one side and they seem right, and then—God!—I talk to the other side, and they seem just as right." McAdoo observed of Harding's speeches that they "leave the impression of an army of pompous phrases moving over the landscape in search of an idea; sometimes these meandering words would actually capture a straggling thought and bear it triumphantly, a prisoner in their midst, until it died of servitude and overwork." Harding himself had a sense of the dignity of his office and a pathetic understanding of his own inability to measure up to it. When Nicholas Murray Butler came to see him at the White House one day, the President looked up and said with a sigh, "I knew that this job would be too much for me."

A pillar of the Chamber of Commerce in Marion, Ohio (where he joined the Rotary and played B-flat cornet in the marching band), Harding, like many other small town folks, shared the values of the business elite, and so did his appointees. With millions suffering in the 1921 recession, Harding announced, "I would have little enthusiasm for any proposed relief which seeks either palliation or tonic from the Public Treasury." When unions sought to retain government operation of the railroads, Harry Daugherty, Harding's lamentable choice for the important post of Attorney General, called the proposal a "conspiracy worthy of Lenin." It raised the prospect, he said, that "our time-tables and freight-rates would be made out in Moscow."

The new Secretary of Commerce, Herbert Hoover, took an assignment that had never amounted to very much and made it the nucleus of an important effort to put government at the service of business. One of his predecessors had told Hoover that as Secretary of Commerce he would have nothing to do save "putting the fish to bed at night and turning on the lights around the coast," but Hoover, an empire builder who more than sextupled the budget of the Bureau of Foreign and Domestic Commerce, energetically fostered trade associations and encouraged greater standardization and efficiency. The spirit of modernization that Hoover nurtured found statutory form in 1921 when Congress approved a Budget and Accounting Act creating the new office of Bureau of the Budget, with a budget director, and a General Accounting Office, headed by a comptroller general charged with auditing government accounts.

Harding had an almost limitless store of liking for and interest in other people, and that quality sometimes served him well, sometimes badly. It was the "liberal" Wilson who removed blacks from federal offices, the "conservative" Harding who restored their limited perquisites. Harding also brought pressure on Elbert Gary, head of United States Steel, to end the punishing twelve-hour day at the blast furnaces. When Wilson received a recommendation that Eugene Debs be freed from prison, he scribbled across it, "Denied," whereas Harding not only approved his release but moved it up to December 24, 1921, "because I want him to eat his Christmas dinner with his wife." He also insisted that the Socialist firebrand stop by to see him at the White House. "Well," said the jovial president, bounding toward him, "I have heard so damned much about you, Mr. Debs, that I am now very glad to meet you personally." A member of the Elks, the Odd Fellows, the Hoo Hoos, the Moose, and the Red Men, Harding brought to his new office both the virtues and the defects of his associations; but in the White House even his virtues were defects, for an uncritical sociability, a virtue understandably cherished in small-town America, was to prove his undoing as president. Years before, his father had unknowingly presaged the disaster that awaited Harding in the White House: "It's a good thing you wasn't born a girl. Because you'd be in a family way all the time. You can't say No."

In some ways akin to the presidency of General Grant, Harding's was one of government by crony. Like Grant, Harding surrounded himself with old friends. For the post of Brigadier General and White House Physician, he named the vainglorious Old Doc Sawyer of Marion, Ohio. For Director of the Mint, the President appointed a man who had been sheriff of Pickaway County. Harding's brother-in-law, a former Seventh Day Adventist missionary to Burma, was selected as Superintendent of Federal Prisons, after the president removed the post from the civil service lists. For Comptroller of Currency, Harding picked a Marion lawyer, Daniel Crissinger, who had spent no more than a few months as head of a small bank. The president later appointed Crissinger, a boyhood chum, to the top banking post in the nation, Governor of the Federal Reserve System. To head the Veterans' Bureau, Harding chose a chance acquaintance, Colonel Charles R. Forbes, who he had met on vacation in Honolulu. With his friends installed in public office, Harding, who felt uneasy with cabinet officers like Hoover, managed to establish in the White House the same atmosphere of informal male conviviality that permeated the backroom of a Marion saloon. Alice Roosevelt Longworth found the White House study filled with the President's cronies, "the air heavy with tobacco smoke, trays with bottles containing every imaginable brand of whiskey, . . . cards and poker chips at hand—a general atmosphere of waistcoat unbuttoned, feet on desk, and spittoons alongside."

In an apartment at the Wardman Park hotel, Harry Daugherty, Harding's Attorney General, lived with his intimate friend Jesse Smith, who was both housekeeper and confidant, and who presided over the headquarters of the Ohio Gang at "the little green house on K Street." Here Daugherty's friends did a flourishing business selling immunity from prosecution, government appointments, liquor withdrawal permits, and pardons and paroles for criminals. Jesse Smith, a regular at Harding's poker table at the White House where he flaunted his flashy jewelry, served as liaison between K Street and Daugherty's Justice Department, and for more than two years he and his confederates ate high on the hog. In a rough, off-key voice, Smith would rumble, "My God, how the money rolls in."

On May 23, 1923, in the Attorney General's Wardman Park

apartment, Jesse Smith committed suicide. It was the beginning of the end for the Ohio Gang. Harding, deeply disturbed by Smith's death, received a series of warnings from Doc Sawyer and others of corruption in the Veterans' Bureau under his friend Colonel Forbes. Harding at first refused to believe them, but by the time he left for a tour of the West, the President had a good idea of how deeply he had been betrayed. "My God, this is a hell of a job!" he told William Allen White before leaving. "I have no trouble with my enemies. . . . But my damned friends, my God-damn friends, White, they're the ones that keep me walking the floor nights!" Harding was spared most of the details of the scandals and the opprobrium that followed. On his western trip he was taken ill; his condition steadily worsened, and on August 2, 1923, he died, probably as the result of a cerebral embolism. The refusal of Mrs. Harding to permit an autopsy fostered unsubstantiated rumors that, enraged by his sexual escapades with other women, she had poisoned him.

In the months after the President's death, the corruption in his administration gradually came to light. In response to protests from the American Legion and private contractors, an investigation was launched into the management of the Veterans' Bureau; it revealed that Colonel Forbes had been operating a gigantic swindle that in less than two years cost the country more than $200 million. At a time when disabled veterans on hospital cots lacked bandages, bedding, and drugs, Forbes condemned carloads of these supplies and sold them off at a fraction of their cost in return for a rake-off. Similar frauds were perpetrated in the purchase of hospital sites and in the construction of hospitals. Forbes was fined $10,000 and sentenced to two years in Leavenworth penitentiary. His legal adviser committed suicide at Harding's former home in Washington.

At the urging of Robert La Follette, a Senate investigating committee headed by Senator Thomas Walsh of Montana probed for the details of government oil leases. The committee found that Secretary of the Interior Albert Fall, with authority given him by Harding and with the acquiescence of Secretary of the Navy Edwin Denby, had leased government oil reserves at Elk Hills, California, which had been set aside for the United States Navy, to Edward Doheny, the president of Pan-American Petroleum. At about the time they were leased, Doheny's son had given Fall a black bag containing $100,000 in exchange for an unsecured note. Fall also leased, without competitive bidding, the reserves at Teapot Dome, Wyoming, to Harry Sinclair. Sinclair's oil firm transferred $233,000 in Liberty bonds to Fall's son-in-law, and Fall himself received $85,000 in cash and a herd of blooded cattle for his New Mexico ranch. Fall was fined $100,000 and sentenced to a year in prison, the first cabinet officer in history to go to jail. Denby, the unwitting agent of the deals, resigned from the cabinet.

The last of the Harding scandals led to Attorney General Daugherty himself. In return for agreeing to sell priceless German chemical patents for a pittance, Harding's Alien Property Custodian, Thomas Miller, received $50,000 in bonds. Miller was convicted and sentenced to eighteen months in jail. Jesse Smith had deposited the bonds in an account Daugherty controlled in his brother's bank in Washington Court House, Ohio. When in 1924, Daugherty denied a Senate Committee access to Justice Department files, he was removed from office. Worse was still to come. Two years later, he refused to testify under oath on the grounds that his confidential relations with President and Mrs. Harding made it impossible. Daugherty's response further besmirched the reputation of the Harding administration, for it indicated either that Harding or his family would be damaged by material in the bank records or that Daugherty was using Harding as a shield to defend himself.

The most striking feature of this corruption in government, the worst in at least half a century, was the public response. Instead of indignation at Doheny and Fall, there was a barrage of abuse at the men who exposed the malefactors. The New York *Tribune* stigmatized Senators Walsh and Wheeler as "the Montana scandalmongers," the *New York Times* called them "assassins of character," and the *Post* labeled them "mudgunners," while the FBI launched a vicious vendetta against Wheeler and harassed prospective witnesses. In part, this reaction derived from the fact that only the Veterans' Bureau corruption became known while Harding was alive. He died a beloved president, mourned throughout the nation. When the thievery became known, Calvin Coolidge was in the White House, and Coolidge personified probity.

Born on a Vermont farm that had been worked by Coolidges for five generations, the new president summoned up images of the democracy of New England town meetings. He had been sworn into office in the Plymouth, Vermont, farmhouse of his family, where his father as justice of the peace read the oath, which Coolidge pronounced by the light of an oil lamp. He spoke with a Yankee twang. Taciturn, unsmiling (it was said that he must have been weaned on a pickle), morose, peevish, even mean-looking, a deeply reserved man, Coolidge was a perfect expression of Puritan asceticism. In years when society was changing at a frightening pace and Americans sought security by incanting their continued allegiance to older virtues at the same time that they were abandoning them, Coolidge was the most usable national symbol the country could have hoped to find. As the historian George Mayer has remarked, "The shy, parsimonious Coolidge was lionized by his free-spending, pleasure-loving contemporaries in the way that the homespun Ben Franklin had been lionized by the jaded aristocrats of eighteenth-century France."

Coolidge served the needs of big business and the Old Guard even better than Harding had. Harding, although his administration was friendly to industry, was primarily a politician, not an ideologue. Coolidge was a man of convictions who deliberately converted his administration into a "businessman's government." He favored industrialists less because he was enamored of profit-making than because he thought they could maintain a condition of prosperity that would be hospitable to his main concern: the preservation of harmony. Financial interests, in turn, exploited Coolidge's idiosyncrasies to their own advantage. His seventeenth-century belief in frugality was used to justify tax cuts, his taciturnity and inactivity in office demonstrated the insignificance of government. H. L. Mencken said of Coolidge, "His ideal day is one on which nothing whatever happens," and no attitude of a president could have suited advocates of laissez-faire better.

Under Coolidge, the Republicans became frankly the business-man's party. "He had the Babbitts' awe of the Dodsworths," his biographer, Donald McCoy, has written. As governor, Coolidge had looked up to Senator Murray Crane, the Massachusetts paper tycoon; as president, he leaned on Secretary of the Treasury Andrew Mellon, multimillionaire financier and aluminum magnate who was one of the country's three richest men (only Rockefeller and Ford had more). In the State House he had been shepherded by Frank Stearns, the Boston department store executive later known as Lord Lingerie. When he entered the White House, Coolidge installed a Massachusetts textile manufacturer as head of the Republican party; at the 1924 convention, Henry Cabot Lodge sat unnoticed and unconsulted.

Coolidge's prescription for government was simple. All prosperity rested on business leadership. What was of "real importance to wage-earners," he wrote, "was not how they might conduct a quarrel with their employers but how the business of the country might be so organized as to insure steady employment at a fair rate of pay. If that were done there would be no occasion for a quarrel, and if it were not done a quarrel would do no good." Under the circumstances, a president's only function was to see that the government interfered with industry as little as possible. Calvin Coolidge, wrote Irving Stone, "aspired to become the least President the country had ever had; he attained his desire."

The 1920 election expressed a yearning for "normalcy," but it was the Old Guard, restored to power by Harding's triumph, who sought to exploit that sentiment for their own ends. After twenty years of Roosevelt's attacks on malefactors of great wealth, Taft's trust-busting, and Wilson's reforms, the Republican right wing was determined to call a halt to social welfare measures and to push legislation favorable to big business. Nor were industrialists who gave $8 million to the GOP in 1920 shy about demanding a return on their investment. Yet despite landslide victories in presidential years, Old Guard Republicans were to find that although they could block most progressive legislation, enacting laws of their own was tough sledding. Stymied by progressives in Congress through much of the decade, the conservative Republican leadership made the most headway in areas lying more directly under executive control, particularly in staffing government agencies, the courts, and regulatory commissions with conservative appointees.

None of these officials labored more single-mindedly to advance the interests of the rich and well-born than Andrew Mellon, who was soon given the droll title of "the greatest Secretary of the Treasury since Alexander Hamilton." Mellon immediately set out to trim government spending (in seven years, it fell from $6.4 billion to $2.9 billion) and reduce taxes. In 1921 he got Congress to repeal the excess-profits tax, but a band of Senate progressives forestalled his efforts to cut taxes on large incomes. In 1924 Mellon's new assault succeeded in lowering the maximum surtax on high incomes, but Congressional insurgents imposed the biggest estate tax in American history, levied a new gift tax, and opened tax returns to full publicity. The bill was such a stunning victory for the progressives that Coolidge thought of vetoing it; in the end, furious at the insurgents, he signed it only with the greatest reluctance. When Mellon set out for a third time in 1926 to slash taxes, progressive forces in both houses had been demoralized by defeats at the polls, and he was finally able to have his way. The Revenue Act of 1926 wiped out the gift tax, halved the estate tax, and scaled down the maximum surtax, which had once been 65 percent, to 20 percent. When Mellon, who served as Secretary of the Treasury under all three Republican presidents (or who, it was said, was the only Secretary of the Treasury under whom three presidents served), got Congress in 1928 to reduce corporation and consumption levies still further, he had rounded out a program that reversed almost completely the progressive tax policies of the Wilson era.

During these same years, business launched a determined campaign to break unions where they existed and to maintain the open shop where they did not. In 1920, the president of Bethlehem Steel announced that even if 95 percent of his workers belonged to a union, he would refuse to recognize it. The Harding administration gave covert and open support to this drive against the unions. In 1922, the Railroad Labor Board, with Wilson's appointees replaced by more conservative Harding men, ordered a wage slash that led to a walkout of 400,000 railroad shopmen. The Board promptly issued instructions to the railroads to set up company unions, as the Pennsylvania Railroad had already done, a practice that would deprive the strikers of seniority rights. When the shopmen stayed out, Attorney General Daugherty obtained the most sweeping injunction ever issued by an American court. "So long and to the extent that I can speak for the government of the United States," Daugherty declared, "I will use the power of the government to prevent the labor unions of the country from destroying the open shop." Contrary to all precedent in periods of prosperity, union membership declined sharply in the 1920s.

Throughout this period, the Supreme Court handed down decisions that staggered organized labor. In 1915 the Court upheld the yellow-dog contract (by which workers agreed, as a condition of employment, not to join a union); in 1919 it approved an assessment of triple damages against the United Mine Workers under the Sherman Antitrust Act; in 1921 it declared illegal a boycott to force unionization and drastically limited picketing. In 1922 in the *Coronado* case, the Court denied labor the protection it thought it had received from the Clayton Act by permitting a union to be sued for damages.

At the same time, other Supreme Court rulings set back severely the movement for social legislation. In a 5–4 decision (*Hammer v. Dagenhart*, 1918), the Court declared the Child Labor Act of 1916 unconstitutional, on the grounds that Congress could not use its commerce power to regulate labor conditions. When Congress then enacted a new law levying a prohibitive tax on products manufactured by children, the Court invalidated that statute too (*Bailey v. Drexel Furniture Co.,* 1922). In 1923 (*Adkins v. Children's Hospital*) the Court struck down a District of Columbia minimum wage law for women. By these decisions the Court made it impossible to adopt the most primitive kind of social legislation, irrespective of whether the federal government or individual states enacted the laws.

The Republican Old Guard, which had little trouble in spiking labor and social reform efforts, found the farm interests, which had serious grievances, much more formidable. During World War I, encouraged both by the lure of profit and by the urging of the government that food would win the war, farmers had plowed up the grasslands and marginal farmlands. With the tremendous wartime demand, crop prices soared to astronomic levels (cotton, which brought 13 cents a pound in 1913, jumped to 38 cents in 1919), and farmers enjoyed a heady prosperity. In 1920 prices crashed, wiping out some farmers, destroying wartime gains for others. By 1924, crop prices were moving upward again, but the farmer, unlike the manufacturer, never regained his wartime prosperity. In the decade after 1919, wheat prices fell from $2.19 a bushel to $1.04, cotton from $1.76 a bale to 85 cents. Farmers were squeezed by a combination of rising production—the consequence of increased mechanization and the liberal application of fertilizer—and lowered demand, as they met world competition from everything from Egyptian cotton to Argentine beef, at the same time that they were carrying a massive burden of debt. The farmer felt that he was losing out, that the country was being industrialized at his expense. Not only did he face a fateful combination of reduced demand and increased supply, but also he had to pay much more of his income for mortgage interest. Moreover, farmers wanted their share of the new appliances and luxuries the city dweller had—electricity, automobiles, and radios—and they were not getting them. In 1919, they had 16 per cent of the national income, by 1929, only 9 per cent. For the first time in the history of the United States, crop acreage decreased; between 1919 and 1924, 13 million acres were abandoned to brush. The farmer believed that the countryside was the basis of the nation's moral grandeur—one powerful farm leader spoke of "the shrines of American farm homes"—and he feared not only that he was in danger of being reduced to peasantry but that the agrarian way of life was being destroyed, often, ironically, by his own desire for profit. In the 1920s farming became increasingly a speculative business enterprise, signifying less and less a permanent tradition of attachment to the soil separate from the commercial world of the city. The farmer was convinced that he had reached a crossroads; only state intervention could save him from being passed by the city man and shunted to a side road.

In May, 1921, a group of western and southern senators led by William Kenyon of Iowa and Arthur Capper of Kansas met in the offices of the American Farm Bureau Federation to organize the "farm bloc," which was to unite farm-district congressmen behind agricultural legislation. With members in both parties and in both houses of Congress, and with the backing of Secretary of Agriculture Henry C. Wallace, the farm bloc in the next two years drove through the Packers and Stockyards Act of 1921, which subjected rates of commission merchants and stockyards to public control and aimed at preserving competition among packers; the Grain Futures Act of 1921, which gave the Secretary of Agriculture control over grain exchanges; the Capper-Volstead Act of 1922, which exempted farm co-operatives from the antitrust laws; and the Agricultural Credits Act of 1923, which created twelve Intermediate Credit Banks to make loans to groups of farmers.

The farm legislation of the Harding administration would at one time have been regarded as a noteworthy achievement, but by the 1920s farmers were no longer content with the old panaceas of government regulation and cheap credit. Under the leadership of George Peek, a farm-implements manufacturer who had been won to the idea of government intervention by his wartime experiences in Washington, farm interests pushed for what amounted to government price supports. Under the so-called McNary-Haugen plan, they sought to dump crop surpluses abroad in order to raise prices in the United States. The Harding and Coolidge administrations, though, under the influence of Secretary of Commerce Herbert Hoover, fought fiercely against all attempts to boost crop prices through government intervention. When Congress passed the McNary-Haugen bill in 1927 and again in 1928, Coolidge vetoed the proposal as "vicious" and "preposterous."

Coolidge's vetoes had something to be said for them, but they did not constitute a farm policy. Since the farmer refused to accept production controls, McNary-Haugenism would have been a failure; increased surpluses and constricted world markets would have frustrated it. As a new instrument of economic nationalism, it would have invited reprisals and still further impeded international trade. At the same time it is true that McNary-Haugenism, for all its faults, was at least a serious effort to improve the lot of the farmer. Some of its ideas—the insistence upon parity (that is, of economic equality of agriculture with industry) and on government responsibility for farm income—would be central to the New Deal legislation of the 1930s. Correct in rejecting this particular proposal, Coolidge put nothing else in its place. Republican leaders in the 1920s dealt cavalierly or unintelligently with the farm problem; they spoke for the urban industrialist and had nothing of value to say to the beleaguered farmer. Two days after he vetoed one of the McNary-Haugen bills, Coolidge raised the tariff on pig iron 50 per cent; several days later the price of pig iron soared 50 cents a ton.

Even before Coolidge took office, the Republican party had become firmly committed to single-interest government. By allying the government with business, the Republicans believed that they were benefiting the entire nation. Alexander Hamilton was their patron saint. The 1920s represent not the high tide of laissez faire but of Hamiltonianism, of a hierarchical conception of society with a deliberate pursuit by the government of policies most favorable to large business interests. No political party, no national administration, could conceivably have been more co-operative with corporate interests. "Never before, here or anywhere else," the *Wall Street Journal* exulted, "has a government been so completely fused with business." If, as Republican orators promised, this alliance succeeded in maintaining prosperity, the wisdom of single-interest politics would be demonstrable. If it failed, a sharp reaction against single-interest politics would be inevitable. This, in essence, became the central question in the politics of the 1920s: whether the business interest, given full support by a co-operative government, could maintain prosperity and develop social policies that would redound to the benefit not merely of itself but of the whole nation.

6

The Reluctant Giant

American foreign policy in the 1920s built on disillusionment with World War I—a dirty, unheroic war which few remembered with any emotion save distaste. There had been earlier wars which, no matter how great the cost, the nation recalled with affection. This was a war it chose to forget. No one sang songs like "Rally Round the Flag" or attended romantic plays like "The Drummer Boy of Shiloh." It was not a war of gallant sorties and dashing cavalrymen; nothing brought home its impersonally unheroic quality more than the Unknown Soldier, the doughboy whose very identity had been obliterated. At no time in our history has the hold of pacifism been stronger than in the interlude between the first and second world wars. ("I can't explain it," said one of Dos Passos's soldiers, "but I'll never put a uniform on again.") Even more important, it bequeathed a deep cynicism about European affairs, for the attitude of the Great Powers appeared to be encapsulated by the statement attributed to Lloyd George at Versailles: "Is it Upper or Lower Silesia that we are giving away?"

Sounding the old theme of American innocence and European wickedness, the United States arraigned Europe as perversely war-loving, decadent, politically unorthodox and economically chaotic, and for welshing on its debts. Before the United States would associate with European nations, they would have to "clean up and pay up." From its perch of insular security, relatively unscathed by the war, the United States lectured to war-shocked countries that feared new invasions. With infuriating smugness, the United States failed to see that the whole structure of the peace, which Wilson and the Americans had helped construct, left a great power vacuum in central Europe—a vacuum that in time would invite a resurgent German militarism unless American power weighed in the balance.

The ghost of the United States sat at every council table of Europe. By taking international responsibilities corresponding to the power it actually held, the United States might have given France the assurance it needed and at the same time have moderated French policies toward Germany, thereby strengthening democratic elements of the Weimar Republic. By stripping France of any hope of American aid in the event of a German invasion, however, the United States intensified a French nationalism which, particularly after France's occupation of the Ruhr in 1923, provided a convenient "foreign threat" with which Adolf Hitler could excite the German people.

In his victory speech following the 1920 election, Harding announced that the League was "now deceased"; in a special message in April, 1921 he told Congress, "In the existing League of Nations, . . . this Republic will have no part"; and in one of his last addresses, he declared that the League issue was as "dead as slavery." Harding not only refused to support something so unpolitical as the health program of the League, but for months a State Department career officer did not even open mail from Geneva. When in the Geneva protocol of 1924 the League attempted to set up a system of collective security defined more precisely than under its original Covenant, Secretary of State Charles Evans Hughes responded to the proposal in the harshest possible fashion. He accused the League of drafting a document which implied "a proposal of a concert against the United States," alleged that League sanctions against an aggressor might be "inimical to American trade," and warned that the United States would maintain the rights of neutrals. In essence, Hughes was saying that the United States would disrupt any attempt of the League to carry out a program of collective security through the use of sanctions.

Yet the United States could not achieve total isolation. The spirit of Wilsonian internationalism never entirely died out, and, to men like Newton Baker and Cordell Hull, Wilson remained a saintly guide. (As Wilson lay dying on the night of February 3, 1924, scores of people knelt in the snow outside his home in prayer.) More important, American wealth and power were so great that the United States found itself inevitably absorbed in world affairs. But American participation was of a singular sort. As Robert Osgood writes, "peace was seen as merely the avoidance of war rather than as a continuous process of political accommodation."

Where national security or extensive economic interests were involved, however, American foreign policy could be militantly interventionist, and that was conspicuously so in Latin America. McKinley had acquired the spoils of victory in the Caribbean after the Spanish-American War; Teddy Roosevelt had boasted that he had taken Panama; and Woodrow Wilson had sought to impose righteousness on Mexico at the end of a sword. When Harding took office, American troops in Nicaragua were upholding a minority regime, and U.S. naval officers were running Santo Domingo and Haiti. Mexico, bent on consolidating its revolution, was infuriating both U.S. oil corporations, who feared expropriation, and American Catholics, outraged by a campaign against the Church, and Washington was being called on to intervene. By 1924, the United States was controlling the financial policies of ten Latin-American nations. Harding landed marines in Honduras, and Coolidge carried American imperialism in the banana republics to its furthest point by conducting a private war in Nicaragua to support a Conservative regime against a Liberal uprising.

Lashed by criticism from Republican progressives in Congress, though, the three Republican presidents gradually moderated their policies. In 1921, the Harding government agreed to pay Colombia the $25 million indemnity it sought for loss of the Panama Canal territory, and in 1924, U.S. forces departed from the Dominican Republic, although officials continued to collect custom duties there right down until 1941. More significant was the retreat Coolidge began to beat in the fall of 1927. He named Dwight Morrow ambassador to Mexico, and Morrow proved a brilliant choice. The ambassador won a settlement of the oil lands dispute, brought a halt to the anticlerical campaign, and, most important, by his friendly demeanor undid much of the damage his predecessors had wrought. For all of their pro-business orientation, neither Harding nor Coolidge, it should be noted, would intervene militarily in Mexico to safeguard the interests of American investors. (Contrary to what some writers have asserted, economic influences on U.S. foreign policy were usually not determinative, unsurprisingly for, at its peak, foreign trade accounted for less than 3 percent of the country's assets.) The Hoover administration, in turn, took a big step toward creating what, under Franklin D. Roosevelt, would be called the Good Neighbor Policy, by coming close to repudiating the "Roosevelt corollary" to the Monroe Doctrine whereby the United States arrogated to itself the right to meddle in Latin American affairs to police unstable governments. By the end of the Republican era, relations with Latin America were better than they had been at any time in this century.

Not only south of the border, but also in the rest of the world, the United States could not escape having an impact for one overwhelming reason: it had become incomparably the dominant economic power on the globe. By 1929 the national income of the United States was greater than that of Great Britain, Germany, France, Canada, Japan, and seventeen other nations combined. The war had produced a revolutionary change in the world economy. In 1914 the United States was a debtor nation; American citizens owed foreign investors three billion dollars. By the end of 1919 the United States was a creditor nation, with foreigners owing American investors nearly three billion dollars. In addition, the United States had lent over ten billion dollars to foreign countries, mostly to carry on the war, in part for postwar reconstruction.

These figures represent one of those great shifts in power that occurs but rarely in the history of nations, a transition with formidable consequences. For three hundred years the American people had been dependent on European capital. The American Revolution was in part a struggle between British lenders and American borrowers; in the nineteenth century it was the stream of European capital into the United States that built the American railway system. For three centuries the country had exported more than it imported, and the American economy had been geared to creating an export surplus—largely of farm products such as cotton and wheat—and selling it abroad. Now, abruptly, the situation had been reversed, and the change demanded a herculean effort to redredge the channels of world commerce.

Unhappily, the United States was ill-equipped for its new position. It was the misfortune of the world and, ironically, a curse for the United States that the American economy was too well balanced to let the nation play the role of creditor. The new leading creditor nation of the world was a country for whom foreign transactions were, relatively speaking, insignificant. Under the circumstances, the boldest, most imaginative kind of leadership was required to prevent world trade from being paralyzed and to avert an economic disaster that would have terrible political results.

Instead, the United States under Harding and Coolidge made an exceptionally difficult situation far worse. If the United States was to function as a creditor nation, it had to import more than it exported. But the country moved in precisely the opposite direction. By an emergency tariff in 1921 and the Fordney-McCumber Tariff Act of 1922, the United States drowned any hope that it would be more receptive to European goods. The Fordney-McCumber Tariff restored the high prewar rates and added a few new tolls of its own, especially on "infant industries" such as chemicals. (Harding dumbfounded one reporter by explaining, "We should adopt a protective tariff of such a character as will help the struggling industries of Europe to get on their feet.") By including farm products—from reindeer meat to acorns—in the new rates, high-tariff advocates quieted traditional rural opposition to protection.

As a gesture toward scientific rate-making, the act empowered the president to raise or lower tariffs by up to 50 percent of the existing rate, but of the thirty-seven times Harding and Coolidge used this authority, they raised rates thirty-two. The five rates that were lowered included tariffs on bobwhite quail and paintbrush handles. Simultaneously, the government operated a great fleet of merchant ships at a heavy loss, thereby reducing still further the number of dollars sent abroad for foreign services. In 1930, neomercantilism (the attempt to export more than was imported, regardless of long-run effect) was carried as far as it could go with the adoption of the Hawley-Smoot Tariff; in the teeth of protests from thirty-four countries and over one thousand American economists, Congress stepped up tariff rates still higher. As the economists had warned, the new law throttled world trade and brought a wave of retaliation from other countries.

With a remarkable capacity for self-delusion, the United States insisted at the same time on collecting its "war debts"—the billions of dollars America had lent to the Allies during and after World War I. Europeans denied they were debts at all. They pointed out that more than 90 percent of the money had never gone abroad but had been spent in the United States, where it had sparked a boom. Furthermore, they claimed that America should have regarded the sum as a modest contribution to the joint war enterprise, one that hardly matched the blood Europe's young men had shed. Nations were not business firms, nor should "bank notes . . . determine the fate of the world," Clemenceau wrote Coolidge. "Come see the endless lists of dead in our villages." When Americans were unpersuaded by this reasoning, the French press renamed Uncle Sam "l'Oncle Shylock." Furthermore, Europeans pointed out, there was no way they could repay the United States save by sending goods and services, and they could not do that as long as the United States erected high tariff walls and refused to accept their goods. Nor would the United States admit that there was any connection between war debts and reparations, even though the best hope America had of being repaid was if Germany honored its reparations requirements.

Not until a disaster ensued did Washington act. In 1923 the

Weimar Republic defaulted on its reparations installment, and runaway inflation, with millions of marks demanded for everyday necessities, threatened to topple the whole financial structure of Europe. At this point, American finance stepped to the rescue. Under the Dawes Plan of 1924, named for the American consultant, Charles G. Dawes, the reparations-debts tangle was unravelled for the moment, and in 1929 the Young Plan, the result of the efforts of another American financier, Owen D. Young, scaled down reparations to a more modest sum. Germany acknowledged its obligations, and the Allies agreed to square accounts with the United States. But what actually happened was that America lent money to Germany; the Germans paid reparations to the Allies; and the Allies sent money to the United States to service their debts. It would have made equal sense for the United States to have taken the money out of one drawer in the Treasury and put it into another.

In the kind of thinking behind the Dawes Plan lay the heart of American financial policy in the 1920s. A creditor nation unwilling to absorb more imports than exports, the United States maintained world trade by private investment of dollars abroad. New York replaced London as the financial capital of the world. American dollars were even used to build a London subway. Once its economic colonial status was ended by World War I, the United States swiftly started colonizing Europe with American plants and investments. American dollars developed rubber plantations in the Dutch East Indies, built American branch factories in Scandinavia, mined tin in Bolivia, and drilled oil wells in the Middle East, where U.S. corporations, given a free hand by their government, carved out a big chunk of the rich oil lands. During these same years, Europeans obtained dollars from the hordes of American tourists who stormed the Continent, and from immigrants to the United States who sent money to relatives across the sea. Moreover, so substantial was America's role in the world economy that, even with tariff barriers, the United States continued to import an impressive amount of goods.

The entire system of finance—reparations and debts, the ability of American farmers to sell abroad, the economic health of European nations—depended on a continual willingness of the United States to lend money outside its borders. In the middle of 1928, American investment overseas started to fall off, probably because there were better opportunities at home, although partly in recognition of the dubious nature of many of the investments that had been made and that were proposed. When, after the crash of 1929, the United States also reduced its direct investments abroad and cut drastically its purchase of foreign goods, the underpinnings of the international economy were pulled out and the system collapsed.

As the United States contemplated policy for the Far East, economic considerations combined with strategic concerns to bring about the most celebrated international conference of the decade. The major powers were all feeling the burden of keeping up with a costly naval arms race, and economy-minded Americans sought some way to bring an end to it. Many also believed that war had come in 1914 not so much because anyone wanted it than because the build-up of arms had readied Europe for it, and there was considerable popular sentiment for disarmament. For a number of years, too, especially after Japan had made the notorious Twenty-one Demands on China in 1915, the United States had been worrying about Tokyo's designs on the Chinese mainland, perhaps even on the Philippines, and it was vexed by the continuation of the Anglo-Japanese defensive alliance that had been negotiated in 1902. These assorted matters led the United States to invite eight countries to take part in a meeting at which both arms limitation and Asian problems would be discussed. Excluded from the talks was one Asian power, the Soviet Union, which America refused to recognize.

When the Washington Conference opened on November 12, 1921, one day after the Unknown Soldier was interred, the delegates settled back to listen to Secretary of State Charles Evans Hughes make the perfunctory remarks expected of presiding officers. As Hughes began his address, delegates nodded to acquaintances around the room and smothered yawns. But they snapped to attention when they realized that the Secretary was making no ordinary talk. The only way to disarm, he said, was to disarm. He proposed a ten year "holiday" on the construction of capital ships, with tonnage for the United States, Great Britain, and Japan set at a 5:5:3 ratio. He not only offered to destroy thirty American battleships, already afloat or partially completed, but went on to tell Great Britain and Japan precisely what they would have to scrap. Hughes declared that Britain should stop construction on the four new "Hoods," and as Lord David Beatty, First Lord of the Admiralty, leaned forward in his chair, Hughes went on to sink the *King George the Fifth* and others of the fleet. (His lordship, said one observer, looked like "a bulldog, sleeping on a sunny doorstep, who has been poked in the stomach by the impudent foot of an itinerant soap-canvasser.") In a few minutes, the Secretary of State annihilated 66 ships with a total tonnage of 1,878,043, including, as one English writer observed, more British battleships "than all the admirals of the world had destroyed in a cycle of centuries." It was an absolutely unique diplomatic episode. Hughes's speech was greeted by a "tornado of cheering" and delegates waved hats, yelled, and hugged one another.

Despite this initial enthusiasm, the conferees reached agreement only with difficulty. Japan objected that accepting the short end of the ratio would both endanger her security and injure her national pride. It read the 5:5:3 ratio as Rolls Royce:Rolls Royce:Ford. To get Japan to yield, the United States was forced to promise not to fortify the Philippines, Samoa, Guam, and the other Pacific possessions, save for Hawaii, and Britain was required to make a similar concession. If America did not fortify its island outposts, there was little chance that it could menace Japan. Once these adjustments were made, the delegates approved the 5:5:3 ratio, with France and Italy each permitted one-third the capital-ship tonnage of the United States or Great Britain. For the first time in history, major powers had actually consented to disarm.

Nor did that exhaust the achievements of the Washington Conference. A Four Power Treaty between the United States, Britain, Japan, and France bound the signatories to respect each other's rights in the Pacific, to negotiate any future disputes in the region, and to consult in case of a threat from another power; most important, the treaty specifically ended the Anglo-Japanese alliance. Under Hughes's remarkable leadership, the conferees went on to conclude a Nine Power Treaty which bound the signatories to respect "the sovereignty, the independence, and the territorial and administrative integrity of China" and to adhere to the principle of equality of commercial opportunity there. In the Nine Power Treaty, Hughes had succeeded where John Hay had failed in securing formal acceptance of the principle of the Open Door. As a result of the meetings, the conciliatory Japanese worked out a series of other agreements too. They restored to China sovereignty over Shantung, withdrew the most noxious of their Twenty-one Demands, granted cable rights on the island of Yap to the United States, and consented to leave Siberia.

In later years, when Japan devastated the American fleet at Pearl Harbor and overran the Philippines, critics charged that Hughes had surrendered American strategic supremacy at the Washington Conference. He was accused of having sunk more of the U.S. fleet than the Japanese demolished at Pearl Harbor. This censure was unrealistic, for the alternative to Hughes's policy was an arms race the country would not have sanctioned. Not until 1938 did Congress authorize a navy even up to the strength permitted by the 5:5:3 formula. Nor would the nation have borne the huge expense required to fortify Guam and the Philippines; on the very eve of Pearl Harbor, such a program was strenuously resisted.

The conference succeeded in halting the construction of battleships and aircraft carriers, which was more than any other disarmament talks had been able to do; it got rid of the objectionable Anglo-Japanese alliance; it reduced tension in the Far East; and it provided a more hopeful atmosphere for peace throughout the world. Without slowing the arms race, there was little likelihood of a political settlement in the Pacific. The deliberations made Japan feel more secure and helped keep the Japanese moderates in power for almost a decade. The treaties did nothing to lessen America's unfavorable position in the Far East, but no treaty could have done that.

It is true, nevertheless, that the American people had unrealistic assumptions about the Washington Conference. Behind the accords lay the idea of peace achieved by self-denying ordinances and, if the peace were broken, by the mobilization of international public opinion. It was as though a world war had never happened. The United States continued to hold excessive expectations in the Far East, overlooking the fact that Japan had come out of the war as one of the great world powers. With its chain of former German islands in the Pacific, Japan could endanger American communications from Hawaii to the Philippines. With the annihilation of German interests in the Pacific and the apparent withdrawal of Russia as a Pacific power, the war had turned the western Pacific into a Japanese lake. All the Washington agreements did was to freeze the status quo. Captivated by the illusion of a democratic, united China open to American trade, the United States was continuing to buy trouble. By committing itself to the cause of Chinese independence and to maintaining Pacific possessions it was unwilling to defend, it stood in the way of Japanese ambitions without developing a power base that Japan would be compelled to respect.

In the period after the Washington Conference, when the United States attempted to prevent war by limiting arms and signing pledges of non-aggression, America carried the idea of a "parchment peace"—a peace built on paper promises—to the ultimate limit. The panacea of a treaty to outlaw war was the brain child of a civic-minded Chicago lawyer, Salmon Levinson, who won the support of Senator Borah and of a group of peace-foundation officials. It was a notion perfectly in tune with Borah's views of foreign affairs; generally regarded as an isolationist, Borah was, as one commentator has noted, actually a "vestigial internationalist" who looked to the power of public opinion and international law to maintain peace and secure justice.

In the early spring of 1927 Professor James T. Shotwell of Columbia University persuaded the French foreign minister Aristide Briand to announce that he was ready to enter into an agreement with the United States for the mutual outlawry of war. Briand was less interested in Shotwell's principles than in drawing the United States into the French system of alliances. Cool to the proposal, Secretary of State Frank Kellogg, after a nine-month barrage of public opinion laid down by Borah, relented and notified Briand he would negotiate such a treaty but only if it was extended to other powers. This was not at all what Briand had in mind (an Assistant Secretary of State noted jubilantly in his diary, "We have Monsieur Briand out on a limb"), but Briand had no choice other than to accept Kellogg's terms.

On August 27, 1928, the United States and fourteen other nations signed the Pact of Paris (popularly known as the Kellogg-Briand Pact). It bound the signatories to renounce war as an instrument of national policy except in the case of self-defense. Most of the countries of the world eventually signed, although Britain insisted on an escape hatch so that it would not be restrained from going to war to defend its overseas empire, the United States reserved freedom of action under the Monroe Doctrine, and France announced that the pact would not apply to its obligations under previous treaties or under the League covenant. The Kellogg Pact, as Frank Simonds observed, was "the high water mark of American endeavors for world peace which consisted in undertaking to combine the idea of political and military isolation with that of moral and material involvement."

When Republican President Herbert Hoover entered the White House on March 4, 1929, the atmosphere was one of universal hope for peace and prosperity. The United States was enjoying boom times, and American investment abroad had unsnarled the debts-reparations tangle and sparked a flourishing world trade. The moderates still held control in Tokyo, and the United States, through the Washington Conference, had apparently worked out a modus vivendi with Japan. The major powers of the world had just agreed to renounce war as an instrument of national policy.

Within three years, the whole system of peace and prosperity would collapse. The stock-market crash of 1929 and the withdrawal of American investments from Europe contributed to world economic disaster. In September, 1931, the Japanese army attacked the Chinese in Manchuria, breaking pledges under the Nine Power Treaty and the Kellogg Pact, and neither the United States nor the League of Nations would do anything about it. Nor did they do anything when in 1932 the Japanese mercilessly assaulted Shanghai. Before Hoover left the White House, Adolf Hitler would come to power in Germany, convinced he had nothing to fear from nations that expected to block war and expansion through documents like the Kellogg Pact.

In retrospect, the folly of American foreign policy in the 1920s is easy to see, but it was not folly alone that produced the breakdown of peace and prosperity. Given the terrible disruption of European society by the war and developments under the surface well before the war, even American entrance into the League and wiser political economic policies might not have prevented the rise of fascism. In the Far East, it is questionable whether the United States could have blocked Japanese expansion save at the price of war. (Whether thwarting Japanese expansion was necessary to American security is, of course, a separate and more difficult question.) Granting that the tariff policies of these years were foolhardy—it is hard to account for the blindness of men of the perspicacity of Hughes on this score—no truly viable economic program was politically feasible.

Any criticism of U.S. foreign policy of this period must take cognizance of the possibilities of the times. In the fall of 1920 Sir Gilbert Murray scolded his fellow Englishmen for "expecting of America more than ought to be expected of any normal agglomeration of human beings." The shift of power to the United States came too quickly; it required a drastic change of attitude at a time when there was no apparent foreign menace to American security, and this was probably too much to expect. Different policies and more enlightened leadership by the United States might have averted some of the worst consequences; it is not clear that they could have avoided the main part of them. The world in the 1920s spun tragically toward the disasters of the 1930s.

7

Tired Radicals

In 1914 the progressive movement had reached its zenith. Two years before, the country had been aroused by a four-party contest in which the conservative Republican incumbent, William Howard Taft, had been overwhelmed by his progressive rivals; Woodrow Wilson, the Democratic spokesman for the New Freedom, had ousted Taft from the White House, while Teddy Roosevelt, the Progressive party candidate, had run a strong second. Even Taft, who in 1912 carried only two states in the Electoral College, had established a record as a reformer—particularly by vigorous prosecution of trusts—that would have seemed improbable a short time before. Most startling of all, Eugene Debs, the Socialist candidate, had polled almost a million votes. Wilson in office had proceeded to carry out the mandate for the New Freedom by driving through Congress an impressive number of reforms. In 1914, progressivism was triumphant; six years later, it was apparently dead as a doornail, buried under the Harding landslide.

The controversies aroused by World War I, and the spirit of chauvinism it unleashed, had a devastating impact on progressivism. In 1912, when social reform was at floodtide, the luminaries of the movement were Roosevelt, Wilson, La Follette, Bryan, and Debs. By 1920, these leaders and their followers were snarling enemies, hopelessly divided by the issues of the war. Bryan had resigned from Wilson's cabinet, to be met by a tirade of abuse from Wilson's supporters, and, although there was a temporary reconciliation in 1916, he was an outspoken opponent of Wilson's strategy on the League three years later. Roosevelt's idolaters viewed Wilson with the angry contempt usually reserved for traitors, and T. R., for his part, had denounced La Follette as a "hun within our gates" and "the most sinister enemy of democracy in America." Wilson kept Debs in a federal prison, and Debs scornfully dismissed Wilson as "the most pathetic figure in the world."

Nothing reveals the damage the war did in splitting the ranks of the progressives so much as the attitude of progressives toward La Follette. No man in America had done more to advance the cause of social reform than "Battle Bob." As governor of Wisconsin, he had found the state a corporation barony and, working with a group of university professors, transformed it into the model social laboratory of the nation. Elected to the Senate in 1905, he quickly became the recognized chieftain of the progressive forces fighting for railroad legislation, conservation, and protection for labor. But once he expressed his reservations about the war—he denounced it as a plot of profiteers and protested that "the poor who are called to rot in the trenches have no organized voice"—none of this counted. The muckraker Charles Edward Russell execrated him as a "traitor in disguise" who was doing "the dirty work of the Kaiser"; La Follette, he said, was "a big yellow streak." During the war, La Follette's old allies at the University of Wisconsin, President Charles R. Van Hise, John R. Commons, Richard T. Ely, and E. A. Ross, signed a statement censuring him for disloyalty, while Ely wrote that La Follette had been "of more help to the Kaiser than a quarter of a million troops."

There had long been a close tie between progressivism and nationalism, particularly among the disciples of Theodore Roosevelt who, not unlike Joseph Chamberlain in England or, to a degree, Bismarck in Germany, stood for a strong state with a sense both of social obligation and of imperial mission. After their defeat in 1912, Roosevelt and his confederates emphasized the nationalist strain in progressivism; they rebuked Wilson for failing to uphold national honor, first in Latin America, then in Europe. As leaders of the Progressive party concentrated their fire on Wilson's foreign policy, they became less and less interested in reform. In December, 1914, the Progressives issued a statement that ignored the reform planks of their 1912 platform and centered on a demand for a higher protective tariff. In January, 1916, the Progressive National Committee denounced Wilson for failing "to deal adequately with the National honor and industrial welfare" and called for "a reawakening of our elder Americanism, of our belief in those things that our country and our flag stands for."

Roosevelt himself gave up on progressivism and turned to preparedness and war. He not only refused to run on the Progressive ticket in 1916 but urged both the Progressives and Republicans to nominate the bleakly conservative Henry Cabot Lodge as a man of "the broadest national spirit," who, Roosevelt told the stunned Progressives, was one of the "staunchest fighters for different measures of economic reform in the direction of justice." The Progressive platform of 1916 was indistinguishable from that of the Republicans, which, as the *New Republic* observed, was a "stupidly, defiantly and cynically reactionary document." When the Republicans nominated Hughes, the Progressives indorsed him too, on the grounds that only he could "serve the two vital causes of Americanism and Preparedness." The 1916 campaign marked the end of the Progressive party.

As Roosevelt and the Progressives merged with the Republicans on nationalist grounds, they adopted the social ideology of the Old Guard too. In September, 1915, Roosevelt decried the "policy of harassing and jeopardizing business"; six months later, he warned that commissions must stand "unflinchingly against any popular clamor which prevents the corporation from getting ample profit." Senator Beveridge, who had a distinguished record as a reformer and especially as a fighter for child labor laws, became a bitter foe of organized labor, attacked the income tax, called for a sales tax, and protested against "persecuting" businessmen. (The Indianapolis Associated Employers, Beveridge wrote enthusiastically, had been highly successful "in the suppression of strikes by force.") In 1918 Roosevelt urged the election to the Senate of four reactionaries, including Albert Fall of New Mexico. "To a peculiar degree," wrote Roosevelt, "Fall embodies the best American Spirit." Delighted by the victories of Fall and other deep-dyed conservatives, Roosevelt was dismayed only by the fact that George Norris and Robert La Follette were needed to form the new Republican majority in the Senate.

The fight over the League and the ugly events of 1919 dealt bruising blows to progressivism. In 1916, Wilson, as spokesman for the progressive wing of the Democratic party, won over a large segment of the Progressives, as well as many Socialists and independent social reformers and intellectuals. By 1920, they had turned against him, convinced that he had cynically betrayed democratic ideals at Versailles and had stamped out dissent at home. Heralded as the hope of the age, Wilson, in Amos Pinchot's words, put "his enemies in office and his friends in jail." Intellectuals who, as Joseph Freeman wrote, had a sense of "craft solidarity . . . with the professor in the White House," had come to distrust all exhorters, soothsayers, and statesmen. Leery of political messiahs, they approached politics with a new wariness. Herbert Croly, who had once written a book with the cheery title, *The Promise of American Life,* spelled out the credo of the postwar liberal: "No more dashes into the political jungle. No more intervention without reservations, without understanding and without specific and intelligent political preparation."

By 1919, the ebullient progressive intellectuals of 1914 had become, as Walter Weyl said, "tired radicals," though, in truth, the progressives were never truly "radical." "The chief distinguishing aspect of the Presidential campaign of 1920," observed Croly, "is the eclipse of liberalism or progressivism as an effective force in American politics." Faced by the victory of political reaction and the disappointment of their hopes for a new international order, they felt an overwhelming sense of their own impotence. The world seemed infinitely less tractable than it once had. The man "who aspired to overturn Society," wrote Weyl, "ends by fighting in a dull Board of Directors of a village library for the inclusion of certain books."

Having lost faith in progress, in man's capacity for reason, and in the malleability of society, the intellectuals could no longer hold to the prewar political solutions. Croly turned from political questions to religious ones, from the problem of changing society to the quest for individual regeneration, and Walter Lippmann attempted to work out a naturalistic ethics. The disillusionment also strengthened the elitist strain in the progressive intellectuals. Since things had turned out so badly, men like Lippmann concluded not that their analyses were mistaken and their assumptions unrealistic but that the people had failed them. In *Public Opinion* (1922), Lippmann emphasized the irrationality of decision-making in politics and argued that men viewed reality in "stereotypes"; in *The Phantom Public* (1925), he attacked the idea that "the compounding of individual ignorances in masses of people can produce a continuous directing force in public affairs" and urged less power for the people and more for experts. The archetypal muckraker Lincoln Steffens gave up on parliamentary democracy entirely ("I can't see why everybody is so anxious to save this rotten civilization of ours") and became a warm admirer of Lenin and Mussolini. There was much more *élan* among the intellectuals who hoped to apply science to politics—John Dewey, Charles Beard, Thorstein Veblen—but they talked a good deal about method and little about concrete political proposals.

If progressivism faltered in the 1920s, radicalism became almost defunct during World War I and its aftermath. Prosecution during the war cut IWW membership in half; government raids in the Red Scare and defection of "Wobbly" leaders to the Communists decimated the remainder while the Palmer raids almost wiped out the Communists. (Ironically, by driving the Communists underground, the government strengthened the conspiratorial sense of the Slavic groups, who fancied themselves as being in the same position as the Bolsheviks under the Czar.) By 1920 there were only 8,000 to 15,000 Communists in the United States (the actual count is probably much closer to the lower figure), of whom only 1,000 to 2,000 were English-speaking. The Socialist party went rapidly downhill. In 1920 Eugene Debs, prisoner 9653 at the Atlanta federal penitentiary, won 900,000 votes on the Socialist ticket, but this figured out as a much smaller percentage than he had received in 1912. In that banner year of socialism, the party had 118,000 members; ten years later, only 11,000. In some states the Socialists virtually disappeared. In Oklahoma, the leading Socialist state in the country in

1914, where merchants had displayed the red flag in their store windows as a commercial expedient, the Socialist party claimed only 14 members in 1924.

In the Great Plains, progressivism had a late Indian Summer brilliance, then died in the first frost, again in no small part because of wartime difficulties. In 1915 the former Socialist A. C. Townley organized the Nonpartisan League in the heavily rural state of North Dakota. Finding the wheat farmers chafing under a government subservient to the millers of Minneapolis and St. Paul, Townley urged them to take the state away from the "sleek, smooth-tongued, bay-windowed fellows that looked well, talked well, lived well, lied well." In 1916 the League elected an obscure farmer to the governorship of North Dakota, and in the next few years it spread through the wheat belt from Minnesota to Washington. With a program that Thorstein Veblen labeled "agrarian syndicalism," the League in North Dakota created a state bank, a state grain elevator, a state flour mill, a compulsory hail insurance fund, and public low-cost housing for farmers and workers. In South Dakota the League added a state cement plant and a state-owned coal mine. Elsewhere, however, the League could never match its success in the wheat area tapped by the Twin Cities. Already under fire as unpatriotic for its coolness or actual opposition to American participation in World War I, the League was crushed by a critical fall in crop prices in 1921. The state bank and many other state projects ran into financial difficulty, and the League discovered that so long as a state was dependent on Minneapolis or Chicago capital, it could not carry on socialistic experiments even within its borders. By 1922 the League was moribund.

The political atmosphere in the 1920s differed from that in 1914 not only because of the impact of the war and its residue, but also because there was considerable congruence between pre-war progressivism and the acquisitive aspirations of the Coolidge era. When Woodrow Wilson declared he was fighting for "the man on the make," when he cried, "just let some of the youngsters I know have a chance and they'll give these gentlemen points," he was talking the language of George Babbitt. Many of the progressives, especially the Wilsonians, had no trouble adapting themselves to the Coolidge era; men such as Newton D. Baker and Joe Tumulty found lucrative jobs with oil companies and private utilities in the 1920s. Businessmen, who had been active in reform groups in many American cities, were excited now by the possibilities of the "new" capitalism. As part of a new managerial class with professional aspirations, they made an easy transition from their prewar interest in "efficiency" in government to the postwar emphasis on scientific management and factory welfare programs. Many progressives were shocked, too, by the militancy of labor in 1919, which offended middle class sensibility, and consequently they aligned themselves with property-conscious conservatives. Some of the people who voted for Wilson and Roosevelt in 1912 flocked to the polls to give landslide majorities to Hoover and Coolidge.

Despite the loud clamor against the trusts and the concerns expressed by the muckrakers about the shortcomings of American society, progressivism had often been less an economic movement than one for moral uplift and more an expression of the self-interest of the old-stock bourgeoisie than the reformers cared to acknowledge, and both aspects became transparent in the 1920s. Prohibition and immigration restriction, which do not seem at all "progressive" to a New Deal liberal, were important aims of many of the prewar reformers, and in the 1920s progressives tended to concentrate almost wholly on such matters, although not without some uneasiness. Prohibition, Richard Hofstadter observed, "was the skeleton at the feast, a grim reminder of the moral frenzy that so many wished to forget, a ludicrous caricature of the reforming impulse, of the Yankee-Protestant notion that it is both possible and desirable to moralize private life through public action." When the immigration-restriction law passed the Senate in 1924, not a single progressive opposed it, and even men like George Norris voted in its favor.

Despite these vicissitudes in the 1920s, however, elements of the prewar progressive coalition that resisted business dominance endured. For a time, the progressives in Congress held the balance of power, and were able to stave off conservative Republican attempts to enact special-interest laws. In the early years, the progressives were even able to pass legislation of their own, notably the Sheppard-Towner Act for instruction in health care for mothers and infants and a new child labor law, subsequently struck down by the Supreme Court. Most impressively, from 1921 to 1925 Senator George Norris almost single-handedly and by brilliant legislative legerdemain stopped the Harding and Coolidge administrations from handing the power site at Muscle Shoals in the Tennessee Valley over to a corporation. By 1928 Norris had won enough congressional support to turn the tide and throw the private utilities on the defensive. Congress twice passed bills for an ambitious government development of the valley; frustrated both times by presidential vetoes, the campaign that would result in the creation of the Tennessee Valley Authority was, by the end of the Republican era, near success.

The Progressives came back from their smashing defeat in 1920 to scare the daylights out of the Old Guard in the 1922 elections, in part as a consequence of a postwar recession. In 1920 the Wilson administration had suddenly reduced spending, ended loans to Europe, and raised taxes; the postwar boom was quickly punctured, prices broke violently, and by 1921 the country experienced hard times. In a single year, America's foreign trade was cut in half and farm prices plummeted. Desperate farmers, not knowing where to turn, used whatever weapons they could improvise, including campaigns to boost prices by holding back crops and thus reducing supply. In the cotton belt, night riders burned cotton gins when owners failed to heed warnings not to buy cotton, and in Kentucky masked riders admonished growers not to send their tobacco to market. In the 1922 elections, farmers resorted to the ballot; progressive Republicans upended Old Guard leaders in the midwestern farm states. In Iowa, irate farmers elected to the Senate Smith Wildman Brookhart, who took pride in the implications of his middle name; in Wisconsin, La Follette was returned with a 300,000-vote margin; in Minnesota, a Farmer-Labor candidate ousted Senator Kellogg. Even in the East, the Harding forces met defeat. In the Old Guard stronghold of Pennsylvania, Gifford Pinchot, the leading conservationist of the Progressive era, beat a reactionary candidate in the Republican gubernatorial primary. "Yesterday," said Senator Moses on hearing the news, "was a bad day for us Tories."

By 1923 midwestern progressives from the farm belt, despairing of both major parties, were talking of launching a national third party in 1924, and they had support among a segment of middle-class intellectuals and reformers and from the Socialists. The one stumbling block was the hesitancy of organized labor. The powerful railroad unions, infuriated by Harding's support of antilabor forces, had decided on political action against the Republicans. Rather than run a third ticket, they preferred to back the Democrat, William McAdoo, who had won their favor by his operation of the railroads during the war. When, however, it was revealed that McAdoo had been employed as counsel by the oil scandals tycoon, Edwin Doheny, at an annual retainer of $50,000, the unions threw over McAdoo, gave up on the Democratic party, and consented to support an independent ticket in 1924.

The Progressive convention of 1924 in Cleveland had much the same spirit of evangelical revivalism that had characterized the 1912 convention of the earlier Progressives. To the convention came veterans of old protest parties: General Jacob Coxey and the 1888 labor party presidential candidate, John Streeter, who wore a flowing beard because he had taken an oath in the 1890s not to shave until populism was victorious; as well as the spokesman for a newer urban progressivism, Fiorello La Guardia, who told the delegates he had come "to let you know there are other streets and other attitudes in New York besides Wall Street. I speak for Avenue A and 116th Street, instead of Broad and Wall." The Progressives named La Follette as their candidate for President and as their Vice-Presidential nominee chose Senator Burton K. Wheeler, the Montana Democrat whose investigation had driven Harry Daugherty from the cabinet. Their platform attacked monopoly, urged that Congress be given the power to override the Supreme Court, supported government ownership of railroads and, eventually, of water power resources, backed collective bargaining, and advocated the direct nomination and election of the President.

The Progressives, although they had a new interest in bread and butter issues, based their 1924 campaign on the old cry of the evil of monopoly. In the postwar years, noted one writer, an attack on the trusts seemed as outdated as the tandem bicycle, and "trust-buster" was a term as much lost in the mists of the past as "free-soiler." In attempting to win public attention to the issue of monopoly, La Follette seemed, as Dos Passos later wrote, "an orator haranguing from the capitol of a lost republic." He appeared to be trying to turn back time to the pre-industrial society of the nineteenth century. The theme song of the 1924 campaign, a La Follette leader later observed, should have been "Tenting Tonight on the Old Camp Ground."

The Progressives waged the 1924 campaign under insurmountable handicaps. They had no state, county, or municipal tickets, for the unions and the farm organizations would not commit themselves to a third party; the Progressive movement of 1924 was, in fact, not a third party but merely a presidential and vice-presidential ticket. The Progressives were crippled by lack of money; for every dollar Coolidge had in campaign funds, La Follette had four cents. Their appeal to the farmer was blunted by a sharp rise in crop prices. The AF of L, which backed La Follette in 1924 and thus broke its tradition of never making an outright indorsement of a Presidential candidate, gave little material aid to the campaign; some unions, notably the Mine Workers under John L. Lewis, even supported Coolidge.

The Progressives found it difficult, though, to forge an enduring tradition of unity between farmers and workers, because the two groups often saw their interests as conflicting rather than co-inciding. Instead of thinking of labor unions as allies in a struggle against Big Business, the more prosperous corn-belt farmers were likely to view them as enemies. When Samuel Gompers called for farmer-labor unity in June, 1921, the farm journal editor Henry A. Wallace, later to be Franklin Roosevelt's Secretary of Agriculture, replied: "The fact is that the farmers are suffering more now from the leaders of labor than from the leaders of industry or finance." He lectured Gompers to urge union labor to submit to a reduction of "exorbitantly high wages" as "an evidence of good faith." Nor did farmers always agree among themselves. Affluent investors in the burgeoning field of "agribusiness" had little in common with dirt poor Mexican field hands, and the truck farmers of the Northeast looked at the world very differently from the cotton planters of the Southern Black Belt or the wheat grower of the Great Plains. Divergence among sections, in fact, would prove to be one of the greatest menaces of the decade to progressivism.

Badly divided on sectional lines, the Democrats could offer little more resistance than the Progressives to the Republicans. In the midst of a dreadful heat wave, delegates to the Democratic national convention at New York's Madison Square Garden battled for seventeen days before they could agree on a platform and candidates. On the convention floor, the heat was insufferable—as much as 100 degrees—and it was made even worse by the fact that the convention had followed immediately on the heels of the circus, and not even seven tons of chemicals could get rid of the stench of the lions.

The year 1924 marked the point in the urbanization of America, and the history of the Democratic party, when an unfortunate equilibrium was struck between the urban Northeast and the more rural South and West. Both the urban and rural elements made a bad showing at the convention. Democrats from the South and West emerged as racial bigots who championed the Ku Klux Klan (Texas delegates had to be dissuaded from burning a fiery cross); New Yorkers appeared to no better advantage as they shouted down Bryan and behaved like rowdies.

Wherever the delegates from the South and West went, their worst suspicions of New York City were confirmed. At Fourteenth Street, they encountered the headquarters of the infamous city machine, Tammany Hall, with its ancient symbol of the Indian above the doorway. Farther downtown they came upon Wall Street, for decades their legendary enemy; on one corner, they even confronted the sinister fortress of the House of Morgan. Yankee Stadium, the Polo Grounds, and Ebbets Field all featured Sunday baseball, a profanation of the Sabbath. In the Columbia University area uptown stood Riverside Church, where modernist preachers denounced fundamentalism from the pulpit. Manhattan was a metropolis, one writer noted, that published books, "some of them less than wholesome," and the home of opera, "sung in a foreign language."

Even efforts at closing the sectional breach misfired. As a welcome sign to the delegates, a statue of Father Knickerbocker was erected on top of the Hotel Astor, but he was holding a conspicuous beer mug. When a block of the city was dedicated to each state delegation, the Texans were appalled to find that their block embraced Saint Patrick's Cathedral, and when, in a gesture of friendship, the convention band picked out a tune to accompany a Southern demonstration, it was "Marching Through Georgia." The attempts of the visitors to make a gesture of good will turned out just as badly. In a conciliatory move, the convention chairman, a Protestant from Tennessee, called upon the renowned Catholic prelate, Cardinal Gibbons, to offer the opening prayer. Unhappily, Gibbons had been dead for three years. The futility of trying to paper over deep cleavages was revealed for the whole country to see when a debate over whether to denounce the Klan erupted into fistfights. At the end, the rival forces were so evenly split that the motion not to mention the KKK by name was adopted 543 3/20 to 542 3/20. The Klan leader, Hiram Evans, boasted, "They were afraid of what we might do."

The convention divided in the same fashion on choosing a presidential nominee. So perfectly did the two leading candidates— New York's Governor Alfred E. Smith, the hero of Catholic city dwellers in the Northeast, and William Gibbs McAdoo, favorite of the Protestant village folk of the South and West—epitomize the urban-rural and sectional divisions at Madison Square Garden that they seemed to have been sent there by Central Casting. The Roman Catholic Smith, graduate of Fulton Fish Market and sachem of Tammany Hall, spoke the argot of the Lower East Side and sported a brown derby which, George Mowry later observed, "rural America had probably never seen outside a vaudeville act." An unapologetic New York provincial, Smith once said, "I'd rather be a lamp post on Park Row than governor of California." McAdoo, a Protestant born in the small town of Marietta, Georgia, where his earliest memory was of the Yankee soldiers on Sherman's march, wore stiff high-standing collars and parted his hair in the middle. He was "the personification," Robert K. Murray has written, "of strait-laced rectitude and sanctimonious moral judgment."

For nine steamy days, the battle between these two contenders deadlocked the convention. (Will Rogers wrote: "This thing has got to come to an end. New York invited you people here as guests, not to live.") When McAdoo moved into the majority, Smith partisans in the gallery sought to deny him the required two-thirds vote by jeering "Oil! Oil! Oil!" and boasting that there was "No Oil on Al." After 95 ballots, Smith and McAdoo withdrew by agreement; on the 103d ballot, the convention named John W. Davis for President and then picked Charles Bryan for Vice-President. Davis, Solicitor General under Wilson and ambassador to Great Britain, was a man of high repute ("the type," noted a political writer sardonically, "that street-railway conductors like to have for a superintendent—that is, 'a mighty fine man'"). As one of the leading corporation lawyers in the country, however, he was a red flag to the Progressive bulls. Moreover, naming William Jennings Bryan's younger brother as the vice-presidential candidate made the ticket look too obviously contrived, not the expression of popular will but the work of backroom politicians—Wall Street and Bryan on the same card. By the end of the convention, neither nomination was worth a lead nickel. Once again the Democratic party had revealed itself to be "merely an aggregation of local interests" resembling "the old Austrian Empire."

The choice of Davis demonstrated how much the progressive emphasis in the Democratic party had diminished. His nomination marked the first time that a major party had nominated a practicing corporation lawyer for the presidency. "I have a fine list of clients," Davis declared. "What lawyer wouldn't want them? I have J. P. Morgan and Company, the Erie Railroad, the Guaranty Trust Company, the Standard Oil Company. . . . I am proud of them." Indeed, his firm—Davis, Polk—was connected by private elevator to the offices of J. P. Morgan. He had been offered an appointment to the United States Supreme Court, but had turned it down because the honor meant less to him than accumulating a fortune. Felix Frankfurter of Harvard Law School commented, "It is good neither for these lads that I see passing through this School from year to year, nor for this country, that we should reward with the Presidency one to whom big money was the big thing." No one summed up better than the Republican Senator, Hiram W. Johnson, what the Madison Square Garden convention had wrought. "How true was Grant's exclamation," he remarked, "that the Democratic Party could be relied upon at the right time to do the wrong thing!"

The Republican party pursued the shrewd strategy of ignoring the Democrats. Calvin Coolidge sat out the campaign in the White House, and left the strenuous barnstorming to his running mate, Charles "Hell and Maria" Dawes, who had given his name to the Dawes Plan. Dawes concentrated his fire on La Follette. Although the Progressive program was on the whole moderate, and although La Follette had flatly spurned Communist support (and was bitterly and unfairly maligned by the Communists), Dawes and the Republicans insinuated that the Senator was a Bolshevik agent. The issue in 1924, declared Coolidge, was "whether America will allow itself to be degraded into a communistic or socialistic state or whether it will remain American." Pointing to the Progressive pledge to tamper with the Supreme Court, and warning that a vote for La Follette might prevent any candidate from winning a majority and might thus throw the election into the House of Representatives, the Republicans argued that the only issue was "Coolidge or Chaos." In this curiously unreal campaign, the Democratic party made less impression on the popular mind than at any other time in its history. Davis could not get the Republicans to notice him, and La Follette could not for long distract the Republican press from the bogus issue of communism. The Republican campaign was a successful application of Philip Guedalla's dictum, "Any stigma would do to beat a dogma."

Calvin Coolidge swept the country with 15 million votes, Davis was second with the unbelievably low total of 8 million (less than 29 percent), and La Follette trailed with somewhat less than 5 million. So great was the Republican margin that Coolidge got more votes than both his opponents put together. Not only were the Democrats engulfed by the Republican party, but, in addition, Davis got only half as many votes as La Follette in seventeen states west of the Mississippi. Unbelievably, in California, Davis, a major party candidate, got less than 10 percent of the ballots. The Democrats, who as recently as 1921 had controlled the White House, seemed to be eliminated as a serious alternative to

Republican conservatism for a long time to come. Democratic national headquarters in Washington, observed a reporter after the election, "are as Romish catacombs or Pompeiian atriums, elegantly preserved but destitute."

The Progressives found the outcome even more discouraging. To be sure, La Follette ran up 17 percent of the vote, one of the better showings for the head of a minor ticket. He carried the city of Cleveland, a stronghold of the railway unions, and won 70,000 votes in San Francisco (Coolidge had 73,000), where Davis polled only 9,800. Yet the Progressives could draw little satisfaction from the election; they had helped produce the Coolidge land-slide, by splitting the opposition and arousing fear of "chaos," and La Follette was able to carry only the single state of Wisconsin, his home, in the Electoral College.

After the 1924 campaign, the movement for a farmer-labor party collapsed. The railway unions pulled out, and only a tiny fragment was left to struggle on for a few more years and then die. (The ideal of a farmer-labor party had always been something of a mirage. An Indiana farmer scolded Coolidge to "get the view-point of the broad prairie farmer. Don't be a narrow minded hill billy from Vermont dominated by selfish money and manufacturing and union labor interests all your life.") Before the war, pro-gressivism had secured its greatest triumphs in an era of prosperity, but in the boom years of the Coolidge era, it got nowhere. When utilities announced high profits, people responded not with indignation but with a rush to buy utility stocks. In Congress, the progressive bloc continued to score Pyrrhic victories, but even there the progressives were dispirited and discouraged.

Baffled progressives looked back nostalgically to their era of influence, unable to puzzle out the reasons for their loss of prestige or to understand why so many of their former leaders had abandoned politics. In a symposium in 1926, the economist Stuart Chase wrote of the prewar era:

Them was the days! When the muckrakers were best sellers, when trust busters were swinging their lariats over every state capitol, when "priviledge" shook in its shoes, when God was behind the initiative, the referendum and the recall—and the devil shrieked when he saw the short ballot, when the *Masses* was at the height of its glory, and Utopia was just around the corner. . . .

Now look at the damned thing. You could put the avowed Socialists into a roomy new house, Mr. Coolidge is compared favorably to Lincoln, the short ballot is as defunct as Mah Jong, Mr. Eastman writes triolets in France, Mr. Steffens has bought him a castle in Italy, and Mr. Howe digs turnips in Nantucket.

Shall we lay a wreath on the Uplift Movement in America? I suppose we might as well.

For the most part, the progressives just waited out the rest of the decade. Although some historians have contended that progressivism flourished in the 1920s, the progressives themselves had no doubt that they were living in a desolate time. "I tell you," said Fiorello La Guardia, "it's damned discouraging to be a reformer in the wealthiest land in the world," and in 1929 the labor lawyer Donald Richberg concluded, "Few indeed are the progressives of my generation who have survived the bludgeoning of these years."

The 1920s did, though, mark a time of transition within progressivism from the old-style evangelical reformism, under leaders like La Follette and Bryan, to a new-style urban progressivism, which would call itself liberalism. Liberalism would be less interested in moral reformation and more in using the power of the federal government to provide specific economic benefits. Unlike progressivism, which drew its strength from the old-stock middle class of the small towns and the cities, with not a little support from rural areas, liberalism would have its base in the urban masses, often the "new" immigrant workers of the great cities. Although the progressives had few accomplishments in the 1920s, they were laying the basis for a change in attitude without which the New Deal would not have been possible. McNary-Haugenism committed the farmer to using the taxing power to subsidize agriculture; the Muscle Shoals fight paved the way for the public power projects of the 1930s; and the Railway Labor Act of 1926 was an important forerunner of the Wagner Act of 1935. At the same time, a corps of economists—men such as Wesley Mitchell, Walton Hamilton, Paul Douglas, and Rexford Tugwell—were hammering out the theoretical foundations of the New Deal.

Yet if the new progressivism launched some forays in the 1920s, it made only small headway. To be sure, there were vivid new figures such as Fiorello La Guardia, who as congressman from New York City's East Harlem delighted in taunting the Old Guard. "I stand for the Republicanism of Abraham Lincoln; and let me tell you that the average Republican leader east of the Mississippi doesn't know anything more about Abraham Lincoln than Henry Ford knows about the Talmud," La Guardia told a reporter in 1922. La Guardia, who as spokesman for the urban immigrant opposed nativism and advanced cost-of-living issues, would link the older progressives with the New Dealers; in the 1920s he was one of the few exceptions to the conservatism of the great cities. The new-style liberalism had not yet gained any considerable strength, while the old-style progressivism was dying out. Some men, such as George Norris and even La Follette and Bryan to some extent, successfully combined elements of both. But in

1925 La Follette and Bryan died, and in 1926 Debs also passed away. ("It is hard," said Senator Borah after hearing of La Follette's death, "to say the right thing about Bob La Follette. You know he lived 150 years.") Until the urban progressives gained greater strength and until they found a national leader who could close the breach between the two traditions, the progressives had little hope of winning national power.

8

A Botched Civilization

A few years before World War I, the only literary tradition America had ever known came to an end. At the time it seemed less like a death than a beginning. "One's first strong impression," recalled Malcolm Cowley, "is of the bustle and hopefulness that filled the early years from 1911–1916. . . . Everywhere new institutions were being founded—magazines, clubs, little theatres, art or free-love or single-tax colonies, experimental schools, picture galleries. Everywhere was a sense of secret comradeship and immense potentialities for change." Intellectuals yearning for a "new republic" founded magazines; painters like John Marin and Marsden Hartley were creating new art forms; Isadora Duncan threw aside the rigid dance patterns of the past; Amy Lowell wrote free verse; and in an old stable on MacDougal Street the American theater got a fresh start with the founding of the Provincetown Players. Woodrow Wilson caught the spirit of the age in the phrase, "the New Freedom." The poet Ezra Pound foresaw an inevitable "American Risorgimento" which would "make the Italian Renaissance look like a tempest in a teapot."

Whenever numerous people speak of a renaissance, of the birth of a new culture, writes T. K. Whipple, "you may be sure that an era is dying. It is a law of literary history that these spectacular outbursts which look as if they were ushering in a new epoch are in truth ushering out an old one." The risorgimento of 1912 aspired to what Edmund Wilson was to call the "liquidation of genteel culture." Mabel Dodge, at whose salon on Fifth Avenue the rebels met, schemed to "upset America . . . with fatal disaster to the old order of things." The rebellious intellectuals of 1912, whether they turned to such philosophers of the irrational as Bergson or Nietzsche or the naturalism of writers such as Zola and Ibsen, bristled at Victorian verities. Holmes assailed formal jurisprudence, Dewey questioned formal logic, and Veblen attacked classical economics. The same currents shook modern art; painters abandoned the effort to represent faithfully the natural world.

The rise of the city created, for the first time in America, a distinct body of intellectuals, large in numbers and pursuing their respective crafts on a full-time, professional basis. For the most part, the intellectuals came from a prosperous urbanized middle class, but because of the anonymity and mobility of city living they could be indifferent to middle-class opinion and not bound by associations to family or region or class. Joining this group were the sons of immigrants in the large cities, often with a background of learning such as European Marxism or Talmudic study, who were educated in public high schools; cut off from their families by their intellectual tastes, they were even more rootless and had fewer ties to American mores than the intellectuals who sprang from the middle class. Out of such groups—it was inevitable even without World War I—arose a literature and an art that expressed a sharp cleavage with traditional American values. Well before the war, the new intellectuals demonstrated that they were drawn not to reason but to emotion, not to stability but to change. Politically, they were attracted not to the rational reforms of the progressives or of the "gas and water Socialists" but to the anarchists and the romantic violence of the IWW.

World War I completed the sense of disintegration. It destroyed faith in progress, but it did more than that—it made clear to perceptive thinkers that they had misread the progressive era and the long Victorian reign of peace, that violence prowled underneath the surface harmony and rationality. "The plunge of civilization into this abyss of blood and horror," wrote Henry James in the first year of the European war, "so gives away the whole long age during which we have supposed the world to be, with whatever abatement, gradually bettering, that to have to take it all now for what the treacherous years were really making for and *meaning* is too tragic for any words." The war, wrote James, was an "unspeakable giveaway of the whole fool's paradise of our past"; he regretted that he had not died before it came. The war, which decimated an entire generation in Europe, including some of its finest artists—the war which appeared to strip life and death of all dignity—was taken as final evidence of the bankruptcy of a civilization. Men had died, wrote Ezra Pound,

> For an old bitch gone in the teeth,
> For a botched civilization.

The war brought to an end four centuries of emphasis on human potentiality and returned men such as Pound and his fellow poet T. S. Eliot to a medieval sense of man's wickedness. Eliot rebelled against nineteenth-century "cheerfulness, optimism, and hopefulness." "The Love Song of J. Alfred Prufrock," completed in 1911 but not published until 1917, is a hymn of weariness and impotence, of failure and loss of will. In 1922 Eliot's *The Waste Land* appeared. Throughout the long poem, deliberately disconnected and fragmentary like the world and the emotions it evoked, are the repeated symbols of sterility and emptiness. *The Waste Land* not only excited the admiration and envy of other poets for its technique; it became the text of despair for a generation of intellectuals. It is, of course, a vulgarization of Eliot's work to view his poetry merely as expressing the despondency of a generation. Apart from the fact that a work of art is not primarily a historical document but has a validity of its own, Eliot sought and achieved an expression of universality beyond any particular period. Nonetheless, his early work is studded with judgments on contemporary culture that clearly represent his conviction of the doom of modern society and were so understood at the time. "The Hollow Men" (1925) carries the sense of desolation and horror even deeper; men meet in a "valley of dying stars," in a world devoid of will or emotion—"shape without form, shade without color, paralyzed force, gesture without motion." Even death no longer has meaning: the world ends not with a bang but a whimper.

This disillusionment found a convenient target in "Puritanism." At least as early as Van Wyck Brooks's *The Wine of the Puritans* (1908), writers argued that American culture had been soured by a Puritan tradition that had suppressed the pursuit of pleasure in favor of a pursuit of things and, ultimately, had diverted all of the nation's energy to technology and utilitarianism. Historically shaky at best, this argument quickly grew so banal that, as Charles Beard wrote, the term Puritan became an epithet for "anything that interfere[d] with the new freedom, free verse, psychoanalysis, or even the double entendre." In like manner, intellectuals seized on Sigmund Freud's conception of "repression" as something unique to American society, as though sex taboos, for example, were known only to modern industrial civilization or to the land of the Puritans.

The literati directed their venom less at seventeenth-century Puritanism than at nineteenth-century Victorianism, which they saw as a blend of prudery, commercialism, and sanctimoniousness that added up to a denial of life. Well before the war, influenced by Oscar Wilde, Frank Harris, and George Bernard Shaw, American writers rebelled against the genteel tradition and in particular against Victorian reticence about sex. They rejected the Victorian era—"the notorious Victorian era," Randolph Bourne called it—both because it was too vulgar and because it was too genteel. Above all, they loathed the "Cambridge ladies who live in furnished souls," that vast middle class which sought "culture" as it would shop for furniture, which measured everything in money.

They despised capitalism as the foul offspring of Puritanism. They rebelled against what Waldo Frank called the "cold lethal simplicities of American business culture." The United States, they argued, was a gadgety, mechanistic society, a place where people were bent only on getting a living, a country hostile to leisure and to art. America, wrote one expatriate, was "the enemy of the artist, of the man who cannot produce something tangible when the five o'clock whistle blows." The country was not without ideals, but its ideals were as vapid as the people who believed in them; American culture, Van Wyck Brooks argued in *America's Coming-of-Age* (1915), had been torn between an absurd Emersonian idealism and "catchpenny opportunism." The great photographer Alfred Stieglitz was even more blunt; on a picture of a horse's buttocks, he placed the title "Spiritual America."

The intellectuals found evidence for their theory of the historical development of American culture and solace for their contemporary plight in the analogy between the United States in the 1920s and the years after the Civil War. Both eras were characterized by materialism, political corruption, and cultural vulgarity. Harding and the Ohio Gang had their counterparts in Grant and his cronies, Teapot Dome and the Veterans' Bureau scandals their forerunners in Credit Mobilier and the Whiskey Ring. In *The Ordeal of Mark Twain* (1920), Van Wyck Brooks wrote of the Gilded Age as "a horde-life, a herd-life, an epoch without sun or stars, the twilight of a human spirit that had nothing upon which to feed but the living waters of Camden and the dried manna of Concord." Puritan, capitalist society, with its distorted values, its insistence on the useful, its hostility to the artist, had succeeded both in crushing and in corrupting Twain, leaving him in his last days a bitter, frustrated man. Such also was the fate confronting the artist in the 1920s.

In 1916, Twain's *The Mysterious Stranger* had been published with its message that life was meaningless; in 1918, *The Education of Henry Adams* had appeared with its deeply pessimistic view of the past and its prophecy of inevitable disaster. American writers, Van Wyck Brooks insisted, were doomed, however great their early promise. "There is no denying," he wrote, "that for half a century the American writer as a type has gone down to defeat."

The intellectuals of these years did not just happen upon a sense of despair; they sought it out. Brooks became obsessed early in life with the great losers ("We were attracted to failure," he later conceded), while writers such as Dos Passos could love only the beaten and scorned—the Wobblies, the Bournes, the La Follettes. "We had begun to develop an idea common to nineteenth century romantics and twentieth century bohemians, the idea that success was synonymous with philistinism," wrote Joseph

Freeman. Quite "unable to distinguish between success and conventional standards of success, we made a cult of failure." The novelist Scott Fitzgerald, in particular, was fascinated by "the beautiful and damned." "All the stories that came into my head," he recalled, "had a touch of disaster in them."

The intellectuals felt cut off from the rest of the country. "What will you say to a man who believes in hell, or that the Pope of Rome wants to run this country, or that the Jews caused the war?" asked Ludwig Lewisohn. "How would you argue with a Methodist minister from an Arkansas village, with a Kleagle of the Klan, with a 'this-is-a-white-man's-country' politician from central Georgia?" Faced with such questions, some writers looked to themselves as leaders of a movement which would regenerate American society. Brooks, in particular, saw the artist as the guide to new directions for American culture; he accepted the Italian poet Leopardi's dictum that "in literature alone the regeneration of our country can have a substantial beginning." But most intellectuals had no such illusions; they felt superior to other men, had no desire to reform them or society, and took pride in their separateness. They admired Flaubert not only for his artistry, but also for his contempt for bourgeois philistines; indeed, the two seemed inseparable. A colloquy in e. e. cummings' *The Enormous Room* (1922) states their underlying conviction:

"What do you think happens to people who aren't artists? What do you think people who aren't artists become?"

"I feel they don't become: I feel nothing happens to them; I feel negation becomes of them."

Sherwood Anderson was the first writer canonized in the religion of art. No legend was more central to the idea that the artist could not survive in a business society, indeed that no worthwhile life could be lived by any man in such a suffocating environment, than the story of Anderson's revolt. On November 27, 1912, it was said, Anderson walked out of his paint factory in Elyria, Ohio, in search of life. At the age of thirty-six, like Gauguin, he turned his back on the bourgeois world for the life of art, for a life with meaning. Such was the legend; in fact, Anderson had suffered a nervous breakdown—the gap between the legend and reality was in itself as savage a commentary as the times could offer.

When so much of tradition seemed barren, when society appeared to be so bleak, the effort to become an artist alone held any promise; and the writers were, if nothing else, devoted to mastering their craft. "I want to be one of the greatest writers who have ever lived, don't you?" Scott Fitzgerald asked Edmund Wilson when they were Princeton undergraduates. The youthful, good-looking, blond, green-eyed Fitzgerald, whose *This Side of Paradise* (1920), as Glenway Wescott said, haunted the decade like a song, typified both the devotion to art and the romantic individualism of the period. "Fitzgerald," observes Lionel Trilling, "was perhaps the last notable writer to affirm the Romantic fantasy, descended from the Renaissance, of personal ambition and heroism, of life committed to, or thrown away for, some ideal of self."

The writers of the 1920s trusted only their own perception of experience; they were determined to write without regard for the public pieties. Yet it was difficult to tell the truth, for it was not easy to avoid using words that expressed what one ought to feel rather than what one did feel. Writers avoided adjectives, which were betraying, and pushed as far as they could with blunt nouns and verbs. In Ernest Hemingway's *A Farewell to Arms* (1929), when a character remarks that the Italians could not have fought the Austrians in vain, a friend observes:

I was always embarrassed by the words sacred, glorious, and sacrifice and the expression in vain. We had heard them . . . and had read them, on proclamations that were slapped up by billposters over other proclamations, now for a long time, and I had seen nothing sacred, and the things that were glorious had no glory and the sacrifices were like the stockyards at Chicago if nothing was done with the meat except to bury it. There were many words that you could not stand to hear and finally only the names of places had dignity.

In repudiating the shibboleths of the day, the intellectuals revolted against the assumptions of progressive politics as well. A few years before the 1920s, men and women such as Golden Rule Jones, the Toledo municipal reformer, and Jane Addams, the Chicago social worker, were exciting figures, insurgents against the accepted notions of their times. After World War I, they seemed to the new generation as dull as Henry Wadsworth Longfellow. H. G. Wells, whose reform writings had stirred the Progressives, was dismissed as a "Fabian schoolmarm." Progressivism had become a kind of orthodoxy, and if you rebelled against orthodoxy, you rejected progressivism as well. Progressive education, recalled Malcolm Cowley, was "a topic that put us to sleep." All the new generation's efforts were bent on a rejection of middle-class values, and it did not matter whether those values appeared in the garb of conservatism or progressivism; nothing seemed worse than what Cowley called "an intolerable utopia of dull citizens."

Intellectuals dismissed progressives as dryasdust nuisances preoccupied with routine matters such as lower streetcar fares for the masses and indifferent to the individual—his soul, his spirit, his imagination. Van Wyck Brooks described the reform movement as having been born middle-aged. There was none of the "tang and fire of youth in it, none of the fierce glitter of the intellect;

there was no joyous burning of boats; there were no transfigurations, no ecstasies." Progressivism was indifferent to religion, other than social gospel religion, and to art. "In a world of electoral reform, plebiscites, sex reform and dress reform," wrote T. S. Eliot, "damnation itself is an immediate form of salvation." For years, bright young intellectuals had attempted to improve society, but what, they now asked, had they in common with society, or society with them? "Society," wrote Malcolm Cowley, recording the beliefs of his generation, "was terribly secure, unexciting, middle class, a vast reflection of the families from which we came. . . . Society was something alien, which our own lives and writings could never affect: it was a sort of parlor car in which we rode, over smooth tracks, toward a destination we should never have chosen for ourselves." Democracy implied the reign of middle-class values; the state was an instrument for suppressing dissent. Why should intellectuals attempt to mobilize new majorities for such sorry ends?

"The great problems of the world—social, political, economic and theological—do not concern me in the slightest," wrote the drama critic George Jean Nathan. "If all the Armenians were to be killed tomorrow and if half of Russia were to starve to death the day after, it would not matter to me in the least. What concerns me alone is myself, and the interests of a few close friends. For all I care the rest of the world may go to hell at today's sunset." Sending money for the relief of starving children abroad, remarked the novelist Joseph Hergesheimer, "was one of the least engaging ways in which money could be spent." "If I am convinced of anything," observed the editor and essayist H. L. Mencken, "it is that Doing Good is in bad taste."

In 1922 Harold Stearns edited *Civilization in the United States,* a symposium of thirty different writers who concluded that American culture was in a desperate and perhaps hopeless state. In a notable article in *The Freeman*, Stearns asked, "What should a young man do?" His answer: There was nothing to do here, nothing at all. Get out of the country. After finishing the manuscript of *Civilization in the United States*, Stearns sailed for France. He was only one of a host of writers who gave up America entirely for some country where, they felt, the artist could breathe more freely; they left the USA, Ezra Pound said, "in disgust." Sitting in sidewalk cafes in Paris, they wrote of Michigan and Wisconsin, especially of the American small town and of the wasted lives there. A few remembered America more fondly and turned out epics such as Stephen Vincent Benet's *John Brown's Body* (1928). Others simply lived the lives of Bohemian artists, following the pattern long since set by the French writer Henri Murger's *Scènes de la Vie de Bohême* (1848).

The exodus to Paris represented a flight not merely from Puritan civilization but from modern industrialism. Although some artists attempted to adapt themselves to the Machine Age (ignoring Edmund Wilson's counsel, "Let the artist attend to his art and the age will attend to his adaptation"), most of the intellectuals of the 1920s saw the machine as a menace to be opposed, circumvented, or outwitted. Elmer Rice's play, *The Adding Machine* (1923), whose characters bear names such as Mr. Zero, and the Theater Guild production of the Czech playwright Karel Čapek's *R.U.R.*, which added the word "robot" to the language, encapsulated a pervasive concern with whether man was being transmogrified into a machine. Lewis Mumford warned that the assembly line was destroying the sense of pride and the sense of self of the craftsman. In fear and dislike of a machine age, many intellectuals turned toward more primitive societies, migrating to Mexico or studying the art of the Congo or centering on the Negro as the symbol of pre-industrial man, uninhibited in his laughter and his sadness. In both the United States and Europe, this sentiment took the form of a cult of jazz, for in a world of synthetic songs mechanically contrived on Tin Pan Alley, the rhythms of New Orleans and the delta had the authentic ring of spontaneity.

Exile appealed most to younger men and women; the somewhat older generation of intellectuals typified by H. L. Mencken remained at home to become devastating critics of American society. Mencken did not merely attack democracy; he made the assault on the majority popular by his barbs at the "booboisie." Mencken's outspoken articles let each reader feel that he and the author (and possibly a few others in the "smart set") were laughing together at the stupid masses. No American institution was safe from these gibes. Mencken declared that a clergyman was *ipso facto* a fraud and to be watched, especially when young girls or young boys were about. He told his readers that all Anglo-Saxons were cowards and that the Civil War was a third-rate war because only 200,000 men were killed in it. He advocated abolishing the public school system, defended prostitution, vivisection, and war, and derided social workers as "settlement sharks." When he announced his candidacy for the presidency, it was on a platform of promising to take the Statue of Liberty beyond the three-mile limit and dump it in the ocean, to create vast stadia in which clergymen would be turned loose upon one another, and to give the Philippines to Japan.

Mencken ridiculed all that "homo boobiens" cherished. In place of courting, he proposed that husbands and wives be matched by the common hangman. "Love," he remarked, "is the delusion that one woman differs from another." He drafted a bill legalizing the assassination of public officials. He ridiculed the pet panacea of the civil service reformers by writing that to urge more gentlemen to go into politics was the same as arguing that the cure for prostitution was to send more virgins into brothels. For a decade, he titillated his readers and enraged the objects of his scorn; no fraternity house was complete without a copy of *The American Mercury.* At best, he was a skeptic who cut through pretentiousness, barbarism, and the false affirmations of Rotarianism. As a critic, Mencken sponsored Theodore Dreiser and Frank Norris and, among Europeans, James Joyce, Gerhart Hauptmann, Havelock Ellis, and his favorite, Nietzsche. Some of these men he took up in the face of a vicious prudery; by his own courage or by his indifference to middle-class tastes, he gained them an audience. Yet, as a fellow editor wrote, Mencken's "gift for literary criticism in the grand sense was very limited. He tended to like only those novelists who 'showed up' Americans." Mencken found everything absurd, the good as well as the bad; he was less a true satirist than a nihilist.

This nihilistic strain is even more pronounced in other writings of the period, most explicitly in Hemingway's "nada hail nada full of nada." Their view of social relations is often so distorted as to deny any kind of mature relationship or enduring tradition. Ezra Pound wrote of the adolescent "smothered in family."

> Oh how hideous it is
> To see three generations of one house gathered together!

Dos Passos' novel *1919* (1932) presents a shallow view of American culture, a crabbed image, which, as Maxwell Geismar has pointed out, breathes death, not life, revealing more about Dos Passos than it does about America. Similarly, Sinclair Lewis's novels, praised for their accurate portrayal of midwestern life, actually presented, as T. R. Fyvel has pointed out, a nightmare vision of American society; with monotonous consistency, Lewis revealed "on the one side a demonic American society from which there is no escape, on the other side a hero or heroine whose solitariness is complete."

Many of the novels of the 1920s are peopled with characters who are neurasthenic, weak, unable to impose themselves on their world, fingering their grievances, nourishing a sentimental melancholia. Often the leading figures have no interest in themselves and are consequently at a handicap in invoking the interest of the reader. The Hemingway hero, as Wyndham Lewis remarked, is the man "things are done to." In the novels of the period, W. H. Auden has pointed out, man is "the absolute victim of circumstance and incapable of choice." Yet, Auden notes, American novelists "produced the only significant literature between the two great wars." There is an odd disparity, Auden observes, between the vitality of the novelists and the "helpless victims" in their novels.

Indeed, the 1920s were years of wonderful creativity and, despite the themes of negation of many of the novels and dramas, of great gusto. Ironically, at the very time when intellectuals were complaining that the arts could not flourish in America, literature, art, and music burgeoned as they rarely, perhaps never, had before. Eugene O'Neill exemplified a revolutionary change in the quality of the theater; in Maxwell Anderson, Paul Green, Elmer Rice, Sidney Howard, and others, more talent was revealed in the 1920s than in all the previous history of the American theater. So prolific was a new generation of gifted black writers—Zora Neale

Hurston, Jean Toomer, Langston Hughes, and a host of others—that critics spoke of a "Harlem Renaissance." The novels of Ernest Hemingway, William Faulkner, Sherwood Anderson, F. Scott Fitzgerald, Willa Cather, Ellen Glasgow, and Sinclair Lewis; the short stories of Ring Lardner; the poetry of Hart Crane, e. e. cummings, Conrad Aiken, Marianne Moore, Robinson Jeffers, and Wallace Stevens; the brilliant New Mexico desert paintings of Georgia O'Keeffe and the haunting urban canvasses of Edward Hopper; the insistent chords and timeless melodies of George Gershwin, who incorporated jazz rhythms in symphonic forms—these comprised just such a risorgimento as Pound had predicted.

The contrast between lament and achievement was especially marked in the Midwest. No theme of the period was more hackneyed than the depiction of the corn belt as a cultural wasteland. The region stood for all that was tedious, humdrum, and false; one could not change it, all one could do was flee. Yet Ford Madox Ford, who edited *Transatlantic Review* in Paris, wrote: "The Middle West was seething with literary impulse. It is no exaggeration to say that 80 per cent of the manuscripts in English that I received came from west of Altoona, and 40 per cent of them were of such a level of excellence that one might just as well close one's eyes and take one at random as try to choose between them."

It is not easy to explain the negativism of the artists of the 1920s in relation to their creativity. The very rejection of tradition and of the earlier idealism, which might have resulted simply in a sterile Nay-saying, appears to have freed writers to experiment with new forms. There may well be a causal connection between intellectual productivity and the alienation of intellectuals. The writer of the 1950s, notes John Aldridge, was able to live "at least on terms of peaceable coexistence with society, and even though that has immensely improved his material circumstances, it has deprived him of that 'something' to push against which seems so necessary to the existence of his art." One thing is certain: the 1920s produced a literature that no era since has been able to match.

9

The Revolution in Morals

The disintegration of traditional values—so sharply recorded by novelists and artists—was reflected in a change in manners and morals that shook American society to its depths. In an increasingly secularized country, religious sanctions no longer had their earlier force. People lost their fear of Hell and had less interest in Heaven; they made more demands for material fulfillment on Earth. Simultaneously, a "status revolution" undercut the authority of the people who had set the nation's moral standards: the professional classes, especially ministers, lawyers, and teachers; the rural gentry; and the urban patricians. The new minorities and *arriviste* businessmen were frequently not equipped—or lacked the desire—either to support old standards or to create new ones. Most important, the authority of the family, gradually eroded through several centuries, was lessened. "Never in recent generations," wrote Freda Kirchwey, "have human beings so floundered about outside the ropes of social and religious sanctions."

When Nora, the feminist heroine of *A Doll's House* (1879) by the Norwegian playwright Henrik Ibsen, walked out into the night, she launched against male-dominated society a rebellion that has not ended yet. The "new woman" revolted against masculine possessiveness, against "over-evaluation" of women "as love objects," against being treated, at worst, as a species of property. The new woman wanted the same freedom of movement that men had and the same economic and political rights. By the end of the 1920s she had come a long way, though with an even longer way still to go. Before the war, a lady did not set foot in a saloon; after the war, she entered a speakeasy as thoughtlessly as she would go into a depot. In 1904, a woman was arrested for smoking on Fifth Avenue; in 1929, railroads dropped their regulation against women lighting up in dining cars. In the business and political worlds, women competed with men, though hardly on equal terms. In marriage, they edged toward a more contractual role, albeit at a glacial pace. Once kept ignorant of financial matters, they moved rapidly toward the point where they would be the chief property-holders of the country. Sexual independence was merely the most sensational aspect of the altering status of women.

Commentators made much of what appeared to be a marked acceleration in the rate of entry of women into the job market. In 1870, there were only a few women secretaries in the entire country; by 1900, 86,000 women held clerical positions; by 1930, more than 775,000 were typing the letters and keeping the records of corporations and countinghouses in every city in the nation, a nearly ninefold increase in one generation. During the war, when mobilization created a shortage of labor, women moved into jobs they had never held before. They made grenades, ran elevators, polished locomotives, collected streetcar fares, and even drilled with rifles. In the years after the war, women flew airplanes, trapped beaver, drove taxis, ran telegraph lines, worked as deep-sea divers and steeplejacks, and hunted tigers in the jungle; women stevedores heaved cargoes on the waterfront, while other women conducted orchestras, ran baseball teams, and drilled oil wells. By 1930, more than ten million women held jobs.

It has been too readily assumed, though, that there was a revolution in women's access to the workplace in the 1920s and that gainful employment resulted in their "liberation." The big gain in the percentage of women who held jobs took place neither in World War I nor in the 1920s but earlier in the century. The proportion of women in the work force was actually less in 1930 than it had been in 1910. They did not come close to receiving equal pay for equal work, and they continued to be cabined in occupations thought appropriate for their sex: domestics, sales clerks, seamstresses. Women made up a smaller proportion of the college student body in 1930 than in 1920, and there were considerably fewer female doctors in 1930 than there had been a decade before. Harvard would not admit women to either its law or its medical schools. Even in the 1920s it was rare for a middle-class married woman to work outside the home. When married women did work, they did so not because they sought emancipation but out of necessity or to augment family income. Most women in the labor force were either blacks or foreign-born whites, who were recruited for menial labor. Furthermore, the traditional attitude about woman's "place" persisted. Women were still expected to assume total responsibility for household chores—to cook, to clean, and to diaper. Vassar even offered courses in "Husband and Wife" and "Motherhood." "If the word 'emancipation' is taken to mean the ability of women to function in the world outside the home on the same basis as men," William H. Chafe has written, "then female workers remained as unemancipated in 1940 as in 1920."

Women's success in gaining access to the ballot also did not turn out as had been predicted, either by advocates or by opponents. The right of women to vote should have required no special justification, but to overcome resistance to approval of the Nineteenth Amendment suffragists, accepting the traditional view of woman's nature, had argued that giving women the ballot would purify politics and initiate a new era of universal peace and benevolence. On the other hand, foes had forecast the disintegration of American society. (The chief result of women's suffrage, Mencken forecast, would be that adultery would replace boozing as the favorite pastime of politicians.) As it turned out, the Nineteenth Amendment had few immediate consequences, for good or evil.

Both friends and enemies of women's suffrage had anticipated that when the amendment was ratified women would seize upon the opportunity and would vote as a bloc. Politicians, fearful of how such developments might affect their survival, initially responded by heeding the desires of women for legislation such as the Sheppard-Towner act, authorizing federal funding of health care for mothers and infants. But it quickly became apparent that women, in common with other newly enfranchised groups, did not vote in the same proportion as men. Asked why they did not vote, numbers of women replied, to the dismay of those who had labored so long to end discrimination at the polls, either that they did not believe in suffrage for women or that they had neglected to do so because their husbands had forgotten to remind them. Nor did women who did vote do so as a female bloc. Wives voted the same way that their husbands did. Once politicians realized that women did not vote as a bloc, they stopped catering to their demands. In 1929, the Sheppard-Towner Act was allowed to lapse. Furthermore, women who did want to mobilize their sex found it hard to define what a "woman's issue" was. Achieving suffrage had the ironic consequence of removing the one cause around which most women could rally. Even the Sheppard-Towner act reflected the traditional role perception of woman as mother. Expected to be a progressive force, women in 1920 had instead bolstered the status quo by swelling Warren Harding's victory margin, because well-to-do women were more likely to vote and the wealthier classes were preponderantly Republican.

Still, significant changes were taking place. Millions of women did vote for the first time, a right too long denied them, and some women were elected to public office (several had gained seats in Congress by the end of the 1920s). As governor of New York, Al Smith depended on the counsel of Belle Moskowitz, and women such as Eleanor Roosevelt were gaining the political experience that would be indispensable in later years. Furthermore, newly enfranchised women provided an invaluable leaven to community activities throughout the land. Though the proportion of women in the labor force in the 1920s remained stable, the actual totals increased 26 percent. By 1930, over ten million women held down jobs, and more than a quarter of all editors, authors, and journalists were female.

These trends, especially the economic changes, also had an impact on the "revolution in morals," though, once again, the connection is not as clearcut as has frequently been suggested. Reformers such as Margaret Sanger, the birth control advocate who championed women's control of their own bodies, disdained the political aspirations of the feminists, while most of the onetime leaders of the suffrage movement deplored promiscuity. Some of the radical feminists preferred, insofar as possible, to dispense with sexual relationships between men and women altogether, because they conceived of sexual intercourse as essentially humiliating to women. "Man is the only animal using this function out of season," protested Charlotte Perkins Gilman. "Excessive indulgence in sex-waste has imperiled the life of the race." Yet, however unintentionally, the rhetoric of liberation and the transition of women out of their homes and into offices, where they associated freely with men, inevitably affected behavior. Wives who took jobs gained greater freedom of motion and choice, though a good deal less than equality, and single women who moved into their own apartments escaped hovering parents. "In the great cities," wrote Alyse Gregory, "in those circles where women twenty-five to thirty-five can control their own purse strings many of them are apt to drift into casual or steady relationships with certain men friends which may or may not end in matrimony."

Men perceived women to be more assertive than ever before and reacted with alarm, often altogether unreasonably, to the implicit and explicit challenges to their dominant roles as the head of the family, the sole breadwinner, and the initiator of sex. Some feminists appeared to believe that women were equal to men, and even more so. "Call on God, my dear," Mrs. Belmont is alleged to have told a despondent young suffragette. "She will help you." Others, chanting slogans such as "Come out of the kitchen" and "Never darn a sock," rebelled against the age-old household tasks assigned women. In Dorothy Canfield Fisher's *The Home-Maker* (1924), the process is taken to its logical conclusion: a woman who has been a failure as a mother succeeds in business while her husband, a failure in business, stays at home and makes a success of raising children. The literature of the time reflects the growing male anxiety, notably in the morbid fear of the British novelist, D. H. Lawrence, that he would be absorbed by woman but even more in a new American character represented by the destructive Nina Leeds of O'Neill's *Strange Interlude* (1928), the husband-exploiting title figure of George Kelly's *Craig's Wife* (1926), and the possessive "son-devouring tigress" of Sidney Howard's *The Silver Cord* (1927).

Greater freedom for women added to the stress on the stability of the family. By the turn of the century, women were demanding more of marriage than they ever had before and were growingly unwilling to continue alliances in which they were miserable. For at least a century, the family had been losing many of its original functions; the state, the factory, the school, and even mass amusements had robbed it of tasks it had once performed. The more that social usefulness was taken away from the family, the more marriage came to depend on the personalities of the individuals involved, and, since many Americans of both sexes entered marriage with unreasonable expectations, such reliance proved a slender reed. In 1914, the number of divorces reached 100,000 for the first time; in 1929, over 205,000 couples ended their marriages in a single year. The rise in divorce probably meant less an increase in marital unhappiness than a refusal to go on with marriages that would earlier have been tolerated.

As the family lost its other social roles, the chief test of a good family became how well it developed the personalities of the children, and parents, distrustful both of their own instincts and of tribal lore, eagerly sought out expert advice to avoid the opprobrium of having raised unhappy offspring. One of the most widely quoted authorities, Dr. John B. Watson, published the first edition of *Behaviorism* in 1914, but it was not until its third edition in 1925 that behaviorism—the idea that man was nothing but a machine responding to stimuli—took the country by storm. "Give me a dozen healthy infants, well-formed, and my own specified world to bring them up in," declared Watson, "and I'll guarantee to take any one at random and train him to become any specialist I might select—doctor, lawyer, artist, merchant-chief, and yes, even beggarman and thief, regardless of his talents, tendencies, abilities, vocations and race of his ancestor." Watson predicted that the time would come when it would be just as bad manners to show affection to one's mother or father as to come to the table with dirty hands. To inculcate the proper attitudes at an early age, Watson warned parents, "Never hug and kiss them, never let them sit in your lap." Most parents appear to have ignored that admonition. Indeed, one of the happier developments of the 1920s was that the middle class family was much more likely than it had been in the past to be child-conscious and affectionate. But Watson's theories were acceptable enough for the Department of Labor to incorporate behaviorist assumptions, including emphasis on rigid scheduling of a baby's activities, in its pamphlet, *Infant and Child Care,* which became the government's best-selling publication.

Great as Watson's influence was, it could not hold a candle to that of Sigmund Freud. In 1909, when the Viennese psychiatrist journeyed to the United States to give a series of lectures at Clark University, he was amazed that "even in prudish America" his work was so well known. The following year, Dr. A. A. Brill published the first of his translations of Freud, *Three Contributions to a Theory of Sex* (previously available only in the German *Drei Adhandlungen zur Sexual-Theorie*), and in 1913, Brill, at the invitation of the precocious Walter Lippmann, explained Freud to a coterie gathered at Mabel Dodge's salon. With startling speed, Freudian doctrine made its way in intellectual circles; along with that of Nietzsche and Bergson, it had strongly influenced Lippmann's *A Preface to Politics* (1914). At the same time, Freudian theories attracted a cadre of practitioners. By 1916, there were some five hundred psychoanalysts, or people who called themselves that, in New York City. Freud's sexual theories, particularly his contention that neurotic symptoms could be traced to sexual disturbances, were not popularly disseminated until after the war. But they were well enough known to New York social workers that, despite hostility and even revulsion at his blunt descriptions of infant sexuality, Brill was able to lecture to the ladies of the Child Study Association on "Masturbation."

American participation in the war made the whole country psychology-conscious, if not Freud-conscious. More than one hundred psychologists served on the Surgeon-General's staff, and there was wide discussion of wartime medical phenomena like "shell shock." Even more important in popularizing psychology were the Army "intelligence" tests; during the war, hundreds of thousands of soldiers were asked to cross out the "g" in "tiger."

In the years after the war, psychology became a national mania. Books appeared on the *Psychology of Golf,* the *Psychology of the Poet Shelley,* and the *Psychology of Selling Life Insurance.* People talked knowingly of "libido," "defense mechanism," and "fixation," confused the subconscious with the unconscious, repression with suppression, and dealt with the tortuously difficult theories of Freud and of psychoanalysis as though they were simple ideas readily grasped after a few moments' explanation. One article explained solemnly that the immense popularity of the song "Yes, We Have No Bananas" was the result of a national inferiority complex. Karl Menninger found himself badgered at parties to perform analyses of the personalities of guests as though he were a fortune teller. "When I refuse," the psychiatrist explained, "my questioners often show me how the thing is done." Neophytes were able to read books like *Psychoanalysis by Mail* and *Psycho-*

analysis Self-Applied, while the Sears, Roebuck catalogue offered *Ten Thousand Dreams Interpreted* and *Sex Problems Solved.* Like the automobile, Freud was brought within reach of everyone.

Freud's popularity had an inevitable effect on what publicists called the "revolution in morals." It was assumed that he was arguing that unless you freely expressed your libido, you would damage your health; by this distortion of his work, a scientific imprimatur was given to sexual indulgence. By a similar but more understandable misinterpretation, it was believed that Freud was denying the reality of love; his name was invoked in support of the dehumanization of sex. "I'm hipped on Freud and all that," observed a Scott Fitzgerald heroine, "but it's rotten that every bit of *real* love in the world is ninety-nine percent passion and one little soupçon of jealousy."

What only the initiate understood was that although Freud did emphasize the strength of unconscious motivation, psychiatry aimed not at enthroning the irrational or at licensing promiscuity but at making it possible for men and women to use their rational powers to control their emotions through a clearer comprehension of their impulses. Freud, in fact, taught that the most "irrational" act had meaning. The vast popularity of Freud in the United States, which was to move the center of psychiatry from Vienna to Park Avenue, alarmed many psychoanalysts. They realized that Freud had become the rage less through an understanding of his ideas than through a belief that he shared the American conviction that everyone has the right not merely to pursue happiness but to possess it. This distortion had a number of unfortunate results, not least of which was the disappointment patients experienced when they came to realize that progress could be made only when self-indulgent fantasies were surrendered; but its ultimate effect was good. In Europe, psychiatry followed a course of near-fatalism in treating mental illness; in the more optimistic and more expectant American environment, psychiatry made greater gains and received far more public support.

Freudian theories made a large impression on American writers, in part because they suggested new modes for the exploration of human motivation, in part because they gave post-war intellectuals an invaluable weapon against the older standards. In some works, the use of Freud was explicit; in others, as in the novels of Sherwood Anderson, where the influence of Freud seems obvious, there was apparently no conscious use of Freud at all. Eugene O'Neill turned to Freudian themes in his ambitious *Strange Interlude* (1928) as well as in his *Desire Under the Elms* (1924) and *Mourning Becomes Electra* (1931). Freud's biggest impact on the form of the novel was in the "stream-of-consciousness" technique, although its most important exponent, the Irish novelist James Joyce, was more directly affected by Jung. Stream of consciousness was employed in America most notably in William Faulkner's *The Sound and the Fury* (1929) and in the works of the novelist and poet Conrad Aiken. "I decided very early," Aiken recalled, "that Freud, and his co-workers and rivals and followers, were making the most important contribution of the century to the understanding of man and his consciousness; accordingly I made it my business to learn as much from them as I could."

Freud's doctrines also opened up a new world to biographers anxious to understand the inner life of their subjects, but most of his effect on biography ran from the unfortunate to the disastrous. His own *Leonardo da Vinci* (1910), which should have served as a warning, became instead a model. In this essay, Freud endeavored with doubtful success to reconstruct Da Vinci's life and to interpret his works from a single fantasy that Da Vinci remembered. With similar fragmentary evidence, psychoanalytically oriented biographers tried to add a new dimension to their work; some of these ventures were serious, others were little more than vendettas on heroes of the past. Emerson and Thoreau, Ludwig Lewisohn contended, were "chilled under-sexed valetudinarians." Even when new information or interpretations were established, it was not always clear what use could be made of them. "The superstition persisted," Alfred Kazin later remarked, "that to have proved one's subject impotent was to have made a critical statement."

In the attempt to work out a new standard of relations between men and women, Americans in the 1920s became obsessed with the subject of sex. Some novelists wrote of little else, in particular James Branch Cabell, whose *Jurgen* (1919), actually a curiously unerotic novel despite its absorption with the subject, was praised for its "phallic candour." Radio singers crooned songs like "Hot Lips," "I Need Lovin'," and "Burning Kisses." Magazines like *Paris Nights, Flapper Experiences,* and *Snappy Stories* covered newsstands. The journalist Frank Kent returned from a tour of the country in 1925 with the conviction that "between the magazines and the movies a lot of these little towns seem literally saturated with sex." Advertising, once pristine, began the transition which, as one writer remarked, was to transmute soap from a cleansing agent to an aphrodisiac and to suggest "that every woman buying a pair of stockings is aiming for an assignation, or at the very least for a rescue via a fire-ladder."

Absorption with sex was the life's blood of the newspaper tabloid. Developed by Lord Northcliffe in England, the tabloid first appeared in America with the founding of the New York *Daily News* in 1919. As a picture newspaper like the *Sketch* and the *Mirror* in England, the *News* caught on immediately; within five years, it had the largest circulation of any publication in New York. Hearst followed with the New York *Daily Mirror,* a slavish

imitation of the *News,* and in 1924 Bernarr Macfadden demonstrated how far sensationalism could be carried with the salacious
New York *Evening Graphic.* The Manhattan tabloids soon had their
imitators in other cities. Although they won millions of readers,
they did not cut into the circulation of the established newspapers; they found a new, semiliterate market.

Not even the tabloids exploited sex with the zeal of Hollywood;
it was movies that created the love goddess. When the "vamp,"
Theda Bara, appeared in *The Blue Flame* in 1920, crowds mobbed
theaters in eastern cities to get in. Producers found that films such
as *The Sheik* drew large audiences, while *Sentimental Tommy* or epics
like *America* played to empty houses. When it was apparent that
sex was infinitely more profitable than the prewar sentimental-
patriotic fustian, the country got a steady diet of movies like *Up
in Mabel's Room, Her Purchase Price,* and *A Shocking Night.* (Cecil B.
De Mille changed the title of Sir James Barrie's *The Admirable
Crichton* to *Male and Female.*) Clara Bow was featured as the "It"
girl, and no one had to be told what "it" was. The only ones in
Hollywood with "it," explained the novelist Elinor Glyn, were
"Rex, the wild stallion, actor Tony Moreno, the Ambassador Hotel doorman and Clara Bow." Movie ads promised kisses "where
heart, and soul, and sense in concert move, and the blood is lava,
and the pulse a blaze."

Threatened by censorship bills in thirty-six states, the industry
made a gesture toward reforming itself. Following the model of
organized baseball, which had made Judge Kenesaw Mountain
Landis its "czar" after the Chicago Black Sox scandal of 1919, the
movie industry hired Harding's Postmaster-General, Will Hays,
to be the "Judge Landis of the movies." All the Hays Office succeeded in doing in the 1920s was to add hypocrisy to sex by insisting on sanctimonious titles and the "moral" ending. Movie ads

continued to entice patrons with "brilliant men, beautiful jazz babies, champagne baths, midnight revels, petting parties in the purple dawn, all ending in one terrific smashing climax that makes you gasp."

As such come-ons suggested, taboos about sex discussion were losing their force. Novelists and playwrights spoke with a new bluntness; in Hemingway's *The Sun Also Rises* (1926), the word "bitch" recurs frequently. Women talked freely about inhibitions and "sex starvation," and men and women told one another off-color stories that a short while before would have been reserved for the Pullman smoker. The woman who once was shocked by everything now prided herself, observed a writer in *Harper's*, on the fact that nothing at all shocked her; "immunity to the sensation of 'recoil with painful astonishment' is the mark of our civilization."

Parental control of sex appreciably diminished; the chaperone vanished at dances, and there was no room for a duenna in the rumble seat of an automobile. The bachelor girl had her own latchkey. Girls petted, and when they did not pet, they necked, and no one was certain of the exact difference; Lloyd Morris observed: "The word 'neck' ceased to be a noun; abruptly became a verb; immediately lost all anatomical precision." At one conference in the Midwest, eight hundred college girls met to discuss searching questions like What do nice girls do? and How far should you go? "Whether or not they pet," said one writer, "they hesitate to have anyone believe that they do not." The consensus of the delegates was: "Learn temperance in petting, not abstinence."

During these years, Victorian dance forms like the waltz yielded to the fast-stepping Charleston, the Black Bottom, or slow fox trots in which, to the syncopated rhythms of a jazz band, there was a "maximum of motion in the minimum of space." Jazz made its way northward from the bordellos of New Orleans to the dance halls of Chicago, crossed the ocean to Paris (where it was instantly taken up as a uniquely American contribution to music), and created its own folk heroes in the lyrical Bix Beiderbecke, the earthy Bessie Smith, and the innovative Louis Armstrong who, legend has it, once played two hundred different choruses of "Sweet Sue." The tango and the fox trot hit the country before the war, but it was not until the 1920s that the more voluptuous and the more frenetic dance crazes swept the nation. Moralists like Bishop Cannon protested that the new dances brought "the bodies of men and women in unusual relations to each other"; but by the end of the period the fox trot was as popular and the saxophones wailed as loudly at the high-school proms of the Bishop's Methodist parishioners as in the dance halls of New York and Los Angeles.

What did it all add up to? "The proportion of frail to virtuous women is probably constant throughout the ages in any civilization," observed the British Lord High Chancellor in 1928. Perhaps, but the meager evidence available suggests otherwise. Researchers have found that women born later than the turn of the century were twice as likely to have lost their virginity before they were married than women of the previous generation, and that the moment of change had come at about the time of World War I and its aftermath. Extramarital sex also became more common. Even George Babbitt had a fling. With more effective contraceptive techniques widely used, the fear of pregnancy was decidedly lessened. ("The veriest schoolgirl today knows as much as the midwife of 1885," wrote Mencken.) At the same time, quite possibly as a consequence, a great many brothels lost their customers and had to close their doors, while itinerant workers in the same field disappeared from the sidewalks.

Not only the American woman but the American girl was reputed to be freer with her sexual favors than she had ever been before. Most college women stopped short of intercourse, but no one doubted that every campus had its Jezebels. Smith College girls in New York, noted Malcolm Cowley, modeled themselves on Hemingway's Lady Brett. Certainly, girls were less reticent than they had been before the war. "One hears it said," lamented a Southern Baptist periodical, "that the girls are actually tempting the boys more than the boys do the girls, by their dress and conversation." They dressed more freely; they wore bathing suits that revealed more than had ever been revealed before. At dances, corsets were checked in cloakrooms; then even this pretense was abandoned. Above all, they were out for a good time. "None of the Victorian mothers," wrote F. Scott Fitzgerald in *This Side of Paradise*, "had any idea how casually their daughters were accustomed to be kissed."

Although Fitzgerald reported that the ideal flapper was "lovely and expensive and about nineteen," the flapper appeared bent on playing down her femininity and emphasizing her boyishness. She used the most ingenious devices to conceal the fact that she had breasts. Even the nudes at the Folies Bergères were flatchested and were picked for that reason, and in England, women wore the "Eton crop" and bound their chests with wide strips of ribbon to achieve a "boyish bust." The flapper wore thin dresses that suggested she had no hips at all; her waistline moved steadily southward. As one writer recalled, "Women not only lost their waists; they sat on them." She dieted recklessly in an effort to remove unwanted protuberances. Girls, noted one physician, were at-

tempting to become "pathologically thin." "A strikingly sad example of improper dieting," he said, "was the case of a shapely
motion-picture actress, who became a nervous wreck and blasted
her career by restricting herself to tomatoes, spinach and orange
juice." The flapper bobbed her hair which she dyed raven black,
and tweezed her eyebrows. She concealed everything feminine but
her matchstick legs. In 1919, her skirt was six inches above the
ground; by 1927, it had edged about to her knees, or even a
couple of inches above. The well-accoutered flapper wore a tight
felt cloche hat, two strings of beads, bangles on her wrists, flesh-
colored hose rolled below the knees, and unbuckled galoshes.
Ironically, the more she adopted mannish styles, the more she
painted her face, daubing her cheeks with two circles of rouge and
her "bee-stung" lips, in the manner of Clara Bow, with "kiss-
proof" lipstick; cosmetics became the chief way of distinguishing
female members of the race.

The flapper was, as Kenneth Yellis has noted, the "utter anti-
thesis" of the "maternal and wifely," ample-breasted but discreetly
covered and corseted, Gibson girl of the 1890s. He explains:

> The Gibson girl was the embodiment of stability. The flapper's aes-
> thetic ideal was motion, her characteristics were intensity, energy, vola-
> tility. While the Gibson girl seems incapable of an immodest thought
> or deed, the flapper strikes us as brazen and at least capable of sin if not
> actually guilty of it. She refused to recognize the traditional moral code
> of American civilization, while the Gibson girl had been its guardian.

What disturbed critics about the flapper, he adds, was "precisely
her modernity," for "when the flapper raised her skirts above the
knee and rolled her hose below it, the naked flesh of the lower
limbs of respectable women was revealed for the first time since

the fall of Rome; the connection of the two events was not seen as coincidental."

The attention paid to flappers, who were never more than a minority, and the alarums over promiscuity beclouded a much more important development. "The sexual revolution of the twenties," Paula Fass has pointed out, "was not a revolt against marriage but a revolution within marriage," characterized by "the sexualization of love and the glorification of sex." Women continued to be denied equality outside of the home, but so long as they accepted their separate sphere as wives and mothers (as, to an overwhelming degree, most women did) they had considerably more authority than ever before to expect that husbands would treat them as equals, especially in the bedroom.

The vogue of the flapper constituted only the most obvious instance of the new cult of youth. "It is the glory of the present age that in it one can be young," Randolph Bourne wrote in 1913. In every age, youth has a sense of a separate destiny, of experiencing what no one has ever experienced before, but it may be doubted that there was ever a time in America when youth had such a special sense of importance as in the years after World War I. There was a break between generations like a geological fault; young men who had fought in the trenches felt that they knew a reality their elders could not even imagine. Young girls no longer consciously modeled themselves on their mothers, whose experience seemed unusable in the 1920s.

Instead of youth emulating age, age imitated youth. Scott Fitzgerald, looking back on the years of which he was the chief chronicler, recalled: "May one offer in exhibit the year 1922! That was the peak of the younger generation, for though the Jazz Age continued, it became less and less an affair of youth. The sequel was a children's party taken over by elders." "Oh, yes, we are collegiate" was the theme song of a generation yearning for the irresponsible, idealized days of youth. Everyone wanted to be young. Gertrude Atherton's *Black Oxen* (1923) described how grandmothers might be rejuvenated through a glandular operation and once more stir up young men. It was the young girl who started the flapper fashion; it was her mother who kept it going.

Americans in the 1920s, at least on the surface, were less sin-ridden than they had ever been before. Many broke the Sabbath apparently without compunction, missing the morning sermon to play golf, driving into the country in the afternoon instead of sitting stiffly in the parlor. The mood of the country was hedonistic; Omar Khayyam's quatrains took the colleges by storm. The ideal of hedonism was living for the moment, and if one can isolate a single spirit that permeated every segment of society in the postwar years, it was the obliteration of time.

Abandoning the notion of saving income or goods or capital over time, the country insisted on immediate gratification, a demand that became institutionalized in the installment plan. The President's Research Committee on Social Trends noted "the new attitude towards hardship as a thing to be avoided by living in the here and now, utilizing instalment credit and other devices to telescope the future into the present." Songs became obsolescent almost as soon as they appeared, and people prided themselves not on remembering the old songs but on knowing the latest. The imitation of youth by age was an effort to foreshorten the years, while youth itself tried to escape the inexorability of time. One of the younger generation, replying to its critics, observed: "The trouble with them is that they can't seem to realize that we are busy, that what pleasure we snatch must be incidental and feverishly hurried. We have to make the most of our time. . . . We must gather rose-buds while we may."

In the magazine *Secession,* a group of intellectuals, including the poet Hart Crane, signed a "Proclamation" declaring "Time is a tyranny to be abolished." Gertrude Stein's concept of a "continuous present" effaced not merely history and tradition but any sense of "time." "The future," she declared, "is not important any more." In Italy, the Futurists had cast out Petrarch and Dante and rejected harmony and sentiment; their present-mindedness had a direct impact on Ezra Pound, who found their chief spokesman, Marinetti, "thoroughly simpatico." The characters in the novels of the day, particularly those of Scott Fitzgerald, gave no thought to tomorrow, while Edna St. Vincent Millay penned the theme of the generation in "My candle burns at both ends." The spirit of the decade, wrote Edmund Wilson, was "letting oneself be carried along by the mad hilarity and heartbreak of jazz, living only for the excitement of the evening."

The obliteration of time carried with it a conscious assault on the authority of history. Carl Sandburg dismissed the past as a bucket of ashes, and the Dada movement, which developed in the war years in Zurich, adopted as its motto: "Je ne veux même pas savoir s'il y a eu des hommes avant moi" ("I do not wish even to know whether there have been men before me"). More remarkably, the very men who were the spokesmen for history and tradition led the onslaught; in this, Henry Ford and Charles Beard were one. Ford's interest in history was actually an anti-history. He took cottages in which Noah Webster and Patrick Henry had once lived and moved them to Dearborn, Michigan, where they had no meaning. He sentimentalized and pillaged the past, but he had no respect for it. "History is more or less the bunk," he said. "We want to live in the present, and the only history that is worth a tinker's dam is the history we make today." As early as 1907, the historians Charles Beard and James Harvey Robinson had deliberately attempted to subordinate the past to the present with the aim of enabling the reader "to catch up with his own times; . . . to know what was the attitude of Leo XIII toward the Social Democrats even if he has forgotten that of Innocent III toward the Albigenses." Beard's emphasis on current history had its counterpart in Veblen's dislike for dead languages, Holmes's skepticism about the value of learning as a guide in jurisprudence, and Dewey's emphasis on the functional in education.

The preoccupation with living in the present had problematic consequences. On the one hand, the revolution in morals routed the worst of Victorian sentimentality and false modesty. It mitigated the harsh judgments of rural Protestantism, and it all but wiped out the awful combination of sanctimoniousness and lewdness which enabled Anthony Comstock to defame Bernard Shaw as "this Irish smut-dealer" and which allowed Teddy Roosevelt, with unconscious humor, to denounce the Mexican bandit Villa as a "murderer and a bigamist." It greatly extended the range of choice; "the conduct of life," wrote Joseph Wood Krutch, had been made "more thrillingly difficult." Yet, at the same time, it raised baffling problems of the relations between husband and wife, parent and child, and, in itself, provided no ready guides to conduct. The hedonism of the period was less a remedy than a symptom of what Walter Lippmann called a "vast dissolution of ancient habits," and rarely did it prove as satisfying as people hoped.

10

The Second Industrial Revolution

In the late eighteenth and early nineteenth centuries the indus-trialization of England accelerated at such a pace that historians have found no term adequate to describe it save one usually re-served for violent political change—revolution. In the late nine-teenth century and early twentieth century the productive capac-ity of the American economy increased at a rate greater than that of the Industrial Revolution. After World War I, the United States, benefiting from half a century of industrial progress, achieved the highest standard of living any people had ever known, though one that still left many millions in poverty. Na-tional income soared from $480 per capita in 1900 to $681 in 1929. Workers were paid the highest wages of any time in the history of the country; essentially unchanged from 1890 to 1918, the real earnings of workers—what their income actually would buy at the store—shot up 22 per cent in just seven years. At the same time, the number of hours of work was cut: in 1923, United States Steel abandoned the twelve-hour day and put its Gary plant on an eight-hour shift; in 1926, Henry Ford instituted the five-day week, while International Harvester announced the electrify-ing innovation of a two-week annual vacation with pay for its employees.

In 1922 the country, already fabulously productive by comparison with other nations, started a recovery from the postwar depression that continued, with slight interruptions, until the fall of 1929. The key to the piping prosperity of the decade was the enormous increase in efficiency of production, in part the result of the application of Frederick W. Taylor's theory of scientific management, in part the outgrowth of technological innovations. In 1914, at his Highland Park plant, Henry Ford had revolutionized production by installing the first moving assembly line with an endless-chain conveyor; three months later, his men assembled an automobile, down to its smallest parts, in 93 minutes. A year before, it had taken 14 hours. During this same period, machine power replaced human labor at a startling rate: in 1914, 30 percent of industry was electrified, in 1929, 70 percent. The electric motor made the steam engine obsolete; between 1919 and 1927 more than 44 percent of the steam engines in the United States went to the scrap heap. Since labor came out of the postwar depression with higher real wages—employers feared a new strike wave if they cut wages as sharply as prices fell—business was stimulated to lower production costs. With more efficient management, greater mechanization, intensive research, and ingenious sales methods, industrial production almost doubled during the decade, soaring from an index figure of 58 in the depression year of 1921 to 110 in 1929 (1933–39 = 100). This impressive increase in productivity was achieved without any expansion of the labor force; manufacturing employed precisely the same number in 1929 as in 1919. The summit of technological achievement was reached on October 31, 1925, when Ford rolled a completed automobile off his assembly line every ten seconds.

The productivity of American industry increased tremendously. Between 1899 and 1929 the total output of manufacturing jumped 264 per cent. Petroleum products—new oil fields were discovered in Texas, Oklahoma, and California—multiplied more than sixteen times in this period, the basic iron and steel industry five times. The number of telephones installed rose from 1,355,000 in 1900 to 10,525,000 in 1915 to 20,200,000 in 1930. Most impressive was the growth of new industries, some of which did not even exist in 1914. Light metals such as magnesium experienced a meteoric rise; the output of aluminum more than doubled between 1914 and 1920. American factories turned out a host of new products—cigarette lighters, oil furnaces, wrist watches, antifreeze fluids, reinforced concrete, paint sprayers, book matches, dry ice, Pyrex glass for cooking utensils, and panchromatic motion-picture film.

Many of the new industries catered to the home. Americans consumed a more varied diet than they ever had before. They thought it commonplace to have fresh fruit and vegetables in midwinter—Louisiana cherries and Arizona melons, Carolina peas and Alabama corn. In 1905, 41 million cases of food were shipped, in 1930, 200 million. Fresh green vegetables, many of them novelties, arrived in northern markets; shipments of lettuce grew from 13,800 carloads in 1920 to 51,500 in 1928, spinach from 2,900 in 1920 to 10,600 in 1927. As people moved into city apartments with kitchenettes, they gave a new spur to the canning industry. Canned fruits and vegetables more than doubled between 1914 and 1929; canned milk almost trebled. In many city homes, the family sat down to a meal that started with canned soup, proceeded to canned meat and vegetables, and ended with canned peaches.

The chemicals industry, which started in the 1880s, got an enormous stimulus from World War I. The war demonstrated how dependent the country was on foreign supplies of potash, nitrates, and dyes. Potash, essential for fertilizers, had come almost entirely from Germany before the war. After supplies were cut off, prices increased ten times, encouraging creation of a domestic potash industry. When the United States could not import German indigo, the Dow Chemical Company's infant industry spurted. The government contributed more to the development of the chemicals industry than to any other industry. It confiscated German dye patents during the war and turned them over to American firms; it advanced nitrogen development by constructing a plant at Muscle Shoals in the Tennessee Valley and by operating a Fixed Nitrogen Research Laboratory in the War Department; and it gave high tariff protection to domestic chemicals and dyes.

The war also sparked the development of a new synthetics industry. Thousands of by-product ovens were built to produce coke needed in manufacturing explosives; after the war, these ovens were used in the production of synthetic chemicals, especially plastics. Synthetic plastics had been developed as early as 1869, with the creation of celluloid, but it was not until the postwar years that synthetic fibers and plastics became an important industry. The output of rayon, which transformed the textile business, multiplied sixty-nine times between 1914 and 1931. Bakelite, which was developed before the war, proved vital to the electrical and radio industries. In 1923, lacquers were introduced; easier to apply than paint, giving better protection and offering a wider range of colors, the quick-drying lacquers reduced the time needed to finish an automobile from twenty-six days to a matter of hours. In 1924, Du Pont established a "cellophane" plant; used to wrap everything from bacon to cigarettes, cellophane at least doubled its sales every year for the rest of the decade. In 1925, a Swiss chemist, who had been invited to America by the government during World War I to build a cellulose nitrate plant, placed "celanese" on the market; an artificial silk superior to rayon, celanese was an important step in the development of synthetic textiles. Scientific geniuses like George Washington Carver found new industrial uses for farm products, many of them surplus crops that were glutting the market. From peanuts, Carver extracted everything from shaving lotion to axle grease; from sweet potatoes, he got shoe-blacking, library paste, and synthetic tapioca.

Construction increased dramatically in the 1920s, in part because building had been halted during the war, in part to meet the drift from country to city and from city to suburbs. During the decade, New York got a brand new skyline. European travelers who in 1910 had been awed by 20-story skyscrapers returned in 1930 to find them dwarfed by new giants; some of the old structures had even been demolished to make way for 60-story towers. The Grand Central section of Manhattan was almost entirely rebuilt; Fifth Avenue resounded with the staccato of riveters and the sharp clash of steel beams. High above the city streets, helmeted gandy dancers balanced themselves on girders; beneath them, men operated mammoth cranes or turned huge drums of concrete. Taller and taller the buildings soared; toward the end of the decade a race to erect the loftiest skyscraper became a fascinating new outdoor sport. On May 1, 1931, the race ended when the Empire State Building climbed past the Bank of Manhattan's 71 stories and the Chrysler Building's 77 stories. Built in less than a year, the 102-story Empire State Building, topped by a graceful mast, was the tallest building in the world.

What New York had, every interior city had to have too. Municipalities the size of Beaumont, Memphis, and Syracuse boasted buildings of at least 21 stories. Tulsa and Oklahoma City, which did not even exist when the first skyscraper was built, had skylines by the end of the decade. Cleveland pointed proudly to its 52-story Terminal Tower, Houston to its Petroleum Building, Chicago to its Tribune Tower. The skyscraper expressed the ebullient American spirit as surely as the Gothic cathedral did that of medieval Europe. Denounced by many American critics as a vulgar evidence of commercialism and an indiscriminate passion for bigness, the skyline was recognized by European observers for what it was—a radiant, defiant display of American energy and optimism. Too often banal in conception, the skyscraper was at its best—as in Raymond Hood's News Building in New York—a symmetrical rectangle of stark beauty.

Outside the great cities, construction went on at an even faster rate, as people fanned out into the suburbs. The borough of Queens, across the East River from Manhattan, doubled its population in the 1920s. Grosse Point Park near Detroit grew 700 percent, Shaker Heights outside Cleveland 1,000 percent, and the movie colony of Beverly Hills 2,500 per cent. Save for the building frenzy in California, the greatest real estate boom in the country took place in Florida. Flivvers with northern license plates clogged Miami's Flagler Avenue in the 1920s; not only the man of wealth, who headed for Palm Beach or Boca Raton, but the man of moderate income decided to winter in Florida. "Realtors" converted swamps into Venetian lagoons, and much of the citizenry of Florida was engaged in selling lots. In Coral Gables, a real estate man hired William Jennings Bryan to sit on a raft under a beach umbrella and lecture on the beauties of Florida climate; Bryan was followed with dancing by the "shimmy" queen, Gilda Gray. The land-speculation mania reached its high point one day in the summer of 1925 when the Miami *Daily News,* crowded with real estate advertisements, printed an issue of 504 pages, the largest in newspaper history. In 1926, after a hurricane had driven the waters of Biscayne Bay over the cottages of Miami, the land boom collapsed. But still the resorts were strung from Jacksonville to Key West. Miami, once a mangrove swamp, grew 400 per cent in the decade.

The construction of roads and highways poured fresh public funds into the economy. While Secretary Mellon endeavored to cut back federal expenditures, state and local governments stepped up spending at a rate that more than offset the Mellon program of deflation. Construction for highways and buildings employed more men and spent more money than any single private industry. In 1914, there were almost no good roads outside of the East, and crossing the continent was an adventure. Automobiles sank to their hubs in gumbo muds; travelers crossing Iowa were often forced to wait several days until the roads dried before moving on to the next town. Perhaps because cars were viewed as pleasure vehicles, parsimonious state legislatures were reluctant to vote public funds to improve roads.

The Federal Aid Road Act of 1916 offered money to states that would organize highway departments and match federal grants. Prompted by this initiative, every section of the country launched ambitious road-building programs in the postwar years. In 1906, local governments appropriated 96 percent of all highway funds; by 1927, they were providing only 53 percent, while the states spent 37 percent, and the federal government 10 percent. Road building gave the auto industry a larger government subsidy than railroads received in their entire history. Florida built the Tamiami Trail through the swamps of the Everglades; Arizona constructed a road across the desert west of Phoenix; Utah laid a highway over a sea of mud, a relic of ancient Lake Bonneville, near the Nevada line; and in Massachusetts the magnificent Mohawk Trail climbed the Hoosac Range. New York pioneered with the construction of the beautiful Bronx River Parkway, which curved its way out of New York City northward through the Westchester countryside. By 1928, the tourist could drive from New York as far west as St. Mary's, Kansas, on paved highways, but it was still not advisable to test the Santa Fé Trail southwest of St. Louis in the rainy season, and mountain passes west of Salt Lake City were seldom open during winter or early spring.

Without the new automobile industry, the prosperity of the Roaring Twenties would scarcely have been possible; the development of the industry in a single generation was the greatest achievement of modern technology. As recently as 1900, Vermont had enforced a law requiring every motorist to employ "a person of mature age" to walk one-eighth of a mile ahead of him bearing a red flag. That year there was not a single filling station in all the country. In 1902, San Francisco, Cincinnati, and Savannah still maintained speed limits of eight miles an hour. While lawmakers were attempting to keep pace with technology, a significant change took place within the industry. Ransom Olds started mass production of automobiles; Henry Leland demonstrated that cars could be made with interchangeable parts; and Henry Ford quickly took over both principles and carried them to lengths that left his competitors far behind.

The production of automobiles soared almost at a geometric rate, and the industry gave a shot in the arm to the whole economy. In 1900, there had been an annual output of 4,000 cars; by 1929, 4,800,000 automobiles were being produced in a single year, and Americans were driving more than 26 million autos and trucks. In the United States, there was one automobile to each five persons—almost one car per family—as compared to one car to 43 persons in Britain, one to 325 in Italy, one to 7,000 in Russia. In America, the possession of an automobile was not, as in Europe, a class privilege. The auto industry was the most important purchaser of rubber, plate glass, nickel and lead; it bought 15 percent of the steel output of the nation and spurred the petroleum industry to a tremendous expansion. There was scarcely a corner of the economy that the automobile industry did not touch; it stimulated public spending for roads, extended the housing boom into the suburbs, and created dozens of new enterprises from hotdog stands to billboards. By opening up hitherto inaccessible land to settlement, the automobile radically altered residential patterns. In the 1920s for the first time, suburbs grew at a swifter rate than central cities.

Detroit became the Mecca of the modern world and Ford its prophet. Russian and German scholars talked reverently of "Fordismus," and industrial missions came from all over the world to study American techniques. "Just as in Rome one goes to the Vatican and endeavours to get audience of the Pope," wrote one British traveler, "so in Detroit one goes to the Ford Works and endeavours to see Henry Ford." "As I caught my first glimpse of Detroit," recorded another Briton, "I felt as I imagine a Seventeenth Century traveller must have felt when he approached Versailles." Ford was worshiped as a miracle-maker: a group of college students voted the Flivver King the third greatest figure of all time, surpassed only by Napoleon and Christ. When Ford announced the Model A early in 1928, 500,000 people made down payments without having seen the car and without knowing the price.

Ford personified the legend of the resourceful American who, by making it to the top on his own, benefits mankind. He was the magical tinkerer who, by bringing the automobile to the masses, revolutionized the way people lived, and he was the progenitor of mass production that promised an end to the curse of poverty. His firm was family-owned; he was hostile to Wall Street; he founded, it was believed, the doctrine of high wages and low prices, of sharing the fruits of his genius with the world—he was, in short, the Good Businessman. The one-time farmer-mechanic become billionaire resolved the moral dilemma of a Puritan-capitalist society by appearing to achieve material success without losing his primal innocence.

Some of this legend had a solid base in fact; some of it did not. It is true that he was the apostle of a high wage-low price economy. In 1914, at a time when the prevailing factory wage was about $3, Ford established the $5 day, and he lowered the cost of a Model T flivver, marketed at $850 in 1908, to only $290 in 1924. But it is also true that he was a despot. He hired thugs to discipline his employees and spies to investigate their private lives. Any worker caught driving a car of any brand other than a Ford was summarily fired. He also held any number of nutty ideas. He believed in reincarnation, hated doctors and Catholics, abominated tobacco because it was "bad for the bowels," and gave wide circulation to the notoriously anti-Semitic and spurious "Protocols of the Elders of Zion." He was so simple-minded that he badgered the creator of "Little Orphan Annie" to send him advance copies of the comic strip because he could not bear the tension of waiting for the next day's episode to appear in the paper.

"Machinery," declared Ford solemnly, "is the new Messiah." Dazzled by the prosperity of the time and by the endless stream of new gadgets, the American people raised business in the 1920s into a national religion and paid respectful homage to the businessman as the prophet of heaven on earth. As government looked only to the single interest of business, so society gave to the businessman social pre-eminence. To call a scientist or a preacher or a professor a good businessman was to pay him the highest of compliments, for the chief index of a man's worth was his income. "Brains," declared Coolidge, "are wealth and wealth is the chief end of man." The half-baked opinions of men such as Ford were accorded the reverent respect due to high priests not only when they spoke on business matters, but also when they made pronouncements on culture and public morals. "The man who builds a factory builds a temple," observed Coolidge. "The man who works there worships there."

Americans increasingly showed less interest in a hereafter than in salvation on earth. Material comfort became not a means to an end but the final end of life itself. People continued to go to church, but religious rituals were sometimes acknowledged less with reverence than with politeness. The functions of the church were gradually replaced by institutions committed to the ideal of service, to "organized altruism." Forced to accommodate themselves, the churches stressed not the divinity but the humanity of Christ. They installed swimming pools, game rooms, and gymnasiums with, as one foreign visitor noticed, "the oxygen of good fellowship" permeating everything. When a British journalist visited one American church, its young preacher invited him to "come and inspect his plant."

The classic statement of the secularization of religion and the religiosity of business came in Bruce Barton's *The Man Nobody Knows,* a best seller in 1925 and 1926. Barton praised Jesus handsomely as a topnotch executive who had "picked up twelve men from the bottom ranks of business and forged them into an organization that conquered the world." Jesus was an A-1 salesman, and the parables were "the most powerful advertisements of all time." No one need doubt that business was the main focus of His concern. Why, Jesus Himself had said: "Wist ye not that I must be about my father's *business?*"

Religion had value not as a path to personal salvation or a key to the riddles of the universe but because it paid off in dollars and cents. Reading the Bible, explained one writer, meant money in your pocket. Insurance men were advised that Exodus offered good tips on risk and liability, while a Chicago bond salesman confided that he had boosted his income by drawing arguments from Ezekiel. "Of all the Plenipotentiaries of Publicity, Ambassadors of Advertising and Bosses of Press Bureaus, none equals Moses," said Elbert Hubbard, for it was Moses who "appointed himself ad-writer for the Deity." Taught to write advertising copy for their churches, pastors billed their sermons after a popular cigarette slogan, "They Satisfy," or after another well-known ad, "Eventually, Why Not Now?" (an appeal for conversion), or "Three-in-One Oil" (the Trinity).

In this ethos of deification of businessmen, the government knew that it could count on a complaisant public when it permitted the concentration of industry to proceed apace. Although the merger movement had reached its apex before the war, it found new areas such as the utilities in the 1920s. Most mergers brought together not competing firms but companies engaged in the same business in different cities. Between 1919 and 1930, 8,000 businesses disappeared. "So long as I am Attorney General," explained Harry Daugherty, "I am not going unnecessarily to harass men who have unwittingly run counter with the statutes." Despite Daugherty's intentions, the Federal Trade Commission occasionally proved obstreperous and interceded to block consolidations and discourage trade associations. But when in 1925 Coolidge appointed the lumber attorney William E. Humphrey to the chairmanship of the commission, large-business interests moved into control of the FTC. Humphrey himself denounced the FTC as a "publicity bureau to spread socialistic propaganda." After Humphrey's accession, the commission approved trade associations and smiled on business agreements to lessen "cutthroat" competition.

In the 1920s, mergers characterized one industry above all others: electric light and power. Between 1902 and 1929, the output of electric power multiplied more than 19 times—from 6 billion kilowatt-hours to 117 billion. Almost as much new hydroelectric power was developed between 1920 and 1930 as in all the years before 1920. By 1929, America was generating more electric power than all the rest of the world combined. As local electric light and power companies, which once served a single town, were interconnected in vast regional grids, financiers used the holding-company device to merge small firms into great utility empires. Between 1919 and 1927, over 3,700 utility companies vanished. Promoters organized a group of utility giants starting with the United Light and Power Company and the American Superpower Corporation in 1923 and ending with the Niagara Hudson Company and the Commonwealth and Southern Corporation in 1929. By 1930, ten holding-company groups controlled 72 percent of the country's electric power.

The most spectacular of the new utility titans, Samuel Insull, started as an office boy in London at five shillings a week and rose to the top of a holding-company empire that controlled gas and electric companies in twenty-three states. Operating out of Chicago, he extended his domain over businesses as remote as the Androscoggin Electric Company in Maine and the Tidewater Power Company in North Carolina. Chairman of the board of sixty-five different firms, Insull was involved in operations in almost every conceivable field, from Mexican irrigation projects to the pathetic attempt to make Port Isabel, Texas, "the Venus of the South." His dairy herd, bathed in ultra-violet rays, was surrounded by electric screens that electrocuted flies. Respected as a philanthropist and a patron of the arts, he built the Chicago Civic Opera an ornate skyscraper opera house. An intimate of mayors and senators, he was accused of suborning public officials.

The merger movement accelerated rapidly in American banking too. Large banks swallowed little banks or established branch banks that took away their business. In 1920, there were 1,280 branch banks; in 1930, 3,516. The greatest of the branch bankers was a newcomer, Amadeo Peter Giannini, who developed a chain of 500 banks throughout the state of California under a single holding company. His Bank of America National Trust and Savings Association in San Francisco became the fourth largest bank in the country, larger than any bank outside New York. In Manhattan, the National City Bank took over the Farmers Loan & Trust Company; Guaranty Trust amalgamated with the Bank of Commerce; and Chase National absorbed the Equitable Trust Company. By 1929, 1 percent of the financial institutions in the country controlled over 46 percent of the nation's banking resources.

Chain stores expanded rapidly in the postwar years. Chainstore units rose from 29,000 in 1918 to 160,000 in 1929; between 1919 and 1927 their sales jumped 124 percent in drugstores, 287 percent in groceries, and 425 percent in apparel. The Great Atlantic and Pacific Tea Company's chain of red-fronted grocery stores grew from 400 in 1912 to 15,500 in 1932. By the end of the period, the A & P was selling a greater volume of goods than Ford at his peak; its billion dollar a year turnover accounted for one-tenth of all food sold at retail in the United States. In these same years, Woolworth "five and tens" crowded out many old neighborhood notion stores; for a dime or less, the customer could buy anything from Venetian Night Incense to Mammoth Tulip Sundaes, Hebrew New Year cards to poker chips, gumdrops to French Guiana stamps. A mammoth holding company, Drug, Incorporated, owned 10,000 Rexall drugstores and 706 Liggett stores, in addition to the Owl chain on the Pacific Coast and huge drug firms such as Vick Chemical, Bayer Aspirin, and Bristol-Myers. By 1932, chain stores accounted for 22 percent of the retail trade in Baltimore, 31 percent in Atlanta, 37 percent in Chicago. In some places, the independent grocery of 1914 had almost disappeared; Philadelphia bought two-thirds of its food in chain stores.

By the end of the decade, the consolidation movement had reached boom proportions. In 1919, there were 80 bank mergers, in 1927, 259. In 1928, the Chrysler Corporation took over Dodge Brothers, Postum Company amalgamated with Maxwell House Coffee, and Colgate merged with Palmolive-Peet. Two advertising agencies combined to form the wonderfully sonorous Batten, Barton, Durstine & Osborn. By 1929, the 200 largest non-financial corporations in America owned nearly half the corporate wealth of the nation, and they were growing much faster than smaller businesses. From 1924 to 1928, their assets expanded three times as rapidly as those of lesser corporations. Four meat packers controlled 70 percent of production in their industry; four tobacco companies accounted for 94 percent of the output of cigarettes.

Many industries—textiles, clothing, and bituminous coal, in particular—remained boisterously competitive, however, and the growth of oligopoly—domination of an industry by a few firms—often meant more rather than less competition. Although consolidation accelerated in the 1920s, there was not as much actual monopoly—that is, domination of an industry by only one company. No longer did a single firm lord it over the steel or the oil industries. Although the chain-store movement spelled national consolidation, it also destroyed the monopoly of the merchant in the small town.

Critics of big business in the 1920s emphasized not only the increase in concentration, but also the fact that the benefits of technological innovation were by no means evenly distributed. Corporate profits and dividends far outpaced the rise in wages, and despite the high productivity of the period, there was a disturbing amount of unemployment. At any given moment in the "golden twenties," from 7 to 12 percent were jobless. Factory workers in "sick" industries such as coal, leather, and textiles saw little of flush times. Nor did blacks in ghetto tenements, or Hispanics in the foul barrios of Los Angeles or El Paso, or Native Americans abandoned on desolate reservations. The Loray Mill in Gastonia, North Carolina, site of a bloody strike in 1929, paid its workers that year a weekly wage of $18 to men and $9 to women for a 70-hour week. At the height of Coolidge prosperity, the secretary of the Gastonia Chamber of Commerce boasted that children of fourteen were permitted to work only 11 hours a day. Perhaps as many as two million boys and girls under fifteen continued to toil in textile mills, cranberry bogs, and beet fields. In 1929, 71 per cent of American families had incomes under $2,500, generally thought to be the minimum standard for a decent living. The 36,000 wealthiest families received as much income as the 12,000,000 families—42 percent of all those in America—who received under $1,500 a year, below the poverty line.

Still, if one focuses exclusively on farm poverty or on depressed

West Virginia coal towns, it is easy to distort the experience of the 1920s. As Henry May writes, "Sometimes even prosperity—an important fact despite its exceptions—is belittled almost out of existence." The wealth of the United States, it should be remembered, was as great as that of Britain, France, Germany, Italy, Russia and all the rest of Europe put together, and never before had Americans had so much discretionary income. If prosperity was by no means as pervasive as Chamber of Commerce publicists claimed, it was still widespread enough to alter markedly the lives of millions of Americans.

The change resulted less from a considerable gain in family income than from the fact that Americans could buy things that they had never been able to purchase before. People could get into their automobile—almost everyone owned a car—and drive into the country or visit neighbors in the next town. For the first time, they saw America, taking trips to distant campsites or historic shrines and most of all discovering the attractions of California and Florida. In 1912, only 16 percent of the population lived in homes with electric lighting; by 1929, more than two-thirds, which is to say virtually everyone outside of the still largely dark countryside. Electricity meant not only electric lights, but also a wide range of electrical appliances—from washing machines to power-driven sewing machines. By 1929, more than a million homes had electric refrigerators, one in five electric toasters, and one in four vacuum cleaners. Women of all classes wore what a short time before would have been luxuries. They discarded cotton stockings and underwear for silk and rayon (in 1900, 12,000 pairs of silk stockings were sold; in 1920, 300 million), and the American woman became known as "America's greatest fur-bearing animal."

In great numbers, Americans went to the sports arena. Organized sport had captivated the country for decades, but not until the 1920s did spectator athletics become a kind of national religion. In the Cathedral of St. John the Divine in New York, a bay was built with windows depicting various sports. On July 2, 1921, 91,000 fans at Boyles' Thirty Acres in Jersey City paid more than a million dollars to watch Jack Dempsey fight "gorgeous" Georges Carpentier. Dempsey knocked him out in the fourth round, but, more important, the country had seen the first "million dollar gate." It was the Golden Age of Sports—of Babe Ruth, Bobby Jones, and Bill Tilden, the era of the Dempsey-Tunney fight, the decade when Ruth hit sixty home runs in a season. The biggest change took place in college football. People who had never been near a campus crowded the vast new college stadiums to cheer the Four Horsemen of Notre Dame or the Galloping Ghost of Illinois, Harold "Red" Grange, who, on one memorable fall afternoon in Urbana, scored four touchdowns against Michigan in the first twelve minutes of the game. By the end of the 1920s, the gridiron had become the site of a major industry, with gate receipts each year of over $21 million.

On any day of the week, people could walk down to the neighborhood theater to see the latest movie. Already flourishing before the war, motion pictures after the war became one of the ten great industries of the country, with an invested capital of a billion and a half dollars. Over 20,000 movie theaters were built in the decade. In 1922, they sold 40 million tickets every week; by 1930, the average weekly attendance was 100 million. The faces of Charlie Chaplin and Harold Lloyd were known in every corner of the globe, and "youngsters playing in the back streets of Hull or Newcastle," noted one British writer, "threatened one another with *the works.*" Movie houses became the temples of a secular society. In New York, Roxy's called itself "The Cathedral of the

Motion Picture," the Capitol described itself as "The Theater with a Soul," and the Fifty-Fifth Street Theater advertised itself as "The Sanctuary of the Cinema."

Radio, an even newer phenomenon, really arrived on the night of November 2, 1920, when KDKA at East Pittsburgh broadcast the presidential election returns. By 1922, there were radios in three million homes; that year the sale of sets was already a $60 million-a-year-industry. Seven years later, $852 million worth of radio sets were sold. Men who bought cone-speakers and amplifiers and talked endlessly about how to eliminate static introduced a whole new vocabulary; soon they were using the terms—"tune in," "network," "airwaves"—so casually that the words lost their gloss of technological novelty. People clamped on earphones to hear Roxy and His Gang, the Clicquot Club Eskimos, the Ipana Troubadours or the A & P Gypsies. Grantland Rice broadcast the World Series, Floyd Gibbons narrated the news with a machine-gun staccato, and Rudy Vallee warbled the latest songs. From speakers in homes all over America came the sound of the ubiquitous ukelele.

In the fall of 1929 two former vaudevillians, Freeman Gosden and Charles Correll, began a radio comic strip called "Amos 'n Andy." Before long, millions of Americans were following avidly the affairs of the Fresh Air Taxicab Company, and Madame Queen and the Kingfish had become household words. Many refused to answer their phones while the two blackface comedians were on the air, and one man inserted an advertisement in a newspaper to ask his friends not to disturb him while the program was being broadcast. Senator Borah even referred to Amos and Andy in a debate on the Philippines.

The growth of popular culture and consumerism reflected economic changes that had important consequences for class structure and life style. Within a decade, the radio and the movie nationalized popular culture, projecting the same performers and the same stereotypes in every section. In movie theaters everywhere, when olive-skinned Rudolph Valentino carried an impeccably blonde heroine across the burning Sahara and flung her into his tent, women swooned. Men scoffed at the Valentino craze, but barbers reported that customers who once had called for bay rum now demanded pomades to make their hair sleek. There was even something of a vogue of sideburns, while dance schools offering the tango did a flourishing business. Endless interviews with Valentino appeared in national periodicals, including one with the inevitable title, "I'm Tired of Being a Sheik."

As the country solved the problems of production, it gave greater attention to distribution. Business developed ingenious methods to transform anxiety about scarcity into a desire for consumer goods. The advertising man and the salesman assaulted the older virtues of thrift and prudence. Behaviorist psychology, with its manipulative view of man, was perfectly adapted to mass advertising; Watson himself left the Johns Hopkins University under fire to become vice-president of an ad agency. Advertisers sold not products but qualities such as social prestige, which the possession of the products would allegedly secure. With debt no longer regarded as shameful, people bought on credit. Three out of every four radios were purchased on the installment plan, as were 60 percent of all automobiles and furniture. Ten years after the war, conspicuous consumption had become a national obsession. When a French perfume would not sell at ordinary rates, the manufacturer raised its price and made a fortune. To staff the agencies of distribution and the "service" industries, a new white-collar class emerged in the cities. Together with the civil servant, the salesman, and the salaried manager, these white-collar employees constituted a "new middle class."

This shift in emphasis produced important changes in the national character. In place of the idea that saving was a virtue, an article of faith as old as the first colonial settlements and the talisman of Benjamin Franklin's Poor Richard, a conviction developed that thrift could be socially harmful and spending a virtue. "We're too poor to economize," wrote Scott Fitzgerald jauntily. "Economy is a luxury." The nineteenth-century man, with a set of characteristics adapted to an economy of scarcity, began to give way to the twentieth-century man with the idiosyncrasies of an economy of abundance. Aggressively optimistic, he was friendlier but had less depth, was more demanding of approval, less certain of himself. He did not knock, he boosted. He had lots of pep, hustle, and zip. He joined the Rotary or Kiwanis, and he believed in "service," a word that was repeated *ad nauseam* during the decade. Sinclair Lewis painted his portrait as George Babbitt, and Babbitt acknowledged that it was a reasonable likeness. "Dare to Be a Babbitt!" urged *Nation's Business*. What the world needed was more Babbitts, "good Rotarians who live orderly lives, and save money, and go to church, and play golf, and send their children to school."

The problem for the twentieth-century man was not the material environment but other people. "Our future," wrote Walter Weyl in 1919, "may depend less on the hours that we work today than on the words or the smile we exchange with some anonymous fellow-passenger in the office-building elevator." Men aimed less at improving their character and more at restyling their personality. Neither health nor education nor even one's own "personality" was valued for itself alone, but for what it would do toward making one a "success," success meaning not merely greater income but the social acceptance necessary to stifle self-doubt. The main social knowledge a man had to acquire was how to "sell himself."

Whereas the nineteenth-century man wanted to make it on his own, the twentieth-century man sought a place for himself in the corporate bureaucracy, which was increasingly taking over during these years. Probably the most important development within corporations was the divorce of ownership from control. In 1900, there were four million owners of stocks; by 1930, twenty million. Determination of business policy passed from owners, many of whom had not the remotest curiosity about or knowledge of the firm in which they held stock, to a salaried bureaucracy. By the end of the decade, a "managerial revolution" had occurred: plant managers and corporation executives, rather than owners, made the chief decisions. Young men no longer aimed to found their own businesses, to be Carnegies or Vanderbilts; they sought to rise to a high position as a hired manager or a salaried executive. The businessman was less interested in risk and more in stability. Unlike the nineteenth-century tycoon with the attitude of "the public be damned," the postwar businessman was extremely self-conscious about how he appeared to others.

Even stubborn Henry Ford had to mend his ways. He had built the Model-T flivver, a sturdy, simply constructed car without grace or beauty, and he had sold millions of them. When he started to lose sales in the 1920s to the more modern General Motors car, he refused to admit that the Model T was no longer marketable. "The customer," he snapped, "can have a Ford any color he wants—so long as it's black." But by the mid-1920s the country had less interest in price than in style and comfort. The purchase of an automobile had been a male prerogative—only men knew what lay under the hood—and men mostly bought cars that offered the soundest mechanical features. As women increasingly decided which car the family would buy, carburetors and gaskets became less important than the color of an automobile and the texture of its upholstery. In May, 1927, Ford surrendered; he halted production on the Model T, and when the Model A came out, it had modern design and construction and could be bought in a choice of colors from Dawn Gray to Arabian Sand.

Industrial relations, too, had a new complexion in some of the more enlightened corporations. During what was called "the New Era," employers embarked on a well-publicized program of welfare capitalism. They built clean, trim, well-lighted factories, with safety devices to forestall injury; they installed cafeterias, complete with trained dieticians, and formed glee clubs and baseball teams. The Hammermill Paper Company sold its employees cut-rate gasoline; L. Bamberger and Company provided free legal service; and Bausch and Lomb set up eye and dental clinics for its workers. In part to avert unionization, employers replaced tyrannical foremen with trained personnel men and organized company unions. They instituted group insurance plans and introduced profit-sharing; probably more than a million workers owned stock by 1929, an innovation that proved of dubious value by the end of the year. "If every family owned even a $100 bond of the United States or a legitimate corporation," declared Franklin D. Roosevelt, "there would be no talk of bolshevism, and we would incidentally solve all national problems in a more democratic way."

Although the new prosperity fostered an exceptionally materialistic view of life, it resulted in more than just increased sales of gadgets. The country spent more than twice as much as it had before the war on libraries, almost three times as much for hospitals. The United States in 1928 paid out as much for education as all the rest of the world. In 1900, a child had only one chance in ten of going to high school; by 1931, that child had one chance in two. In 1900 a teenager had only one chance in thirty-three of going to college; by 1931, he or she had better than one in seven. In part as the result of increased wealth—which financed research, improved sanitation, and made possible better nutrition—science in the first third of the twentieth century increased American life expectancy from 49 to 59 years, cut infant mortality two-thirds, and slashed the death rate of typhoid from 36 to 2 per 100,000, of diphtheria from 43 to 2, of measles from 12 to 1.

In December, 1928, President Coolidge declared: "No Congress of the United States ever assembled, on surveying the state of the Union, has met with a more pleasing prospect than that which appears at the present time." By 1928, Coolidge had the assent of many of the New Era's former faultfinders. "The more or less unconscious and unplanned activities of business men," asserted Walter Lippmann, "are for once more novel, more daring, and in general more revolutionary than the theories of the progressives." "Big business in America," concluded Lincoln Steffens, long a fierce critic of American capitalism, "is producing what the Socialists held up as their goal; food, shelter and clothing for all. You will see it during the Hoover administration."

New Era publicists argued that a new kind of "economic democracy" had been established. The businessman, enjoying substantial profits, shared them in high wages with his worker, who, in turn, by investing in the stock market, open to all, could own a share of industry. "We are reaching and maintaining the position," declared Coolidge as early as 1919, "where the property class and the employed class are not separate, but identical." The consumer, spending his dollars, it was said, cast votes to determine what should be produced. Soundly based on technological

innovations, its gains widely dispersed, administered by enlightened businessmen, a new civilization appeared to be emerging.
Without the class hatred or bureaucratic despotism of communism, the United States, it seemed, was on its way toward the
final abolition of poverty.

11

Political Fundamentalism

Despite prosperity, the United States in the postwar years felt deeply threatened from within. The American people suddenly had thrust upon them the responsibilities of war and the making of peace, and their contact with Europe and power politics was bitterly disillusioning. In a world of Bolshevik revolutions and Bela Kuns, of general strikes and Mussolini's march on Rome, there was danger that America, too, might be infected by the social diseases of the Old World. Yet the threat of foreign contagion was not as terrifying as the menace of change from within. In part the danger seemed to come from enclaves of the foreign-born, not yet adapted to American ways, in part from the rise of the metropolis, with values different from those of nineteenth-century America, in part from the new currents of moral relativism and cosmopolitanism. Not a little of the anxiety arose from the disturbing knowledge that Americans themselves no longer had their former confidence in democracy or religion. "They have," observed André Siegfried, "a vague uneasy fear of being overwhelmed from within, and of suddenly finding one day that they are no longer themselves."

Political fundamentalism attempted to deny real divisions in the nation by coercing a sense of oneness. Celebration of the Constitution became a tribal rite; in the 1920s, Americans, as one English writer noted, were "a people who, of all the world, craved most for new things, yet were all but Chinese in their worship of their Constitution and their ancestors who devised it." Constitution-worship was a kind of magical nativism, a form of activity in which, as the anthropologist Ralph Linton writes, "the society's members feel that by behaving as the ancestors did they will, in some usually undefined way, help to recreate the total situation in which the ancestors lived." Efforts toward social change were condemned as un-American. "Individualism?" cried an American Legion commander in California. "Down with all Isms!" This resistance to change and this insistence on conformity intertwined with the desire of rural churchmen to turn back modernism in religion and compel morality by statute. In 1924, Protestant fundamentalists wove together both movements in a "Bible-Christ-and-Constitution Campaign," while the Ku Klux Klan's warcry was "Back to the Constitution."

Many felt hostile to anything foreign. Isolationism had its counterpart in a determination to curb immigration, to avoid alien contamination and to preserve the old America ethnically before it was too late. In the late nineteenth century and the early years of the twentieth century, the drive for immigration restriction had foundered on presidential vetoes. Restrictionism could not overcome the industrialists' demand for cheap labor or, more important, America's confidence in its ability to absorb large numbers of foreign-born. World War I badly shook that confidence. The war revealed that the sympathies of millions of Americans were determined by their countries of origin, and the fight over the League of Nations reflected the animosities of Irish-Americans, German-Americans, and other "hyphenated Americans." In his defense of the Versailles Treaty, Wilson charged:

"Hyphens are the knives that are being stuck into this document."
By the end of the war years, many agreed with Walter Hines Page:
"We Americans have got to . . . hang our Irish agitators and
shoot our hyphenates and bring up our children with reverence
for English history and in the awe of English literature."

The drive for immigration restriction after the war was based,
to a far greater degree than before, on a pseudo-scientific racism.
Men with little knowledge of either science or public affairs were
accepted as experts on "race," although their writings revealed
neither insight nor good judgment. In *The Passing of the Great Race*
(1916), Madison Grant contended that race was the determinant
of civilization and that only Aryans had built great cultures. "The
man of the old stock," alleged Grant, "is being crowded out of
many country districts by these foreigners, just as he is to-day
being literally driven off the streets of New York City by the
swarms of Polish Jews. These immigrants adopt the language of
the native American, they wear his clothes, they steal his name
and they are beginning to take his women, but they seldom adopt
his religion or understand his ideals." Lothrop Stoddard in *The
Rising Tide of Color* (1920) and Professor Edwin East of Harvard
warned that white races were being engulfed by the more fertile
colored races. Most influential of all were the widely read articles
by Kenneth Roberts in the *Saturday Evening Post.* Roberts urged
that the immigration laws be revised to admit fewer Polish Jews,
who were "human parasites"; cautioned against Social Democrats,
since "social democracy gives off a distinctly sour, bolshevistic
odor"; and opposed unrestricted immigration, for it would inevitably produce "a hybrid race of people as worthless and futile as
the good-for-nothing mongrels of Central America and Southeast-
ern Europe."

In the first fifteen years of the century, an average of one million immigrants a year had entered the United States. Slowed to a trickle by the war, the stream of immigration became a swollen torrent after the armistice. From June, 1920, to June, 1921, more than 800,000 persons poured into the country, 65 percent of them from southern and eastern Europe, and consuls in Europe reported that millions more were planning to leave. By February, 1921, Ellis Island was so jammed that immigration authorities had to divert ships to Boston. Alarmed almost to the point of panic, Congress rushed through an emergency act to restrict immigration; it passed the House in a few hours without a record vote and was adopted by the Senate soon after by 78–1.

Despite initial opposition, sentiment for a more lasting form of immigration restriction soon gained increasing strength. For a time, industrialists continued to set themselves against the movement. T. Coleman du Pont protested that critics of the immigrant were suffering from "sheer Red hysteria, nothing more," while Judge Gary denounced the 1921 law as "one of the worst things that this country has ever done for itself economically." With the new prosperity of 1923 and increased mechanical efficiency, which reduced the need for mass labor, however, the chief obstacle to permanent immigration restriction was removed at the same time that industrialists, agitated by the Red Scare, grew increasingly nativist. So did unions, largely confined to skilled craftsmen, who for some time had wanted to limit new entrants into the labor market, thereby enhancing the market value of their members by reducing supply.

In 1924, Congress passed, over scant opposition, the National Origins Act, which drastically cut down the total of newcomers to be admitted each year and established quotas to be calculated on the basis of the proportion of descendants of each nationality resident in the United States at an earlier time. Under that proviso, the more "Nordic" lands of northern and western Europe got 85 percent of quotas. In addition, the law forbade all Oriental immigration—a gratuitous insult which was marked in Japan with a day of national mourning. "It is a sorry business," wrote Hughes, "and I am greatly depressed. It has undone the work of the Washington Conference and implanted the seeds of an antagonism which are sure to bear fruit in the future."

The law, reflecting racist warnings about a threat to "Anglo-Saxon" stock, aimed at freezing the country ethnically by sharply restricting the "new" immigration from southern and eastern Europe. In the debate on the bill, Congressmen reviled the foreign-born of the great cities, particularly New York, to whom were attributed every evil of the day. "On the one side," asserted a Kansas congressman, "is beer, bolshevism, unassimilating settlements and perhaps many flags—on the other side is constitutional government; one flag, stars and stripes." For three hundred years, English squires and cutthroats, French Huguenots, Spanish adventurers, pious subjects of German duchies, and, above all in recent years, peasants from Calabria to the Ukraine had come to America in search of gold, or land, or freedom, or something to which they could not put a name. Now it was over. One of the great folk movements in the history of man had come to an end.

While the immigration restriction movement drew on the apprehension that America might be transformed ethnically by an invasion of alien elements from without, the Ku Klux Klan preyed on the feeling that the country was already in peril from elements within. The KKK was organized on Stone Mountain in Georgia on Thanksgiving night, 1915, in the light of a blazing cross, by William J. Simmons, a former Methodist circuit rider and organizer of fraternal associations. Modeled on the hooded order of Reconstruction days that murdered blacks, the Klan admitted "native born, white, gentile Americans" who believed in white supremacy; by implication, they could not be Catholics. Although it took the name of an old Southern society, the Klan owed more to the nativist tradition of Know-Nothingism, having its greatest appeal not to the deep South but to the Midwest, Southwest, and Far West, where people were worried less by blacks than by the encroachment of "foreigners," especially if they were papists.

The Klan attracted its chief support from the sense of desperation experienced by old stock Protestants who felt themselves being eclipsed by the rise of the city with its polyglot masses. Though the Klan had a following in some cities, especially ones undergoing rapid growth, two-thirds of its members lived in places with a population of less than 100,000, and the KKK found metropolises with large proportions of the foreign-born hostile territory. In cities such as Boston and San Francisco, the Klan got nowhere, and in New York it did not dare show its face at a public gathering.

"The reason there is a Klan in America today," said Colorado's grand dragon, "is to make America safe for Americans." Those attracted to the KKK thought themselves engaged in a battle which their falling birth rates doomed them to lose. "The dangers," Simmons explained, "were in the tremendous influx of foreign immigration, tutored in alien dogmas and alien creeds, slowly pushing the native-born white American population into the center of the country, there to be ultimately overwhelmed and smothered." In its elaborate ritual, its stark pageantry, its white-hooded sheets, its titles of "Exalted Cyclops," "Klaliff," "Klokard," "Kligrapp," and "Klabee," the KKK appealed to the lodge vogue of blue collar and middle-class America. When the Klansman sang "klodes" with his neighbor and klasped his hand in a secret grip, he felt reassured.

In the early years of the 1920s, the Klan, which had less than 5,000 members as late as 1920, experienced a phenomenal growth, and, with probably a few million adherents at one time or other during this period, made its weight felt in politics. In Youngstown, Ohio, the KKK elected the mayor and the entire city government, and in Texas, where it ousted a four-term U.S. Senator, the Klan dominated the legislature and the cities of Dallas, Fort Worth, and Wichita Falls. Candidates running with KKK backing were elected to the United States Senate in six states, and the Klan controlled municipal governments in cities such as Denver and El Paso. In Oklahoma, the governor called all the citizens of the state into military service and declared martial law in an effort to put down the organization; the Klan-controlled legislature retaliated by impeaching him and removing him from office in November, 1923. In staunchly Republican Oregon, a state settled by Eastern and Midwestern Protestants, the Klan helped elect a Democratic governor, Walter Pierce, by the largest majority in state history and supported a law that wiped out parochial schools by requiring parents to send all children between eight and sixteen to public schools. (In 1925, the Supreme Court [*Pierce v. Society of Sisters*] declared the law unconstitutional.) For the most part, though, the Klan did not know, once it had power, what to do with it, for it was more a vehicle to express resentment than a movement with coherent policy aims.

Where the Klan entered, in its wake too often came floggings, kidnappings, branding with acid, mutilations, church burnings, and even murders. In the South, the Klan sometimes used terror to preserve a social system that was swiftly changing. Yet even in the South, intimidation, although it was used against blacks (a bellhop in Texas was branded on the forehead with the initials "KKK," and black homes were burned in Florida to discourage voting), was employed more often against Catholics or political enemies or bootleggers or, most important, against individuals deemed immoral. In Birmingham, a Klansman murdered a Catholic priest in cold blood and was acquitted; in Naperville, Illinois, two hours after a monster Klan ceremony, a Roman Catholic church was torched. When the mayor of Columbus, Georgia, ignored demands of the KKK that he remove the city manager, his home was dynamited. After the triumph of the Klan ticket in Alabama in 1927, a black woman was flogged and left to die; a white divorcee was punched into unconsciousness; a naturalized citizen was lashed for marrying a native-born woman; and a black was beaten until he sold his land to a white man for less than it was worth.

Such episodes did not characterize the everyday routine of the KKK, but they were symptomatic. Most Klansmen never participated in violence, and not a few viewed the organization as an interest group for white Protestants or a fraternal association that sometimes carried on benevolent activities. When the Klan did resort to flogging or social ostracism, it was less likely to do so against ethnic minorities than to people thought to have broken some moral code—by trafficking in liquor, or gambling, or carrying on an extramarital affair. (One of its avowed aims was to "break up roadside parking.") Yet, as an organization exclusively of white Protestants, there was no mistaking its hostility to Catholics and Jews and to anyone it defined as "alien." The Klansmen, who thought white Protestants were being victimized, had no comprehension of the fact that it was not they but Catholics and Jews who faced blatant discrimination in employment, and blacks who, when they were not at the mercy of lynch mobs, were denied the most fundamental Constitutional rights. Furthermore, as Don Kirschner has pointed out, while there were any number of fraternal associations that promised conviviality and solace, "the one thing that the Klan offered that was uniquely its own was extra-legal or even illegal action."

Opponents of the KKK fought fire with fire. Especially in northern cities, the order encountered resistance not only from Catholics, Jews, and liberals, but also from bootleggers and other elements of organized crime. When in Chicago a Klan organizer boasted that his group would soon be strong enough to drive out the bootleggers and maintain law and order, the bullet-ridden body of an outspoken Protestant clergyman was discovered in Cicero, headquarters of the gangland boss, Al Capone. After the Imperial Wizard spoke in Carnegie, Pennsylvania, thousands of armed foes of the KKK massed at a bridge, and when Klan marchers pushed on, several fell dead. Elsewhere, KKK halls from Texas to Indiana were bombed or set ablaze.

The Klan reached the heights in Indiana, and in Indiana it toppled to its death. Hundreds of thousands of white-sheeted Klansmen took over the state. Many of them sauntered brazenly through town with their hoods flung back, not even bothering to conceal their identity. On parade nights in Kokomo, the police force vanished and white-sheeted figures, bearing a striking resemblance to the absent patrolmen, directed traffic. The Grand Dragon of the Indiana KKK, David Stephenson, extended his influence in the Klan beyond the borders of the state and into the Republican party, especially through his association with the governor of Indiana, Ed Jackson. A gross, corrupt man, who was a boozer, a womanizer, and a violent brawler, Stephenson made himself a political power and a multimillionaire overnight through his Klan activities. Finally, he overreached himself: he forced a twenty-eight-year-old State House secretary onto a Chicago-bound train and brutally assaulted her. When she took poison, his henchmen spirited her to a hotel and held her for several days without medical aid; a month later she died. In November, 1925, Stephenson was convicted of second-degree murder and sentenced to life in prison. When his crony, Governor Jackson, refused to pardon him, Stephenson opened a "little black box" which sent a congressman, the mayor of Indianapolis, and other officials to jail; Jackson was indicted for bribery but escaped because of the statute of limitations.

As early as 1924, the Klan had been put on the run in Oklahoma, Louisiana, and Texas, and the conviction of Stephenson sealed its doom. It brought into bold relief both the hypocrisy of the Klan (Stephenson had denounced petting parties and had warred on vice) and the corruption that threaded the history of the order. Many of the KKK leaders had joined the organization primarily for personal profit; many who preached righteousness were corrupt. Feeding on a millennial lust for rule by a league of the pure, the Klan, once in power, sometimes licensed the very evils it said it would exterminate. Its ugly side lay in the fact that it appealed to many who were frustrated by the rigid moral code of the small town. Klansmen often felt tempted by that which they were condemning—sexual freedom, modernity—and their frustration sometimes took a sadistic turn, as when they stripped "fallen" women naked and whipped them. The Stephenson episode revealed everything that was seamy about the organization. The KKK never recovered.

To a considerably greater degree than the Klan, the prohibition movement, which was often the focus of KKK activities, centered in the rural areas of the country, especially in the villages where the preacher could speak with authority on matters of politics and morals. Prohibition was a way that rural Americans could impose their mores on city folk; that Baptists and Methodists could badger people of other faiths, especially Catholics; that old stock Americans could compel newer arrivals to conform; and that the middle class could get workingmen to give up their favorite beverages. The Eighteenth Amendment, Andrew Sinclair has observed, was a victory for the "Corn Belt over the conveyor belt," and prohibition and a pervasive anti-urbanism went hand in hand. Prohibition, claimed one of its advocates, would permit the "pure stream of country sentiment and township morals to flush out the cesspools of cities."

Though prohibition found supporters in the urban middle class, most city people regarded it as a punishment inflicted on them by mirthless rubes. What underlay such "crazy enactments," Mencken said, was "the yokel's congenital and incurable hatred of the city man—his simian rage against everyone who, as he sees it, is having a better time than he is." The precept "thou shalt not" had no attraction for Irish Catholic teamsters nursing their gin on Boston's dockside or German Lutheran workers guzzling ale in Milwaukee's breweries. Nor did it appeal to the Episcopalian hostesses of cocktail parties on Chicago's Gold Coast or San Francisco's Nob Hill. Some of the wets even claimed that consuming liquor was a public good. "The more advanced a country is," asserted Congressman George Tinkham of Massachusetts, "the higher its alcoholic content," while the president of Washington and Lee University called prohibition "the longest and most effective step forward in the uplift of the human race ever taken by any civilized nation."

The fanaticism of the extreme drys permitted their urban critics to caricature prohibition, often unfairly. It has become commonplace to say that the prohibition experience demonstrates that you cannot alter people's behavior, but, in fact, during these years drinking declined. Arrests for public drunkenness fell, and there were fewer deaths from alcoholism. The zealotry of many of the drys, however, opened the experiment to ridicule. They viewed the immensely complex problem with which they were dealing primarily in moral terms, and their picture of the world of drink was a nightmare vision. The Anti-Saloon League had invited incredulity when it reported earlier that "nearly 3,000 infants are smothered yearly in bed by drunken parents," and not even the triumph of the prohibition movement with the ratification of the Eighteenth Amendment tempered its hyperbolic rhetoric.

In the cities, and even in the countryside (where moonshiners operated stills in mountain hollows), people devised ingenious means to outwit the efforts of the drys. Redistilling industrial alcohol was one source, prescriptions from compliant druggists another. (One cunning gangster bought a chain of drug stores in the Midwest so that he could order liquor legally for medicinal purposes, then hijack his own trucks.) Many Americans made their own home brew; in large cities, hardware stores openly displayed copper stills along with yeast, hops, and other ingredients. Others bought their whiskey from bootleggers who claimed they were selling the best imported brands from Canada or Scotland, and sometimes did. More often, they passed off inferior products—at worst substances such as Jamaica ginger, better known as "jake," which paralyzed thousands; Jackass Brandy, which caused internal bleeding; Soda Pop Moon from Philadelphia, containing poisonous isopropyl alcohol; Panther Whiskey, based on esters and fusel oil; or Yack Yack Bourbon from Chicago, which blended iodine and burnt sugar.

Schooners plied Rum Row off the New Jersey coast, and ice

sleds ran booze across Canadian rivers in winter. Bootlegging in Detroit, which had the advantage of being just across a border river from Ontario, became the Motor City's second leading industry. In more than one town, saloons disguised themselves as private associations with names like "The Bombay Bicycle Club." E. B. White slyly proposed that the government nationalize speakeasies (illegal saloons operating covertly.) "In that manner," he wrote, "the citizenry would be assured liquor of a uniformly high quality, and the enormous cost of dry enforcement could be met by the profits from the sale of drinks."

When the Eighteenth Amendment was ratified, the drys forecast that since "90 percent of adult criminals are whiskey-made," prohibition would reduce or eliminate crime, whereas, in fact, bootlegging became the main source of income for gangs which infested the large cities and frequently bought or coerced their way into municipal governments. In 1920, "Scarface" Al Capone, a New York hoodlum from the Five Points Gang, moved to Chicago and set up an empire in alcohol, gambling, prostitution, and drugs. By 1927, he was operating a $60 million business and had a private army of close to one thousand hoodlums who "rubbed out" rival bootleggers attempting to cut into Capone's "territory." In 1926 and 1927, there were 130 gang murders in Cook County, and not a single murderer was apprehended. Capone drove the streets of Chicago in a $30,000 armor-plated automobile, convoyed by scout cars, and went to the theater with a score of bodyguards. On one occasion when the police brought Capone in for questioning, the Detective Bureau was besieged by nearly one hundred gangsters.

The gangsters in many of the great cities either infiltrated the government or were permitted to create their own private governments. In Chicago, the Terrible Gennas had five police captains and four hundred policemen on their payroll. In New York, speakeasies paid "protection" to gangsters like Dutch Schultz, who were allied with Tammany Hall sachems. By consolidating independent units, observed Lloyd Morris, tongue in cheek, Schultz "eliminated waste, promoted efficiency, and replaced the disorder of obsolete individualism with rigorous discipline." In Philadelphia, bootleggers established an inner government with a judge before whom attorneys practiced and whose decisions were enforced by gunmen.

Against such formidable power, and charged with administering a law that millions abhorred, enforcement agencies had a nearly impossible assignment. They never had enough officers, and their agents were often venal political hacks, quick to resort to violence. Public fury was aroused at the agents, who on occasion sprayed bullets over waterfront streets or invaded the premises of minor offenders; they appeared to be as lawless and reckless as the men they were pursuing. Before long, millions of Americans sided with the lawbreakers. On one occasion, thousands of bathers at Coney Island watched an encounter between Coast Guard cutters and rumrunners: they cheered the rumrunner as it opened a lead on the pursuing government boats. In areas hostile to prohibition, agents were almost helpless. In wet cities such as New York and San Francisco, the easiest way for a stranger to locate a speakeasy, it was said, was "to ask the nearest cop," who could usually point out one to him just a few doors away. In 1929 Mabel Walker Willebrandt, who had been Assistant Attorney-General of the United States in charge of prohibition prosecutions, conceded that liquor could be bought "at almost any hour of the day or night, either in rural districts, the smaller towns, or the cities."

Throughout the 1920s, a swelling chorus called for repeal of the Eighteenth Amendment. The president of Carnegie Tech testified at a Senate committee hearing that rum was "one of the greatest blessings that God has given to men out of the teeming bosom of Mother Earth," and Mencken complained that prohibition had caused suffering comparable only to that of the Black Death and the Thirty Years' War. "The government which stands against the founder of Christianity cannot survive," Senator David I. Walsh of Massachusetts told a rally. "The Volstead law has put every Christian on the defensive, for they are forbidden to do something which the founder of their religion sanctioned. If Christ came back to earth and performed the Cana miracle again, Walsh said on another occasion, "he would be jailed and possibly crucified again."

The demand for repeal centered in urban industrial states and was led by Governor Alfred E. Smith of New York and Governor Albert Ritchie of Maryland. New York had repealed its "Baby Volstead Act" as early as 1923, while feeling was so strong in Maryland, which never passed a state enforcement law at all, that in June, 1922, a mob of wets stormed the jail at Ocean City and freed two men arrested for drunkenness. Increasingly, the wets found allies among those who were worried by the contempt for law that prohibition bred, and by the great gap between profession and practice, which applied even to many of the prohibitionists. In Virginia, prohibition had been enacted when a state senator, ill with a hangover from carousing the night before, cast the decisive vote in its favor. By the end of the decade, prohibition still appeared to have the support of the majority of the nation, but its days were numbered.

The campaign to preserve America as it was, which characterized both the Klan and prohibition, came to a head in the movement of Protestant fundamentalism climaxed by the Scopes trial.

Although the publication of Darwin's *Origin of Species* in 1859 had touched off a controversy between science and theology that rocked the Western world for the next two decades, men such as Asa Gray in the United States and Charles Kingsley in England had succeeded in reconciling evolution and Christianity; by the time of World War I, an assault on Darwin seemed as unlikely as an attack on Copernicus. When in 1922 the Kentucky legislature came within a single vote of banning the teaching of evolution in the schools, though, the nation suddenly awoke to a deep-seated hostility to Darwinian assumptions in rural America that it thought had been scotched a half-century before.

In farmlands and small towns, particularly in the mountain country of the South, many Protestant ministers had never subscribed to Darwinism; they continued to believe that the only true account of the origin of the world could be found by a literal reading of the first two chapters of Genesis. The attempts of modernists to accommodate religion to scholarly criticism of the Bible had, the fundamentalists argued, shattered the chief tenets of Christianity. One fundamentalist wrote: "The Modernist juggles the Scripture statements of His deity and denies His virgin birth, making Him a Jewish bastard, born out of wedlock, and stained forever with the shame of His Mother's immorality." To attempt to preserve religion while denying the truth of Christ's resurrection, wrote the editor of a Baptist periodical, "is like saying that the title to the house which you prepared as a habitation for your old age is a fraud. . . . If Jesus Christ did not rise from the dead, we cannot depend upon a word of what he said."

Strengthened by popular anger against Germany (the home of modernist religion) and by the Red Scare (which linked atheism with communism), fundamentalism made modest gains during and after the war, but it amounted to little until William Jennings Bryan joined the anti-evolution movement. The Peerless Leader was a man to reckon with; for three decades, he had been the folk hero of the Mississippi Valley heartland. A man of transparent sincerity, courageous in the face of repeated defeats, a man whose belief in democracy was instinctive, Bryan was the authentic representative of the tradition of Jacksonian democracy (with a leaven of nineteenth-century evangelical Christianity) in his suspicion of the expert and the university-educated as members of a privileged class. "It is better," wrote Bryan, "to trust in the Rock of Ages than to know the age of rocks; it is better for one to know that he is close to the Heavenly Father than to know how far the stars in the heavens are apart."

Always a factionalist, Bryan threw himself into the anti-evolution campaign with the same zeal he had marshaled against the "goldbugs" in 1896. Bryan, wrote Heywood Broun, "has never lived in a land of men and women. To him this country has been from the beginning peopled by believers and heretics." Under Bryan's leadership, the campaign to compel the teaching of a biology that conformed to the account of the origin of man in Genesis quickly caught the attention of the nation. It was a war of country and small town against the city, a war largely centered in the South. In the Northeast, the anti-evolutionists got nowhere, even though fundamentalists held a number of city pulpits. When a bill was introduced in the Delaware legislature to forbid teaching that man evolved from lower animals, it was referred facetiously to the Committee on Fish, Game, and Oysters. In many Southern states, too, anti-evolution efforts were turned back by counterattacks from university presidents and urban newspapers, but in Oklahoma, Florida, and North Carolina the anti-evolutionists won partial victories. When the Texas legislature turned down a bill to censor textbooks, Governor "Ma" Ferguson took matters in her own hands and blacklisted or bowdlerized books to remove any mention of Darwinism. "I am a Christian mother," the Governor declared, "and I am not going to let that kind of rot go into Texas textbooks."

The first smashing victory for the anti-evolutionists came in Tennessee, where a farmer who was also a part-time school teacher and clerk of the Round Lick Association of Primitive Baptists was elected to the legislature on the single plank of advocating an anti-evolution law. Bryan and a powerful fundamentalist lobby moved in on Nashville to support him; in March, 1925, the legislature made it illegal "for any teacher in any of the universities, normal, and all other public schools of the state, to teach any theory that denies the story of the divine creation of man as taught in the Bible and to teach instead that man has descended from a lower order of animals."

That spring, in the mountain town of Dayton, Tennessee, John T. Scopes, a slim, bespectacled young biology teacher at Central High School, a man of engaging modesty and wit, was sipping lemon phosphates at Robinson's Drug Store with several of his friends, and in particular with George Rappelyea, manager of the local mine, and druggist Robinson, chairman of the county schoolbook committee. They talked about the law, of which they disapproved, and about the fact that the American Civil Liberties Union had offered counsel to any Tennessee teacher who challenged it. More in the spirit of fun than of social protest, the mine manager and the teacher hatched a scheme. The next day Scopes lectured from Hunter's *Civic Biology* and Rappelyea filed a complaint with local officials; the police brought Scopes before the justices of the peace, and he was bound over to a grand jury.

To Scopes's defense came Clarence Darrow, the most famous defense lawyer in the country and an avowed agnostic, Arthur

Garfield Hays, a civil liberties attorney, and Dudley Field Malone, who in other years had campaigned with Bryan for the Democratic cause. Retained by the World's Christian Fundamentals Association to assist the prosecution was William Jennings Bryan, who announced that the trial would be a "duel to the death" between Christianity and evolution. "He gave the impression," observed *Le Matin,* "of one returned to the earth from the wars of religion."

The Scopes trial is usually seen simply as a struggle of champions of truth pitted against Tennessee Hottentots. Certainly, academic freedom and respect for the findings of science constituted the most important feature of the case, and nothing is to be said for the attempt to force teachers to give their students a wholly inaccurate account of the evolution of man. It should be noted, though, Tennessee had no intention of enforcing the law, which many legislators went along with not because they doubted Darwin but because they did not want to become enmeshed in a controversy that might imperil university appropriations. Nobody ever interfered with Scopes's teaching until he and his fellow conspirator contrived their scenario, in part as a way to put their town on the map, which the "monkey trial" surely did. Quite apart from its singular origin, the case was never simply a morality play between the good forces of intellectual liberty and the evil spirits of obscurantism. In the Scopes trial, the provincialism of the city was arrayed against the provincialism of the country, the shallowness of Mencken against the shallowness of Bryan, the arrogance of the scientists against the arrogance of the fundamentalists.

The very faith in science, as C. E. Ayres pointed out, had reached the point where it, had become "superstition, in another guise." In the 1920s, the nation was captivated by electricity, by the new world of radioactivity, even by more mundane matters like calories and vitamins; science, many people believed, was a universal balm that would answer every human need. High priests of the science cult dismissed traditional concerns as remnants of an irrational age. "No one," declared Watson, the behaviorist psychologist, "has ever touched a soul, or has seen one in a test tube." Churchgoers were understandably concerned about a dogma that stripped away myths, presented no adequate system of ethics, offered little sustenance in times of grief, and provided a partial, limited glimpse of man and the universe.

Fundamentalism made sense to men and women in isolated rural areas still directly dependent on nature for their livelihood; they put their trust in divine intervention and depreciated human capacity because it had been their experience that people were all but helpless when disease struck or when their corn withered in a drought. They were much less likely than city folk to believe that life had the predictable rhythm of an assembly line and more willing to hope and pray that a benign Providence would spare them the caprices of nature. Their adversaries in the city found fundamentalism incomprehensible because the rational methods of production in the factory and life in the metropolis suggested that man, through science and education, could solve the major problems of living and might even be able someday to solve the ultimate questions of human existence.

At the Dayton trial, the court maintained that the only issue properly before it was whether Scopes had violated the law, which he clearly had. The defense attempted to shift the emphasis to the questioning of the law itself. Scopes's attorneys, who argued that a belief in evolution was consistent with Christian faith and that Genesis was allegorical, were frustrated in their efforts to demonstrate that the statute was either wicked or foolish, until Hays hit upon the idea of calling Bryan to the stand as an expert on the Bible.

In the suffocatingly hot courtroom, Darrow and Bryan, each in shirtsleeves, faced off against one another in one of the most dramatic confrontations of the twentieth century. In response to Darrow's grilling, Bryan declared that the whale had swallowed Jonah (although he thought it was a fish rather than a whale), that Eve had been made from Adam's rib, that all languages derived from the collapse of the tower of Babel, and that Joshua had literally made the sun stand still. Professing himself an authority on religion and science, Bryan was revealed by Darrow's devastating probing to be a man of dense ignorance. Bryan made a fatal admission: he conceded that when the Bible said the world had been created in six days, it did not necessarily mean that a "day' was twenty-four hours long; it might be a million years. Thus Bryan, whose position was grounded on the conviction that the Bible must be read literally, had himself "interpreted" the Bible, thereby destroying the basis for opposition to modernism.

The Dayton trial ended in victory for the fundamentalists, but it was a hollow one. Scopes was found guilty, as had been anticipated from the first, and fined $100. The Tennessee supreme court later threw out the fine on a technicality, thereby blocking his attorneys from testing the constitutionality of the law. (Scopes himself received a scholarship to attend the University of Chicago, where he was trained as a geologist.) Scopes had lost, but, in another sense, he had won. In the last minutes of Darrow's cross-examination, there was raucous laughter at Bryan, derision from his own followers. A terrible pathos filled Bryan's last days; soon after the trial, he died—after having written an autobiographical statement to prove that he was neither an ignorant nor an uneducated man. The anti-evolutionists won in three more southern states, but with Bryan's death the heart went out of the movement, and it quickly subsided.

The aftermath of the Scopes trial is symbolic of the fate of political fundamentalism in the 1920s. Immigration restriction, the Klan, prohibition, and Protestant fundamentalism all had in common a hostility to modernity and a desire to arrest change through coercion by statute. The anti-evolutionists won the Scopes trial; yet, in a more important sense, they were defeated, overwhelmed by the tide of cosmopolitanism. Such was the fate of each of the other movements. By the end of 1933, the Eighteenth Amendment had been repealed and the Klan was a dim memory. Immigration restriction, which apparently scored a complete triumph and certainly did win a major one, was frustrated when (since the law did not apply to the Western Hemisphere) Mexicans, French Canadians, Cubans, and Puerto Ricans, most of them "swarthy" Catholics, streamed in. Ostensibly successful on every front, the political fundamentalists in the 1920s were making a last stand in a lost cause.

12

The Sidewalks of New York

The United States in the 1920s neared the end of a painful transition from a country reared in the rural village to a nation dominated by the great metropolis. In 1910, 54.2 percent of the country lived in villages of fewer than 2,500 inhabitants; by 1920, only 48.6 percent—for the first time in our history, less than half the people dwelt in villages and on farms. During the decade, some six million people abandoned the farm for the city. Los Angeles jumped from 319,000 in 1910 to more than 1,238,000 in 1930. By 1930, the United States was only 44 percent rural.

Not only were the cities outstripping the villages and small towns in population, but these years saw a conscious rejection of rural values. In *Spoon River Anthology* (1915), Edgar Lee Masters pictured small-town life as mean and narrow; in *Winesburg, Ohio* (1919), Sherwood Anderson painted a series of haunting portraits of the human spirit stifled by an Ohio town; in *Main Street* (1920), Sinclair Lewis held up to public inspection the faults of a typical prairie community; in *Look Homeward, Angel* (1929), Thomas Wolfe took a far more savage look at a southern town. Scattered across the continent, wrote Van Wyck Brooks, were thousands of villages, "frostbitten, palsied, full of a morbid, bloodless, death-in-life." No theme of American literature of the period was more pervasive than what Carl Van Doren called "the revolt from the village." In the last chapter of the representative novel of the day, the hero went to the railroad depot of a midwestern town to buy a one-way ticket to Chicago or New York, the bright metropolises shiny with promise.

The city made no effort to conceal its contempt for rural mores. Mencken contended that the farmer was not a member of the human race. The *New Yorker,* founded in 1925, the epitome of urban wit light-years removed from country foolery, boasted that it was "not for the old lady in Dubuque." In Dorothy Parker's epigrams at the Hotel Algonquin, in the joyously raucous nasality of Al Jolson, and in the Manhattan provincialism of Jimmy Walker and Texas Guinan, the city created a world in which the traditions of small-town America were almost unrecognizable.

Rural leaders in turn attacked New York as the modern Gomorrah. The Broadway theater, expostulated the Methodist Board of Temperance, Prohibition and Public Morals, was "naked, profane, blasphemous and salacious." The city, rural traditionalists expounded, harbored hordes of aliens indifferent or hostile toward fundamental American values. "New York," wrote the *Denver Post* in 1930, "has been a cesspool into which immigrant trash has been dumped for so long that it can scarcely be considered American any more." New York was, as Bryan had long ago said of the East, "the enemy's country." It was cruel and impersonal, the abode of the rootless, a place where, as one writer noted, "nobody seemed to have parents."

Critics viewed the city as a great incubus sucking the life's blood of the countryside. Sociologists raised the nightmare of a barren urban society that could not reproduce itself, dooming America to depopulation and decay. The German philosopher Oswald Spengler, who enjoyed a vogue in the 1920s, warned that urbanization spelled the degeneration of Western culture. In 1915, the nation's birth rate was 25.0; by 1932, it had skidded to 17.4. During the first four decades of the twentieth century, city dwellers did not bear enough children to maintain a stable population in the next generation. Yet the population of urban America increased 27 per cent between 1920 and 1930 while rural America grew only 4 per cent. The cities outdistanced rural areas chiefly by depopulating the countryside.

The war between the country and the city had been fought for decades; what was new in the 1920s was the tension within each camp as well. On the one hand, people on farms and in the small towns could not help but sense, even if they would not always admit, how deeply their own lives were affected by the appeal of the city. They knew that not merely was America changing but that they themselves were changing. As Don Kirschner has noted, farmers were casting a vote for the urban way of life every time they tuned in a Chicago radio station, and "thousands of farmers, or children of farmers, . . . chose the bright lights of cities to the economic uncertainties of the soil." Farm papers that at the beginning of the decade featured ads for chick mash were by the end of the 1920s enticing readers with sketches of automatic toasters and glamorous hotel weekends in Kansas City or even Palm Beach. The protagonist of an autobiographical novel by Floyd Dell could not get out of his head something he had seen on the wall of a railroad station in a small Midwestern town: "a map with a picture of iron roads from all over the Middle West centering a dark blotch in the corner. . . . 'Chicago!' he said to himself."

On the other hand, the very men who symbolized the triumph of the city were among the most reluctant to see the death of the old order. Mencken's celebration of the virtues of New York was so boisterous because deep down he felt uneasy whenever he was in the big city; he was always happiest when he was headed home to the quieter confines of Baltimore. Beneath Sinclair Lewis's satire of Gopher Prairie lay a deep love of the place. "If I seem to have criticized prairie villages," Lewis wrote in 1931, "I have certainly criticized them no more than I have New York, or Paris, or the great universities. I am quite certain that I could have been born and reared in no place in the world where I would have had more friendliness."

In no writer is this ambivalence more apparent than in Sherwood Anderson. The main character of *Winesburg, Ohio* turns his back on the small town, true enough. But no one can read Anderson's stories without being aware of his abiding affection for the small town and its skilled craftsmen and his loathing of the "filth and disorder of modern civilization." The harness maker Joe Wainsworth, who in his hatred of machinery kills his assistant, is the symbol of the earlier order venting its wrath on the modern age. The same Anderson who wrote of the thwarted lives in "the little frame houses, on often mean enough streets in American towns" could also recall fondly "men and lads together on chairs and upturned boxes before livery-stable doors or before country-town hotels at evening, breeding lines being discussed and fought over, great names mentioned, the master reinsmen, Murphy, Budd Doble, Walter Cox, and the great master of them all, Pop Geers." With not a little sadness, Anderson protested: "We never did get a fair break from our writers on some of the sweeter sides of our American life."

Some men sought not merely to retain the nation's rural character, but to turn back the clock and restore the pristine America of yesteryear. At the head of this movement was Henry Ford, who collected a great variety of Americana at "Greenfield Village" and constructed a replica of a nineteenth-century rural community. Critical of modern dancing as immoral because it occurred "mostly above the feet," Ford revived old-fashioned folk dancing, importing dozens of fiddlers to Dearborn and turning up old folk tunes like "Arkansas Traveler." He also subsidized a printing of selections from the *McGuffey Readers* and distributed them to libraries around the country. Yet at the same time, Ford in his massive automobile factories was doing more than any man to destroy rural America beyond recall. Despite his celebration of rural values (he even supported a back to the soil movement) Ford himself had turned toward tinkering with machines because he loathed farm work.

Until the 1920s, city and rural values had not clashed head-on in the national political arena. For more than a century, American politics had been dominated by the country; no asset was greater than that of birth in a log cabin. Even when, in the years after the Civil War, the United States moved rapidly from an agrarian to an industrial nation, its chief political figures were cut from the familiar mold. They were farmboys, or men from the small town, or, if they came from the city, they had not cut their ties with rural America and were as acceptable to the crossroads town as to the metropolis. In the 1920s, for the first time, a man who was unmistakably of the city made a bid for national power; in the career of Alfred E. Smith and the campaign of 1928 all the tensions between rural and urban America reached their highest pitch. "For the first time," wrote the *New Republic*, "a representative of the unpedigreed, foreign-born, city-bred, many-tongued recent arrivals on the American scene has knocked on the door and aspired seriously to the presiding seat in the national Council Chamber."

Born in 1873 in a tenement on New York's Lower East Side in

the shadow of the Brooklyn Bridge, Smith lived the life of a boy in a great city. Instead of currying his pony or shooting squirrels on a smoky October afternoon, Al climbed among packing crates and boxes along the waterfront. Instead of playing one o'cat in the old apple orchard, he cuffed handballs against a warehouse wall. Instead of splashing in a swimming hole of a sylvan brook, Al leaped from dirty wharves into the East River. From the age of seven until he was fourteen, he served seven o'clock Mass as altar boy in the neighborhood Catholic church. At the age of fifteen, he was forced to quit school to go to work; four years later, he was hired as salesman and assistant bookkeeper in the Fulton Fish Market at $12 a week and all the fish he wanted.

Smith joined Tammany Hall, as inevitable an institution as one could find in the Fourth Ward, and, after a long apprenticeship, moved steadily up the ranks of political preferment. Leaving the fish markets behind him, he worked for eight years in the commonplace patronage job of subpoena server. In 1903, at the age of thirty, as a reward for faithful service, Smith was sent to the New York state legislature where he made a brilliant record. He handled the bills resulting from the insurance probe conducted by Charles Evans Hughes and investigated the terrible Triangle Fire that took the lives of 145 girls in a shirtwaist factory, and he awakened the country to the need for social legislation. Ultimately he became, as Elihu Root said, the best-informed man on legislative matters in the entire state. In 1918, he was elected governor; save for 1920, when he was submerged in the Harding landslide, Smith remained in the Albany State House until 1928.

Smith personified the desire of the sons of urban immigrants to make a place for themselves in the world, and politics was one of the few avenues of social mobility open to them. Smith was not the first to discover this. He was part of a tradition at least as old as the election of the German immigrant John Peter Altgeld to the governorship of Illinois in 1892, a tradition that embraced in the early years of the century Irish boys like David I. Walsh in Massachusetts and Joe Tumulty in New Jersey. But he was the first to ask acceptance by the people for the highest office in the land. It was for this reason that Smith was so taken to heart by the Irish of the Northeast; he was a test case of how far an Irish Catholic boy from the big city could go, and how soon. "Al Smith," wrote William Allen White, "must rise or fall in our national life, if ever he should enter it, as our first urbanite."

One of the ablest state officers in American history, a man with an impressive record of electoral success, four times chosen governor of the most populous state in the country, Smith was the logical candidate for the Democratic presidential nomination in 1928. Despite lingering bitterness over the Madison Square Garden convention, even many of the old McAdoo supporters recognized that if Smith could not win in 1928, no Democrat could. "In my present state of mind," wrote a West Virginia Democrat, "I am for 'Rum, Romanism and Rebellion.'" Although he was opposed by a variety of southern rivals, Smith won the Democratic nomination handily.

When Coolidge announced laconically, "I do not choose to run," the Republicans turned to Herbert Hoover, born in Iowa, as their presidential candidate and named Senator Charles Curtis of Kansas as his running mate. For the first time in history, both candidates of a major party hailed from west of the Mississippi. After a rewarding career as a mining engineer and promoter in every corner of the earth, Hoover had first caught national attention in the war years as Food Administrator and administrator of Belgian relief. John Maynard Keynes observed that he was "the only man who emerged from the ordeal of Paris with an enhanced reputation," while Justice Brandeis remarked that he was "the biggest figure injected into Washington life by the war." As Secretary of Commerce, Hoover epitomized the new capitalism, with its emphasis on efficiency, distribution, co-operation, and "service." Smith could make the appeal of a humanitarian and a friend of business interests at the same time; it was his misfortune to run against a man in 1928 who could make precisely the same claims and did not have Smith's liabilities.

The Democratic party faced a dilemma. If it attempted to compete with the Republicans by showing it was just as conservative, it had little chance of success, because the GOP had established itself too firmly as the party of business. On the other hand, if it attempted to take a more radical line, it ran smack against the circumspect mood of the decade. Either way, it was licked. It could hope for success only through a change in the national temper, something it could not bring about on its own.

For the most part, the Democratic party in 1928 chose to take a "me too" position. After their resounding defeat in 1924, the Democrats grew even more cautious than they had been before. In 1925, John W. Davis wrote a follower: "When will we get done with the fool idea that the way to make a party grow is to scare away everybody who has an extra dollar in his pocket? God forbid that the Democratic party should become a mere gathering of the unsuccessful!" To head his campaign in 1928, Smith named John J. Raskob, a Republican who had voted for Coolidge in 1924, who had run the Finance Committee of General Motors, and who listed himself in *Who's Who* as "capitalist." Raskob made a deliberate attempt to identify the Democratic party with business interests and to assure the country there was no real difference on this score with the Republicans. He proudly announced that Harkness of Standard Oil, Spreckels the sugar titan, and James the New York financier were supporting Smith; not one of them "considers that his interests are in the slightest degree imperilled," Raskob told the nation. On almost every important issue, the Democratic platform of 1928 paralleled that of the Republicans. As Newton Baker ruefully observed, "McKinley could have run on the tariff plank and Lodge on the one on international relations."

Smith's inability or unwillingness to establish a progressive position sharply different from Hoover's permitted the campaign to focus on religion, prohibition, and personalities. Well before the battle began, foes of Smith warned that his election would mean the control of the White House by a foreign pope, and after his nomination they spread vicious rumors against him. They whispered that if Smith were elected all Protestant children would be declared bastards; circulated scurrilous pamphlets with titles such as "Traffic in Nuns" and "Alcohol Smith"; and distributed photographs of him at the dedication of the Holland Tunnel under the Hudson River with the warning that Smith planned to extend the tunnel to the basement of the Vatican. As the Democratic campaign train moved across Oklahoma, the candidate could see fiery crosses burning in the fields.

"No Governor can kiss the papal ring and get within gunshot of the White House," announced a Methodist bishop of Buffalo, while Methodist Bishop Cannon of Virginia referred contemptuously to Raskob as "this wet Roman Catholic Knight of Columbus and chamberlain of the Pope of Rome." The minister of the First Methodist Church of Lynn, Massachusetts called Smith "the greatest menace that has faced America since the Civil War," and in Oklahoma City, the pastor of that city's largest Baptist church cried, "If you vote for Al Smith, you're voting against Christ and you'll all be damned." (Implicit in the latter statement is the bizarre denial that Catholicism is Christian, much like the KKK attack on "*pagan* Papist priests.") It was not merely extremists who injected the religious issue into the campaign; the liberal Protestant publication, *Christian Century,* observed that Protestants could not "look with unconcern upon the seating of a representative of an alien culture, of a mediaeval Latin mentality, of an undemocratic hierarchy and of a foreign potentate in the great office of President of the United States."

This assault by Protestant clergymen on Smith was closely linked to hostility to the foreign born in northern cities and to the conviction that the Catholic Church was an alien institution. "Elect Al Smith to the presidency," declared one southern churchman, "and it means that the floodgates of immigration will be opened, and that ours will be turned into a civilization like that of continental Europe. Elect Al Smith and you will turn this country over to the domination of a foreign religious sect, which I could name, and Church and State will once again be united."

Rivalling religion in importance in alienating the South was the prohibition issue. Hoover was to call prohibition a "great social and economic experiment, noble in motive and far reaching in purpose," while Smith's skepticism about prohibition was highlighted by his choice of Raskob, the leading wet in the country, as his campaign manager. In the 1920s, prohibition was the most avidly discussed question of the day, a subject of far more popular concern than any issue of foreign policy, and the drys were well organized and politically powerful, centered in the Methodist Church under the fanatical leadership of Bishop Cannon. As Will Rogers observed: "A Preacher just can't save anybody nowadays. He is too busy saving the Nation. . . . Every Crossroad Minister is trying to be a Colonel House." For Bishop Cannon and his followers, the campaign resolved itself into one overwhelming question: "Shall Dry America elect a 'cocktail President'?"

The prohibition issue, in turn, fused with anti-urban sentiment, especially in Southern parishes. An editorial in *Christian Endeavor World* called "City against Country" proclaimed:

> The wet city is trying to impose its will on the dry country. The wet north on the dry South!
> What is to be done about it?
> . . . The Christian vote must be got out on election-day.

If Christians did not go to the polls, "we shall see our towns and villages rumridden in the near future and a whole generation of our children destroyed."

Hoover won the election with 21 million votes to Smith's 15 million, taking the Electoral College by a decisive 444 to 87. Smith won fewer electoral votes than any Democratic candidate since Horace Greeley in 1872 and a smaller proportion of electoral votes than any Democrat since General McClellan in 1864. For the first time since Reconstruction, the Republicans split a large segment of the Solid South, taking Virginia, Texas, Tennessee, North Carolina, Florida, Kentucky, and almost capturing Alabama as well. The election, explained Bishop Cannon, was a repudiation "of the wet sidewalks of our cities, aided and abetted by a selfish, so-called liberal element of high society life."

In later years, historians were to contend that buried in the election returns was a shift of allegiance of such significance that rather than speak of the "Roosevelt Revolution" of the 1930s one should demarcate an "Al Smith Revolution" in 1928 as the decisive moment when the Democrats became the country's majority party, especially in the great cities. In swinging 122 Republican counties into the Democratic column, Smith lifted the Democratic Party from the 34 percent of the vote Cox had polled in 1920 and the less than 29 percent that Davis had received in 1924 to a more respectable almost 41 percent, a higher proportion than any Democratic nominee save Wilson had won in the twentieth century.

By far the most important transition took place in communities with large proportions of working-class "Newer Americans." One of the outstanding features of the election was the exceptionally high turnout, 67.5 percent of those eligible, a decided increase over the 51.1 percent of 1924, in part the result of an outpouring of Catholic women casting their first ballots. In Boston, the vote was a staggering 44 percent heavier than in 1924. The Catholic vote in 1928 was formidable enough to move both Rhode Island and Massachusetts into the Democratic column. In Massachusetts, a chiefly Irish ward gave Smith 2,257, Hoover only 135, but Smith's appeal was not confined to Irish-American neighborhoods. A precinct in Boston's Italian North End counted 2,325 for Smith, 134 for Hoover, and in a French Canadian ward in western Massachusetts, where the New York Yankees' rookie shortstop, Leo Durocher, campaigned for Smith, New York's governor garnered over 84 percent of the ballots.

If there was an "Al Smith revolution," though, it did not move beyond these purlieus. Smith did not do nearly so well in old-stock cities with a substantial middle class. In Los Angeles, he got a miserable total of less than 29 percent, and in New South metropolises, Hoover was welcomed as spokesman for a chromium-shiny new capitalism. Smith lost Dallas, Fort Worth, Birmingham, Nashville, Chattanooga, Winston-Salem and other southern cities with high aspirations. Overall, Smith's nearly 41 percent could be viewed as an improvement, but it still meant that he was a badly beaten candidate.

Given the temper of the 1920s and the success of the Republican party in identifying itself with prosperity, given the aura of legitimacy about the Republican party since the days of the Civil War, Smith's setback was only to be expected. If Smith had been Protestant, dry, and born in a log cabin of good yeoman stock, he still would have been defeated on the Democratic ticket. In the atmosphere of the 1920s, the Republicans, the nation's majority party in the prevailing party system, were invincible.

Historians have been more perplexed by why Smith lost normally Democratic areas, especially in the South. Was prohibition or anti-Catholicism the determining cause? Religious prejudice has been the answer offered by scholars most recently, but the question may well be fruitless, for the campaign reflected a deep antagonism between rural and urban America that went beyond any single issue. The rural voter or the city voter loyal to small town values did not stop to ask himself whether he was dismayed by Smith's religion or by his views on alcohol; he responded to Smith as the embodiment of a great many attitudes that differed from his own. Once this tension developed, every episode in the campaign tended to exacerbate the sense of alienation non-urban and non-eastern voters felt toward Smith. His use of the word "ain't," his pronunciation of "raddio" and "horspital," even the way he smoked his cigar, marked Smith as an outlander with little of the sensibility of the countryside or an older America. Mencken said of him that his world "begins at Coney Island and ends at Buffalo."

Hoover, on the other hand, established the image of himself as an Iowa farmboy steeped in the folkways of rural America. He recalled his boyhood days of gathering walnuts in the fall, of carting grain to the mill, of planting corn and sawing wood, of cavorting in the swimming hole under the willows, of finding "gems of agate and fossil coral" on the Burlington track, and of bellywhopping down Cook's Hill on winter nights. He remembered being taught by a neighboring Indian boy how to bring down pigeons and prairie chickens with bow and arrow, and of fishing for catfish and sunnies. He sang the praises of "the willow pole with a butcher's-string line, fixed with hooks ten for a dime, whose compelling lure is one segment of an angleworm and whose incantation is spitting on bait." His family had woven its own carpets, made its own soap, preserved "meat and fruit and vegetables, got its sweetness from sorghum and honey." In his response to the telegram notifying him of his nomination in 1928, Hoover said, "In no other land could a boy from a country village, without inheritance or influential friends, look forward with such unbounded hope."

Smith, by contrast, was seen as the agent of the foreigner, a man who, if elected, would flood the nation with a new tide of European immigrants, a man who had gained the nomination only because he held the suffrage of big-city aliens plotting to take over the country. "I'll tell you, brother, that the big issue we've got to face ain't the liquor question," the Reverend Bob Jones told a Birmingham meeting. "I'd rather see a saloon on every corner in the South than see the foreigners elect Al Smith President!" George Fort Milton, the Tennessee editor and historian, wrote that Smith's appeal was "to the aliens, who feel that the older America, the America of the Anglo-Saxon stock, is a hateful thing which must be overturned and humiliated; to the northern negroes, who lust for social equality and racial dominance; to the Catholics who have been made to believe that they are entitled to the White House, and to the Jews who likewise are to be instilled with the feeling that this is the time for God's chosen people to chastise America yesteryear. . . . As great as have been my doubts about Hoover, he is sprung from American soil and stock."

At the beginning of the campaign, Elizabeth Tilton, a Boston reformer who had been active in causes such as the struggle against child labor, wrote in her diary that the choice between Hoover and Smith was one "between two levels of civilization— the Evangelical, middle-class America and the Big City Tammany masses." In mid-summer, she added: "It is the old American, Puritan-based ideals against the new Latin ideals. . . . It is old stock agin the loose, fluctuating masses of the Big Cities. It is dry agin wet. It is Protestant against Catholic." On the eve of the election, increasingly frantic, she saw the conflict as "My America against Tammany's. Prairie, Plantation and Everlasting Hills against the side-walks of New York!" When on Election Night the radio reported that Smith had gone down to defeat, she set down in her diary, "We are saved!"

In a rabidly nationalistic time, America insisted that the country be represented by a symbol of the old values; Smith could not fulfil this function as the United States viewed itself in 1928. "It is not that Governor Smith is a Catholic and a wet which makes him an offense to the villagers and town dwellers," wrote William Allen White in 1928. "The whole Puritan civilization which has built a sturdy, orderly nation is threatened by Smith." One of Smith's supporters of 1928 was later to report: "Recently I spent a pleasant weekend in Virginia. I visited the tombs of Thomas Jefferson, Robert E. Lee and 'Stonewall' Jackson to renew my faith. I feel that it did so, and I have reached the conclusion that neither Jefferson, Lee or Jackson could have been born on the East Side in New York."

Smith, with his East Side mannerisms, when placed alongside the marble figures of Jefferson or Lee frightened rather than reassured a nation trying to come to terms with the city. As Walter Lippmann observed: "Quite apart even from the severe opposition of the prohibitionists, the objection to Tammany, the sectional objection to New York, there is an opposition to Smith which is as authentic, and, it seems to me, as poignant as his support. It is inspired by the feeling that the clamorous life of the city should not be acknowledged as the American ideal." After the election, a Minnesota newspaper concluded gratefully:

America is not yet dominated by the great cities. Control of its destinies still remains in the smaller communities and rural regions, with their traditional conservatism and solid virtues. . . . Main Street is still the principal thoroughfare of the nation.

A man of ability, Al Smith arrived too early on the political scene to be accepted as a national symbol. His rejection, particularly the manner in which he was denied, not only embittered Smith, but also left a wound that would not heal until the 1960 election admitted to the White House a much more urbane Irish Catholic, John Fitzgerald Kennedy.

13

Smashup

The prosperity of the 1920s encouraged the contagious feeling that everyone was meant to get rich. The decade witnessed a series of speculative orgies, from "get-rich-quick" schemes to the Florida real estate boom, climaxed in 1928 and 1929 by the Great Bull Market. Before the war, stock market investment had been almost wholly a preserve of the wealthy; in the 1920s, clerks and bootblacks talked knowingly of American Can or Cities Service and bought five shares "on margin." In later years, it was frequently said that by the end of the twenties "everyone was in the market," though there were actually fewer, probably far fewer, than a million people involved. What is closer to the truth is that millions of Americans followed the market with avid interest; it became, as J. Kenneth Galbraith remarks, "central to the culture."

No one can explain what caused the Great Bull Market. It is true that credit was easy, but credit had been easy before without producing a speculative mania. Moreover, much of the speculation was carried on at rates of interest that by any reasonable standard were tight. More important was the spirit of optimism that permeated the decade. "We grew up founding our dreams on the infinite promises of American advertising," Scott Fitzgerald's wife

Zelda once remarked. "I still believe that one can learn to play the piano by mail and that mud will give you a perfect complexion." The faith people had that they, too, could be rich was deliberately cultivated by people in positions of responsibility—bankers and heads of investment trusts, who gave every indication of believing what they were saying. In an article called "Everybody Ought to Be Rich," John J. Raskob argued in the *Ladies' Home Journal* that anyone who saved fifteen dollars a month and bought sound common stocks would in twenty years be worth $80,000. Since commodity prices were remarkably stable throughout the boom, economists were confident that, despite the speculative fever, the economy was basically sound.

The volume of sales on the New York Stock Exchange leaped from 236 million shares in 1923 to 1,125 million in 1928. That was a year when everything one touched seemed to turn to gold: industrial stocks went up a then astonishing 86.5 points. Customers borrowed money, bought more stock, watched the stock go up, and borrowed still more money to buy still more stock. By 1928, the stock market was carrying the whole economy. If it had not been for the wave of speculation, the prosperity of the twenties might have ended much earlier than it did. Coolidge's deflationary policies had withdrawn government funds from the economy, consumers had cut spending for durable goods in 1927, and the market for housing had been glutted as early as 1926. But with the economy sparked by fresh funds poured into speculation, a depression was avoided and the boom continued.

The stock market frenzy began in March, 1928. On Saturday, March 3, Radio sold at 94½. By the next Friday, it had surged to 108. On the following day it bounded to 120½. It seemed impossible, but when the market closed on Monday morning, Radio had gained another 18 points and was selling at 138½. The next morning, Radio opened at 160, a gain of 21½ points overnight. And it did not stop. After a few days of relative quiet, Radio jumped 18 points on March 20. The Big Bull Market was under way. Not long before he left office, President Coolidge announced that stocks were "cheap at current prices." The summer of 1929 not only bore out his dictum but made the gains of 1928 look modest in comparison. In three months—from June to August—industrials climbed 110 points; in a single summer, the value of industrial stocks increased by almost a quarter.

Even by the summer of 1928, the market had drawn people who never dreamed they would be caught in the speculative delirium. How much longer could you hold out when your neighbor who bought General Motors at 99 in 1925 sold it at 212 in 1928? There were stories of a plunger who entered the market with a million dollars and ran it up to thirty millions in eight months, of a peddler who parlayed $4,000 into $250,000. The Bull Market was not simply a phenomenon of New York and Chicago; there were brokerage offices in towns such as Steubenville, Ohio, and Storm Lake, Iowa. In an era of prohibition, as Charles Merz points out, the broker's office took the place of the barroom; it had "the same swinging doors, the same half-darkened windows." In midmorning, men would slump into the mahogany chairs of the smoke-filled room to search the blackboard or the hieroglyphics of the chattering ticker tape for news of the fate of Anaconda or Tel. and Tel. and remain until closing time.

In early September, 1929, the stock market broke, rallied, then broke again. By early October, Radio had tumbled 32 points, General Electric over 50 points, U.S. Steel almost 60 points. Still there was no panic. "Stock prices," announced Professor Irving Fisher of Yale, in what was to become a classic statement, "have reached what looks like a permanently high plateau."

In the last week in October, the situation turned suddenly worse. On October 23, rails and industrials fell 18 points. On Thursday, October 24, prices broke violently, and a stampede set in. The gains of many months were wiped out in a few hours. Radio opened at 68¾, closed at 44½. After a brief respite, the downward plunge resumed with reckless fury. On Monday Steel lost 17½, Westinghouse 34½, General Electric 47½. The next day, Tuesday, October 29, was one of sickening disaster. The ticker closed two and a half hours behind; when the last sales had been listed, industrial stocks had zoomed down 43 points.

On November 13, the market reached the lowest point it was to hit that year, but this was only the beginning of the end. On that day, industrial stocks were 228 points lower than they had been in early September; their value had been cut in half. In September, industrials had stood at 452; in November, 1929, they were 224. On July 8, 1932, at the bottom of the depression, they would sink to 58. In three years General Motors plummeted from 92 to 8, U.S. Steel from 262 to 22, Montgomery Ward from 138 to 4.

One can assign no single cause to the crash and the ensuing depression, but much of the blame for both falls on the foolhardy assumption that the special interests of business and the national interest were identical. Management had siphoned off gains in productivity in high profits, while the farmer got far less, and the worker, though better off, received wage increases disproportionately small compared to profits. As a result, the purchasing power of workers and farmers was not great enough to sustain prosperity. For a while this was partly obscured by the fact that consumers bought goods on installment at a rate faster than their income was expanding, but when the time came that they had to reduce purchases, the cutback in buying sapped the whole economy. With no counteraction from labor unions, which were weak, or from government, business increased profits at twice the rate of the growth in productivity. So huge were profits that many corporations no longer needed to borrow, and as a result Federal Reserve banks had only minimal control when profits were then plunged into the stock market, fueling a runaway speculation.

The policies of the federal government in the 1920s were disastrous. Its tax policies made the maldistribution of income and oversaving by the rich still more serious. Its oligopoly policies added to the rigidity of the market and left business corporations too insensitive to changes of price. Its farm policies sanctioned a dangerous imbalance in the economy. Its tariff policies made a difficult foreign-trade situation still worse. Its monetary policies were irresponsible, and at critical junctures the fiscal policy of the Coolidge administration moved in precisely the wrong direction.

The market crash played an important, but not the critical, role in precipitating the Great Depression. It shattered business confidence, ruined many investors, and wiped out holding company and investment trust structures. It destroyed an important source of long-term capital and sharply cut back consumer demand. Yet business would have been able to weather even the shock of the crash, if business had been fundamentally sound. The crash exposed the weaknesses that underlay the prosperous economy of the twenties—the overexpansion of major industries, the maldistribution of income, the weak banking structure, and the overdependence of the economy on consumer durable goods.

Developments in the construction and automobile industries foreshadowed what was to come. Residential building, which had stood at five billion dollars in 1925, was down to three billion by 1929. Auto manufacturing continued to grow, but after 1925 at a much slower rate, which meant cutting back purchases of steel and other materials; the cycle of events, whereby an increase in car production stimulated the steel, rubber, glass, and other industries, now operated in a reverse manner to speed the country toward a major depression. By 1929, the automobile industry—and satellites such as the rubber-tire business—were badly overbuilt. Since there was no new industry to take the place of automobiles and no policy of federal spending to provide new investment (Mellon, in fact, was working in the opposite direction), it was inevitable that as investment fell off and the rate of production slackened, there would be a serious slump.

Furthermore, no other industrial nation in the world had as unstable or as irresponsible a banking system. "The banks," noted one writer, "provided everything for their customers but a roulette wheel." During these years, wrote Joseph Schumpeter, "a new type of bank executive emerged who had little of the banker and looked much like a bond salesman"; these banker-promoters financed speculation and loaded the banks with dubious assets. By the time the banking crisis reached its height in Hoover's last three weeks in office, nine million savings accounts would be wiped out. Nothing did more to turn the stock market crash of 1929 into a prolonged depression than the destruction of business and public morale by the collapse of the banks.

By 1932, manufacturing output had fallen to 54 percent of what it had been in 1929; it was a shade less than production in 1913. All the gains of the golden twenties were wiped out in a few months. By the last year of the Hoover administration, the automobile industry was operating at only one-fifth of its 1929 capacity. As the great auto plants in Detroit lay idle, fires were banked in the steel furnaces on the Allegheny and the Mahoning. By the summer of 1932, steel plants operated at 12 percent of capacity, and the output of pig iron was the lowest since 1896.

Between 1929 and 1932, freight shipments were cut in half, and major railroad systems such as the Missouri Pacific, the Chicago and North Western, and the Wabash passed into receivership.

In heavily industrialized cities, the toll of the depression read, as one observer noted, like British casualty lists at the Somme— so awesome as to become in the end meaningless, for the sheer statistics numbed the mind. By 1932, there were 660,000 jobless in Chicago, a million in New York City. In Cleveland, 50 percent were unemployed; in Akron, 60 percent; in Toledo, 80 percent. In Donora, Pennsylvania, only 277 of 13,900 workers held regular jobs. In the three years after the crash, 100,000 people were fired on the average every week.

Like a chill bay fog, fear of the bread line drifted up into the middle class. Detroit counted 30 former bank tellers on its relief rolls. Universities graduated thousands of engineers, architects, and lawyers who had not the slightest prospect of a job. With no hope of employment, young people postponed marriage or, if they were married, did not have children. In 1932, there were 250,000 fewer weddings than in 1929, and the birth rate slipped from 18.8 to 17.4 per thousand. Hundreds of thousands of working women had to go back to their homes. Economy-minded school boards halted building projects and slashed teachers' salaries. Chicago teachers, unpaid for months, lost their savings, had to surrender their insurance policies, and were forced to borrow from loan sharks at 42 percent annual interest. By the middle of 1932, over 750 had lost their homes.

Farmers, who had not known the best of times in the 1920s, were devastated by the depression. The crash—and the ensuing financial debacle—destroyed much of what remained of their foreign markets. American trade abroad declined from $10 billion in 1929 to $3 billion in 1932. Foreign capital issues fell from

$1500 million in 1928 to an abysmally small $88 million in 1932. As other nations erected additional barriers to U.S. products and unemployment cut heavily into the domestic market, crop prices skidded to new lows. Wheat dropped from $1.05 a bushel in 1929 to 39 cents in 1932, corn from 81 cents to 33 cents a bushel, cotton from 17 cents to 6 cents a pound, tobacco from 19 cents to 10 cents a pound. The result was catastrophic. Gross farm income fell from nearly $12 billion to the pitiful sum of $5 billion.

The depression touched every area of American life. Bergdorf Goodman slashed sables 40 per cent, Marcus and Company offered a $50,000 emerald ring for $37,500, and the Pullman Company reduced rates on upper berths 20 percent. The Yankees mailed Babe Ruth a contract for the 1932 season with a $10,000 salary cut, and the Giants offered their star first baseman, Bill Terry, 40 percent less. The United Hospital Fund reported that donors not only reneged on pledges but even asked that the previous year's contributions be returned to them. On Broadway, theater lights were darkened; on Fifth Avenue, strollers no longer heard the sound of riveters. The managers of the Empire State Building ended all pretext that its offices were rented; elevators stopped running from the 42d to the 67th floors.

The first response of the nation's leaders to the depression was fatalistic. Business cycles were inevitable, it was said, and there was nothing to do but wait out this latest disaster. Any attempt to interrupt the process would only make matters worse. The *New York Times* contended that "the fundamental prescriptions for recovery [were] such homely things as savings, retrenchment, prudence and hopeful waiting for the turn." Businessmen, especially bankers, demanded ruthless deflation. "To advise people to spend," declared one banker, "would be seditious." Above all, governments must reduce expenditures, and budgets for relief of the jobless must be cut to the bone. The depression revived an emphasis on Puritan virtues which the 1920s had rejected, and bankers linked their insistence on deflation to Calvinist morality. President John E. Edgerton told the National Association of Manufacturers in the autumn of 1930 that people must understand that the suffering of the unemployed was not the product of an economic breakdown but of their own moral infirmity.

The financial community purported to see the depression as a blessed occurrence that would improve the national character by chastening the spirit. The crash, announced the leading banking periodical, "should be highly beneficial." Nevertheless, as Gilbert Seldes dryly remarked, "No one ever proposed to continue the depression in order to continue its benefits." Even hard-shelled British Tories were shocked by the tenacious resistance of American businessmen to unemployment insurance. "I do not sympathize," wrote Winston Churchill, "with those who think that this process of compulsory mass saving will sap the virility and self-reliance of our race. There will be quite enough grind-stone in human life to keep us keen."

Financiers and politicians hoped to lick the depression through magical incantation and by showing the same kind of booster spirit that had made Zenith hum. "Just grin," urged Charles M. Schwab, "keep on working." Thousands of people in Cincinnati wore buttons reading: "I'm sold on America. I won't talk depression." The vice-president of one Wall Street firm took a bunch of white carnations to his office every morning for each of his department heads, so that they would exude confidence, and New York's Mayor Jimmy Walker asked movie theaters to show only cheerful films. Businessmen and government officials issued periodic bulletins declaring that the depression would be over in 30 or 60 or

90 days. Julius Rosenwald even announced that he was afraid there might soon be a serious labor shortage. These conjurations met with indifferent success. "Some leading Republicans are beginning to believe there is some concerted effort on foot to use the Stock Market as a method of discrediting the Administration," complained the Republican National Chairman. "Every time an Administration official gives out an optimistic statement about business conditions, the market immediately drops."

President Hoover insisted on a more activist role. Hoover has been flayed by his critics as a tool of Wall Street and as a "do-nothing" President. He was neither. He strongly disapproved of the bankers' insistence on deflation, and he used governmental power to check the depression in an unprecedented manner, though still too modestly. Hoover had little patience with men like Secretary Mellon, who urged him to "liquidate labor, liquidate stocks, liquidate the farmers, liquidate real estate." The President stepped up federal construction, urged state and local governments to accelerate spending, and gained promises of increased capital investment from the railroads and utilities. He summoned the leading businessmen of the country to a White House conference and obtained a pledge from them to maintain wage rates. Earlier in 1929, Congress had passed the Agricultural Marketing Act, which aimed to stabilize agriculture through federal encouragement of farm co-operatives. By 1930, a Grain Stabilization Corporation and a Cotton Stabilization Corporation were invading the market to bolster prices.

Unhappily, however, after these shrewd steps, Hoover's approach to the problems of the Great Depression was essentially orthodox, and nothing revealed how far short he fell of his boldness a decade before in dealing with the suffering of the destitute than his attitude toward the plight of the unemployed. To provide relief for the jobless, Hoover relied on local governments and private charity. He created national committees of volunteers to solicit funds for those who were down and out, but he set himself rigidly against all proposals for federal relief expenditures. A federal dole would invite reckless spending on "pork-barrel" projects and would unbalance the budget and thus jeopardize the national credit, he thought. Most important, federal grants, Hoover argued, would destroy the character of the recipients and create a class of public wards. Fortunately, he claimed, they were not required for local initiative was taking care of the needy.

By 1932, the assumptions on which Hoover based his relief policies had been shot to bits. Private charity proved wholly inadequate, and local governments soon exhausted their treasuries. Relief payments were $2.39 a week in New York and still less elsewhere. Dallas and Houston gave no relief at all to Mexican or black families. Detroit's relief rolls were swelled by thousands of discharged auto workers, but Detroit could tax neither Ford nor Chrysler, because their plants were beyond the city line. When Detroit's Mayor Frank Murphy tried to borrow, he could obtain funds from the auto companies only by agreeing to slash welfare funds drastically. Detroit dropped more than one-third of the families on relief. The worse the depression got, the less the cities did. More than 100 cities had no relief appropriations at all for 1932.

Unable to pay rent or meet mortgage payments, many families lost their homes. In empty lots on the edge of industrial cities, homeless men, sometimes with families, built crude shelters of packing crates and old pieces of metal. In the larger cities, whole colonies of these "Hoovervilles" were established. In New York's Central Park, a group of squatters nested in "Hoover Valley," the bed of a drained reservoir; in Arkansas, men were found living in caves; by the Salt River in Arizona, miners camped under bridges. In the great cities, girls slept on subways. Thousands wandered the country aimlessly, in quest of a job, or relief, or just a sense of motion. In 1929, the Missouri Pacific counted 13,745 migrants; in 1931, 186,028. By 1932, there were from 1 to 2 million men, including a few hundred thousand young boys, roaming the country.

In many cities, long queues of hungry men, their shoulders hunched against December winds, edged along sidewalks to get a bowl of broth from charity "soup kitchens." Though most families were able to make out on shorter rations, the plight of the utterly destitute—and by 1932 they numbered millions—was appalling. In the St. Louis dumps, small groups of men, women, and children dug for rotten food. In Chicago, they stood outside the back doors of restaurants for leavings or scoured the market districts for spoiled fruit and vegetables. In the coal hills of Pennsylvania, families were fed on weeds and roots. Though the Hoover administration claimed that nobody actually starved to death, 238 persons suffering from malnutrition or starvation were admitted to New York hospitals alone in 1931. Forty-five of them died.

In the three years after the crash, factory wages shrank from $12 billion to $7 billion. From the first, bankers declared relentless war on the high-wage philosophy. "The man who relies upon the wage he receives for his daily toil," declared the *Commercial and Financial Chronicle,* "must realize that employers have suffered even as has the employee; and much beyond the same." For a time, manufacturers kept their promise to Hoover to maintain wage *rates,* even though total wages were falling. On September 22, 1931, though, U.S. Steel announced a 10 percent wage cut; General Motors, Bethlehem Steel, and other corporations immediately followed. The wage front was broken. Within a year, sweatshops had mushroomed all through the East. In one factory, 13-year-old packing girls were paid 50 cents a day; in another plant, apron girls received a daily wage of 20 cents.

To alleviate the misery of the depression and to use public funds to revive investment, a group of Senate progressives demanded federal action, but to no avail. Senator Robert Wagner of New York introduced bills to create a federal employment service and an agency to gather unemployment statistics, and together with Senators Robert M. La Follette, Jr., of Wisconsin, Edward P. Costigan of Colorado, and Bronson Cutting of New Mexico advocated federal spending for public works and direct relief. Hoover peremptorily opposed all these bills. With the relief situation rapidly nearing the point of total breakdown, he issued sanguine statements minimizing the number of unemployed and the degree of suffering. When the President's own relief experts reported that unemployment was mounting to unprecedented heights, he would not believe them. When they urged him to launch a huge public works program, he disregarded them. Because of "an aroused sense of public responsibility," Hoover claimed, "those in destitution and their children are actually receiving more regular and more adequate care than even in normal times."

In the spring of 1931, at a time when a slow upturn led some economists to believe that the United States was pulling out of the depression, disaster struck from abroad. The withdrawal of American dollars from Europe after the 1929 crash had created serious financial stringency on the Continent. In March, 1931, French bankers called in short-term German and Austrian notes, a move made partly for political reasons. Unable to meet the demands, the Kreditanstalt in Vienna buckled. The collapse of the greatest bank in Austria in turn set off a chain reaction. Heavy withdrawals of gold from Germany forced the Weimar Republic to default on its reparations payments. Fearing Germany would go Communist, President von Hindenburg appealed to Hoover for help.

In June, 1931, Hoover proposed a one-year moratorium on reparations payments and intergovernmental debts. It was a sensible move, but the president received so little cooperation from the French that much of its value was dissipated. In August, the British, who had gone to the aid of both Austria and Germany, were caught short themselves. In September, Great Britain abandoned the gold standard. This decision marked the virtual end of the system of international exchange of nineteenth-century capitalism.

The American banking system was exceptionally vulnerable to these financial upheavals. In 1929, 659 banks failed; in 1930, 1,352; in 1931, 2,294. In November, 1930, a panic, starting in Nashville, swept through the Middle South and closed 129 banks. The following month, a little before Christmas, the Bank of the United States in New York City, an institution with 400,000 depositors, collapsed. The ruin of the Bank of the United States, which held the life savings of thousands of recent immigrants, affected a third of the people of New York City and was the worst bank failure in the history of the republic. Millions of Americans who in 1929 had regarded banks as the epitome of security withdrew their money and hid it under flagstones. By the fall of 1931, a billion dollars had been taken from banks and put in safe deposit boxes or stuffed in old mattresses.

The European financial debacle created a fresh crisis in the United States. As Europeans demanded gold, American banks in turn had to call in their loans to American businesses, and a new wave of liquidations followed. Bankers carried out the policy of deflation so relentlessly that they were caught in their own web. The endless downward spirals of liquidation reached the point where they threatened the existence of the banks themselves. Once deflation threatened the financial structure, bankers were curiously unwilling to experience the spiritual benefits of chastening, and they demanded government protection from the consequences of their actions. Fearing that if the policy of deflation was not arrested, bankers would pull their own houses down, Hoover, in December, 1931, proposed the creation of a Reconstruction Finance Corporation. Based on the War Finance Corporation of World War I, the RFC was chartered by Congress in January, 1932, to lend funds to banks, railroads, building and loan associations, and similar institutions. In addition, in July, 1932, after Hoover vetoed the Garner-Wagner relief bill, which provided direct aid to the jobless and vast public works, Congress passed a new law authorizing the RFC to lend money to states and municipalities for self-liquidating public works and to lend a smaller sum for relief to the jobless to states whose resources were exhausted.

The RFC, and a series of other anti-deflationary programs, all much too small in scale, failed to get the economy rolling again. Although the RFC helped shore up railroads on the verge of bankruptcy and reduced, at least for a time, bank closings, bankers viewed the RFC not as a way to expand the volume of credit but as a means of preserving their own and other institutions from bankruptcy. The RFC, virtually ignoring its role as a public works and relief agency, moved with exasperating slowness in spending the appropriations Congress granted it. The rest of Hoover's program met with even less success. The railroads and utilities, which had promised to expand construction, contracted their operations instead. New capital issues—investment in stocks and bonds—fell from $10 billion in 1929 to $1 billion in 1932. This was not enough new capital even to maintain the country's industrial plant. Although Hoover slightly increased federal spending on public works, state and local governments cut back so sharply that total public construction declined. The grain and cotton corporations accumulated huge warehouses of surpluses they could not sell. Despite their efforts, the prices of grain and cotton plummeted, and the Federal Farm Board wound up with losses of $184 million. Disgusted with Hoover's insistence on voluntarism, the Board advocated federal compulsion to reduce farm production in order to raise prices by diminishing supply.

In the months after the crash, people continued to look to the business leaders they had revered in the 1920s to lift them out of the depression, but as the outlook darkened, the financial titans fell from their pedestals. Businessmen, who had claimed credit for the prosperity of the 1920s, were now blamed for producing the depression of the 1930s. Andrew Mellon, who had been all but canonized in the 1920s, was mocked as "the greatest Secretary of the Treasury since Carter Glass," his immediate predecessor. In April, 1932, Hoover, convinced that a malicious conspiracy of bears was driving down the market, instigated a Senate investigation of Wall Street. The Senate probe revealed that J. P. Morgan and his nineteen partners paid no federal income taxes for 1931 and 1932 and that Morgan kept a list of insiders who were allowed to buy at less than the market price.

Spectacular scandals added to the disillusionment. In March, 1932, Ivar Kreuger, one of the most respected international financiers, committed suicide in his Paris apartment. When his affairs were disentangled, it was found that the Swedish Match King had fleeced American investors of a quarter of a billion dollars. American financiers had permitted Kreuger to take $50 million in securities from the vaults of the International Match Company without anyone knowing it, and Lee, Higginson had sold Kreuger's issues to the American public without insisting on the elementary step of an independent audit. That same month, Samuel Insull's utility empire collapsed, with a total loss to investors of nearly $700 million. The stock of Insull Utility Investments fell from 107½ in 1929 to 1⅛ in March, 1932. Soon it was completely worthless. The scapegoat for other businessmen, Insull fled to Paris and crossed the Mediterranean in a dirty Greek steamer to avoid extradition to face a Cook County jury.

Nothing struck a harder blow at the prestige of business than the phenomenon of want in the midst of plenty. While people went hungry, granaries bulged with wheat no one could sell. While people froze for lack of fuel in winter, snow drifted over the mouths of idle coal pits. With billions of dollars locked up in banks, Iowa towns issued scrip and stores in the state of Washington issued and accepted wooden money. Knoxville, Atlanta, and Richmond printed their own currency.

Abundance stalked the canefields and the grain belts. "From Ocala south and east to Orlando and the fertile Indian River region," reported one writer after a tour of Florida, "oranges and grapefruit hang heavy on the trees and cover the ground beneath." When a terrible drought struck the country in 1930, many farmers rejoiced, and stock prices soared on Wall Street. The Federal Farm Board urged southern planters to plow under every third row of cotton, and even the boll weevil was viewed with a friendlier eye. Brazil burned thousands of bags of coffee and shoveled scowloads of the beans into the Atlantic. Rubber planters were jubilant when they discovered a new pest was attacking their trees.

Men relentlessly sabotaged the technology on which they had

preened themselves in the Coolidge years. In the winter of 1930, Newark abandoned machines for hand excavation, Minneapolis resorted to picks and shovels, and Boston stored its snow-loading machines to give men work with shovels. In 1932, Representative Hatton Sumners of Texas urged that the Patent Office cease giving patents on labor-saving devices. When Henry Ford, who had done as much as any man to mechanize agriculture, hired hands to harvest crops on his farms, he equipped them only with old-fashioned hoes. Kansas, the most highly mechanized agricultural state, restored hitching racks in front of courthouses.

Many Americans who had never had a radical thought before in their lives began to question the virtues of capitalism. How, critics asked, could one justify a system that wilfully destroyed its crops and cast aside its machines? "When I think of what has been happening since unemployment began, and when I see the futility of the leaders," declared Father John A. Ryan, "I wish we might double the number of Communists in this country, to put the fear, if not of God, then the fear of something else, into the hearts of our leaders." Even that insouciant exemplar of the apolitical 1920s, Scott Fitzgerald, who by the summer of 1932 was reading Karl Marx, wrote, "To bring on the revolution, it may be necessary to work inside the communist party."

As the bread lines lengthened, the mood of the country became uglier. In July, 1931, 300 unemployed men stormed the food shops of Henryetta, Oklahoma. An army of 15,000 pickets marched on Taylorville, Illinois, and stopped operations at the Christian County Mines in 1932. In Washington, D.C., 3,000 Communist "hunger marchers" paraded. None of these demonstrations matched in importance the farm rebellion. From Bucks County, Pennsylvania, to Antelope County, Nebraska, farmers banded together to prevent banks and insurance companies from foreclosing mortgages. When sheriffs attempted to carry out fore-closures, mobs brandishing pitchforks and dangling hangman's nooses persuaded them to retreat. In Iowa—the center of stable rural Republican life—once prosperous farmers, leaving their neat white houses and rich lands behind, barricaded highways to prevent milk from getting to market in a vain effort to force up prices. In a national radio broadcast, the president of the National Farmers' Union denounced the wealthy as "cannibals that eat each other and who live on the labor of the workers."

Nothing seemed more unreasonable to farmers than to deprive them of their land when, through no fault of their own, they could no longer meet their obligations, and, on this one question, farmers were almost beside themselves. The president of the Farmers' Union of Wisconsin told a Senate committee: "They are just ready to do anything to get even with the situation. I almost hate to express it, but I honestly believe that if some of them could buy airplanes they would come down here to Washington to blow you fellows all up. . . . The farmer is naturally a con-servative individual, but you cannot find a conservative farmer today. . . . I am as conservative as any man could be, but any economic system that has in its power to set me and my wife in the streets, at my age—what can I see but red?" For the first time in history, Lloyd's of London sold large sums of "riot and civil commotion insurance" to Americans.

No "civil commotion" attracted as much attention as the march of the "bonus army." Demanding immediate and full payment of bonuses for their service in World War I, 15,000 to 20,000 un-employed veterans moved on Washington in the spring of 1932. The House passed the bonus bill, but when the Senate voted it down by an overwhelming margin, half the men stayed on; they had no jobs, no homes, no place else to go. Most of them lived in mean shanties on the muddy Anacostia flats, some camped in unused government buildings. General Glassford, the head of the District police, treated the men decently and with discretion, but, as the men stayed on day after day, federal officials panicked. On July 28, 1932, the government decided precipitately to evict bonus marchers from vacant buildings on Pennsylvania Avenue. Two veterans were killed and several District police were injured in a scuffle that followed. President Hoover summoned the U.S. Army to take over.

With machine guns, tanks, and tear gas, brandishing sabers and drawn bayonets, the Army, in full battle regalia, advanced on the ragged group of bonus marchers. Led by the Army Chief of Staff, Douglas MacArthur (Dwight Eisenhower and George Patton were two of his junior officers) the Army dispersed the marchers and burned their billets. Hoover, whose attack on the veterans had aligned much of the country against him, made matters worse by releasing a report of the Attorney General accusing the bonus army of being composed of Communists and criminals. General MacArthur, who called the veterans "a mob . . . animated by the essence of revolution," added to the impression that the government had lost its sense of proportion. If Hoover had "let it go on another week," MacArthur declared, "I believe that the institutions of our Government would have been very severely threatened."

By the summer of 1932, much of the nation viewed Hoover with open contempt. None of his efforts seemed to do much good, and a great deal that he had said was less than frank. The country was convinced that Hoover, who more than any man of his generation had won the reputation of Great Humanitarian, was cold-hearted and indifferent to suffering. Scurrilous biographies were circulated accusing Hoover of having indulged in slave-trading, profited from Belgian relief, and even having caused the execution of Nurse Edith Cavell. His name became a trademark for every artifact of the depression. Men who slept on park benches dubbed the newspapers with which they covered themselves "Hoover blankets." A pocket turned inside out was a "Hoover flag." In the Southwest, jobless harvest hands sang "Hoover made a souphound outa me."

A man of great administrative ability, Hoover possessed almost no political gifts. He had an aversion to the tortuous practices of democracy. Lacking skill at political maneuver, he met every situation with the directness of a rhinoceros. No one could question his devotion to his office. Hoover, observed Allan Nevins, worked "as hard as any resident of the White House since James K. Polk worked himself to death there." But, apart from his political failings and his questionable economic policies, he did not have the personality to inspire the people. In his early years he had traversed the globe from the Transvaal to the Malay Peninsula, from western Australia to Mandalay, living the life of a Richard Harding Davis hero. Yet Hoover, as Arthur Schlesinger, Jr., observed, "transmuted all adventure into business as a Davis hero would transmute all business into adventure." When asked to stir the people, President Hoover would tell his friends glumly: "I have no Wilsonian qualities."

Since it seemed almost certain that the Republicans would pay the price for Hoover's shortcomings and, even more, for being the party in power during hard times, a keen contest developed for the Democratic presidential nomination in 1932. When New York's Governor Franklin D. Roosevelt won re-election by a landslide in 1930, he immediately established himself as the leading contender. A distant cousin of Theodore Roosevelt, he had much of Teddy's gusto. Although he took some time to grasp the seriousness of the depression—he dismissed it at first as a "little Flurry down town"—he soon was meeting it with Rooseveltian vigor. He established the first state relief agency in the country, spoke out for public development of electric power, and by 1932 had won almost every progressive in the party to his cause. In his humanitarian approach to governing, in his love of experimentation, and in his impatience with economic fatalism, Roosevelt suggested that beneath his cautious platitudes lay the promise of an audacious program.

The fight for the Democratic nomination quickly settled down to a stop-Roosevelt campaign. Al Smith, piqued by FDR's rise to eminence while Smith's fortunes were declining and riled at Roosevelt's refusal to retain Smith's advisers in Albany, led the opposition. Although the conflict was essentially a clash of personalities, Smith injected an ideological note as well, for he was aligned with the most conservative elements in the Democratic party. When Roosevelt in April, 1932, pleaded for "the forgotten man at the bottom of the economic pyramid," Smith, his face red with anger, retorted, "This is no time for demagogues." It seemed unlikely that Smith could win the presidential nomination himself, but it was quite conceivable that he could muster enough votes to block Roosevelt's nomination and throw the honor to someone else. Of the myriad of other candidates, John Garner, the Speaker of the House, had the strongest support, but astute observers believed that, if the convention deadlocked, the nomination might well go to Wilson's Secretary of War, Newton D. Baker, an internationalist who was conservative on economic issues.

At the Democratic convention, Roosevelt took a sizable lead over his nearest rivals, Smith and Garner, but when, after three ballots, he was unable to obtain the two-thirds vote necessary for victory, it appeared that he might be denied the nomination. At this critical juncture, California threw its Garner votes to Roosevelt. The reasons for this action are not certain, but there is a persistent belief that it was based on the determination of the newspaper titan, William Randolph Hearst, to prevent the convention from turning to the internationalist Baker. Even more important was Garner's refusal to permit his party to deadlock and destroy itself as it had in 1924. On the fourth ballot, Senator William McAdoo, whose presidential hopes had been frustrated by Smith in 1924, announced California's switch. As he stalked to the platform, he allegedly whispered: "Here's where I even up scores." The California votes turned the tide for Roosevelt; Garner, possibly as the result of an informal deal, gained the vice-presidential nomination.

The 1932 contest rarely addressed in a constructive way the critical issues of the Great Depression. Neither convention appeared to be as concerned about hard times as about prohibition. "Here we are in the midst of the greatest crisis since the Civil War," wrote John Dewey, "and the only thing the two national parties seem to want to debate is booze." Save for prohibition—the Democrats were wringing wet, while the Republicans hedged—few important differences separated the parties. The one major distinction established during the campaign was that Roosevelt, who, for an old Wilsonian, had become strongly nationalist, traced the depression to domestic causes, while Hoover emphasized its European origins. At times, too, Roosevelt's campaign speeches anticipated the New Deal; he indorsed social welfare legislation, outlined the idea of the Civilian Conservation Corps, and urged government regulation of utilities. But a great deal of what he said was double talk. At the same time that he promised expensive national reforms, he pledged a 25 percent cut in the budget and censured Hoover for heading "the greatest spending administration in peace times in all our history"—one which had "piled bureau on bureau, commission on commission." His tariff policy was contradictory; his farm speech at Topeka was designed to mean all things to all men. Running safely ahead, Roosevelt saw no point in unnecessary specificity. On Election Day, the country gave Roosevelt 22,800,000 votes to Hoover's 15,750,000. Roosevelt captured all but six states; he carried every state south and west of Pennsylvania.

The vote reflected less a triumph for Roosevelt than a rejection of Hoover, and in the weeks after the election, as another depression winter approached, the country plunged deeply into gloom. "For after a three years' deflation of the smart man, who is there in whom we can put our confidence?" asked Elmer Davis. "The leaders of industry and finance? They are about as thoroughly discredited as any set of false prophets in history and most of them know it. . . . Confidence in the politicians? The mere suggestion is enough to make anybody laugh." America no longer seemed a land of hope and promise. In 1932, 36,000 immigrants entered the country; 103,000 emigrants left. "Has the prophecy of Henry Adams, that we are all on a machine which cannot go forward without disaster and cannot be stopped without ruin, come true?" asked William Dodd. Of all the losses wrought by the depression, the ebullient optimism of 1914 was the chief casualty.

Epilogue

Never was a decade snuffed out so quickly as the 1920s. The stock market crash was taken as a judgment pronounced on the whole era, and, in the grim days of the depression, the 1920s seemed a time of irresponsibility and immaturity. "It was an easy, quick, adventurous age, good to be young in," wrote Malcolm Cowley, "and yet on coming out of it one felt a sense of relief, as on coming out of a room too full of talk and people into the sunlight of the winter streets."

Time dealt ruthlessly with the heroes of the decade. In 1929, with horrible appropriateness, Zelda Fitzgerald suffered a mental breakdown. Scott Fitzgerald aged like Dorian Gray; he wrote excellent work which, in the serious-minded thirties, was dismissed as trivia. Fitzgerald himself entered that "dark night of the soul" where it was "always three o'clock in the morning." The incorrigible Jimmy Walker continued to make the rounds of Manhattan nightclubs, but in the depression days his antics no longer amused, and he was driven from office. Mencken, the savant of the college generation of the twenties, was brushed aside by the college generation of the thirties, if they read him at all, as an antiquated reactionary.

In 1933, the nation repealed the prohibition amendment, and

with it went the world of the speakeasy; that same year, Texas Guinan died. Sound movies ended the careers of many of the silent stars. Clara Bow, who recalled halcyon days—"I'd whiz down Sunset Boulevard in my open Kissel (flaming red, of course) with seven red dogs to match my hair"—entered a sanitarium. Hollywood's greatest lover, John Gilbert, failed to make the transition from the silent screen; at 38 he was dead, the sound era's most conspicuous victim. In 1931, the Ziegfeld Follies opened for the last time; in 1932, bankrupted by the depression, Florenz Ziegfeld died. Vaudeville went to the grave when the Palace gave its last all-vaudeville bill in the spring of 1932. The law caught up with Al Capone in 1931, and he was sentenced to eleven years in prison for federal income tax evasion. The underworld caught up with Dutch Schultz and riddled him with bullets in a Newark barroom; dying, he uttered the baffling metrical sentence: "A boy has never wept, nor dashed a thousand kim." Dempsey's defeat, Gene Tunney's retirement, and the death of Tex Rickard brought the golden age of boxing to an end in 1929. In 1934, Babe Ruth, a pathetic waddling figure, tightly corseted, a cruel lampoon of his former greatness, took off his Yankee pinstripes for the last time.

The depression years killed off the icons of simplicity the 1920s had cherished. In January, 1933—eight weeks before Franklin Roosevelt took office—Calvin Coolidge died. Henry Ford, the folk hero of the Coolidge era, was damned in the 1930s as a tyrannical employer. When he instituted the five-dollar day, he had been honored as the laboring man's warmest friend. In the depression days, Ford was hard put to defend the actions of his private police headed by a former prize fighter, Harry Bennett, a mean-tempered man close to the Detroit underworld. Charles A. Lindbergh, the tousled blond airman whose flight to Paris in 1927 made him America's golden boy, suffered the trials of Job in the 1930s. On the night of March 1, 1932, his twenty-month-old son was kidnapped from his crib. Seventy-two days later, the child's body was found in a patch of woods. Cruelly badgered by the press and exploited by publicity-seekers, Lindbergh and his family abandoned America for Europe in December, 1935. The magnificent Lone Eagle of the 1920s, Lindbergh, by 1940, was detested as an associate of Nazis and an avowed racist.

Throughout the 1920s, demure Mary Pickford had remained the curly-locked Pollyanna of prewar American innocence. She refused to play "bad girl" roles. Spurning the flapper fashions of the time, she would not cut her hair. In 1927, she wrote: "Sometimes it is a dreadful nightmare, when I feel the cold shears at the back of my neck, and see my curls fall one by one at my feet, useless, lifeless things to be packed away in tissue paper with other outworn treasures." In the first year of the depression, her curls were shorn, and she appeared on the screen portraying bad women.

In the 1920s, the events of half a century finally caught up with America. Ever since the Civil War, the United States had been industrializing at an astonishing rate—erecting mammoth factories, filling up the empty spaces of the West, expanding its cities to gargantuan size. In the years after World War I, the productive capacity of the American economy exploded at the very same time that, in large part because of the growth in productivity, the United States became the world's greatest economic power, and the city disputed the pre-eminence of the countryside. All the institutions of American society buckled under the strain.

It was a time of paradoxes: an age of conformity and of liberation, of the persistence of rural values and the triumph of the city, of isolationism and new internationalist ventures, of laissez faire but also of government intervention, of competition and of merger, of despair and of joyous abandon. Many of the apparent paradoxes can be explained by the reluctance of the American people to accept the changes that were occurring and by their attempt to hold on to older ways of thought and action at the same time that they were, often against their will, committed to new ones. The very men who were taken as the epitome of the old order were the ones who undermined it—the Victorian statesman Woodrow Wilson, who presided over the transition to a strong state and the breakdown of isolation; the antiquarian Henry Ford, who disrupted the nineteenth-century world with revolutionary industrial technology; even Herbert Hoover, whose triumph in 1928 over Smith appeared to be a rejection of urban mores, but who was, in fact, an architect of modernization. Although Republican ideologues like Hoover sounded the praises of laissez faire, the state continued relentlessly to augment its power, with the civil and military functions of the federal government doubling between 1915 and 1930.

The 1920s have been dismissed as a time when America was hell-bent on the "gaudiest spree in history," but there was a great deal more to the era than raccoon coats and bathtub gin. "The world broke in two in 1922 or thereabouts," wrote Willa Cather. The year may not be accurate, but the observation is. The United States had to come to terms with a strong state, the dominance of the metropolis, secularization and the breakdown of religious sanctions, the loss of authority of the family, industrial concentration, international power politics, and mass culture. The country dodged some of these challenges, resorted to violence to eliminate others, and, for still others, found partial answers. The United

States in the period from 1914 to 1932 fell far short of working out viable solutions to the difficulties created by the painful transition from nineteenth-century to modern America. But it is, at the very least, charitable to remember that the country has not solved these problems yet.

Important Dates

1914   Outbreak of World War I
First moving assembly line with endless-chain conveyor
Strand Theatre in New York begins exclusive showing of motion pictures
T. S. Eliot abandons Boston for London

1915   Sinking of the *Lusitania*
Great Migration of blacks begins
Ku Klux Klan organized
Nonpartisan League formed
H. L. Mencken popularizes English term: flapper

1916   Preparedness movement
Sussex affair
Louis Brandeis named to Supreme Court

1917   Wilson's "peace without victory" speech
Zimmermann telegram
American declaration of war
Creation of war economy
First United States troops land in France
Bolshevik Revolution in Russia

1918   *Hammer v. Dagenhart*
Wilson announces Fourteen Points
Sedition act

Battle of the Argonne
Victorious end of World War I

1919 Peace conference and Versailles pact
Eighteenth Amendment (prohibition)
Senate rejects United States membership in League of Nations
Race riots in Chicago and East Saint Louis
Red Scare
Founding of American Communist parties
First ads showing woman holding a cigarette

1920 Nationwide Palmer raids
Senate rejects United States membership in League of Nations
for second and final time
Nineteenth Amendment (women's suffrage)
Sinclair Lewis's *Main Street*
F. Scott Fitzgerald's *This Side of Paradise*
Start of postwar depression
KDKA broadcasts news of Harding's victory
Studebaker stops making horse-drawn wagons

1921 Emergency immigration restriction law
Organization of the farm bloc
Washington conference on disarmament and Far East

1922 Fordney-McCumber tariff
Bailey v. Drexel Furniture Co.
T. S. Eliot's *The Waste Land*
Recovery from postwar depression
WEAF New York airs first radio commercial

1923 United States Steel abandons twelve-hour day
Death of President Harding
Adkins v. Children's Hospital
Revelation of scandals of Harding administration

1924 National Origins Act (immigration restriction)
Dawes Plan on reparations
Progressive ticket headed by Robert La Follette

1925   Scopes trial
Third edition, Watson's *Behaviorism*
The New Yorker founded
F. Scott Fitzgerald's *The Great Gatsby*
Bryn Mawr rescinds rule against smoking by students in college buildings

1926   Ernest Hemingway's *The Sun Also Rises*
First radio network, National Broadcasting Company

1927   Lindbergh flies the Atlantic to Paris
Execution of Sacco and Vanzetti
The Jazz Singer — first feature sound film
Start of "Good Neighbor Policy" in Latin America

1928   The Big Bull Market
Kellogg-Briand Pact

1929   Thomas Wolfe's *Look Homeward, Angel*
Wall Street Crash

1930   Hawley-Smoot Tariff Act

1931   Empire State Building
Hoover moratorium on intergovernmental debts
Japan invades Manchuria
Stromberg v. California
Near v. Minnesota

1932   Reconstruction Finance Corporation
Bonus Army episode
Election of Franklin D. Roosevelt

Suggested Reading

Every account of this period begins with Frederick Lewis Allen, *Only Yesterday* (1931), a lively social history. Isabel Leighton (ed.), *The Aspirin Age* (1949), collects ten essays on America between Versailles and the crash, including a hilarious article on prohibition by Herbert Asbury, the fantastic life story of Aimee Semple McPherson by Carey McWilliams, and a moving account of the Klan in Indiana by Robert Coughlan. A more scholarly collection is John Braeman, ed., *Change and Continuity in Twentieth-Century America: The 1920s* (1968).

Some three decades of research have produced John D. Hicks, *Republican Ascendancy* (1960); Paul A. Carter, *The Twenties in America* (1968), and his *Another Part of the Twenties* (1971); Gilman Ostrander, *American Civilization in the First Machine Age, 1890–1940* (1970); and Ellis Hawley, *The Great War and the Search for a Modern Order* (1992). Otis L. Graham, Jr., *The Great Campaigns* (1971), perceptively links progressivism to the instinct for war, and Stanley Coben, *Rebellion Against Victorianism* (1991), offers an original perspective on cultural change during these years. George B. Tindall, *The Emergence of the New South, 1913–1945* (1967), is invaluable.

The most substantial study of American society in this period is The President's Research Committee on Social Trends, *Recent Social Trends in the United States* (1933). David Riesman, *The Lonely Crowd* (1950), presents a stimulating study of the American character. Although Riesman does not fix precise dates, his "other-directed" man moved onto the national stage for the first time in the 1920s. So did the "new" middle class which is the subject of C. Wright Mills, *White Collar* (1951). Supporting evidence for both Riesman and Mills can be found in Richard

Walsh, "The Doom of the Self-Made Man," *Century,* CIX (1924), and Irvin Wyllie, *The Self-Made Man in America* (1954). Robert and Helen Lynd in *Middletown* (1929) dissect a "typical" American town, Muncie, Indiana.

Reports on America by European travelers have usually been a prime source for American historians. In this period, they are, for the most part, unrewarding. Of the British accounts, one of the best is J. A. Spender, *Through English Eyes* (1928). Stephen Graham, "The Spirit of America After the War," *Fortnightly Review,* CXIII (1920), and James Muirhead, "America Revisited After Ten Years," *The Landmark,* III (1921), vividly sketch the United States after Versailles. Eric Linklater, *Juan in America* (1931), is an engaging satire; at times, it is uproariously funny. Colonel J. F. C. Fuller, *Atlantis* (1926), is a tedious diatribe which revives the nineteenth-century tradition of contempt for America. Colonel Fuller observes: "Spiritually, the country is a corpse, physically, a terrific machine." C. E. M. Joad, professor of philosophy at the University of London, preserves his objectivity by writing about the United States without ever visiting it. America, Joad is convinced, is *The Babbitt Warren* (1926). British critiques of American civilization are summed up in George Knoles, *The Jazz Age Revisited* (1955). Continental accounts are generally more discerning, although André Siegfried, *America Comes of Age* (1927), is overrated. Moritz Bonn, "The American Way," *Atlantic Monthly,* CXLII (1928), is a searching German interpretation of the United States as a "man-made, not time-made commonwealth." Richard Müller-Freienfels, *Mysteries of the Soul* (1929), discusses with considerable understanding the impact of mechanization on American culture, a subject which fascinated the Germans.

Arthur Link's ambitious multi-volume biography is the standard source on Woodrow Wilson. Link also gives the most lucid account of the first Wilson administration in *Woodrow Wilson and the Progressive Era, 1910–1917* (1954). John Blum, *Woodrow Wilson and the Politics of Morality* (1956), and John Garraty, *Woodrow Wilson* (1956), are masterful brief biographies. The most judicious biographies of the men around Wilson are John Blum, *Joe Tumulty and the Wilson Era* (1951), and Frank Freidel, *Franklin D. Roosevelt: The Apprenticeship* (1952). George Mowry, *Theodore Roosevelt and the Progressive Movement* (1947), concludes with a superb analysis of the strangulation of the Progressive party.

The literature on the causes of American entrance into World War I is so mountainous that early on an impressive literature of bibliographies of literature of the topic developed. The more important of these are Bernadotte Schmitt, "American Neutrality, 1914–1917," *Journal of Modern History*, VIII (1936); D. F. Fleming, "Our Entry into the World War in 1917," *Journal of Politics*, II (1940); and Richard Leopold, "The Problem of American Intervention in 1917: An Historical Prospect," *World Politics*, II (1950).

Although important historical writing on the origins of U.S. intervention appeared soon after the war, it has been largely displaced by sophisticated diplomatic history often drawing upon archives in more than one country. Ernest R. May, *The World War and American Isolation* (1959), is the book to turn to first. Other valuable sources are Daniel M. Smith, *The Great Departure* (1965); John A. S. Grenville and George B. Young, *Politics, Strategy, and American Diplomacy, 1873–1917* (1966); John M. Cooper, Jr., *The Vanity of Power* (1969) and *The Warrior and the Priest* (1983); and Ross Gregory, *The Origins of American Intervention in the First World War* (1971).

Those interested in the subject, though, should not neglect earlier works such as Harley Notter, *The Origins of the Foreign Policy of Woodrow Wilson* (1937), and Charles Seymour, *American Diplomacy during the World War* (1934). Seymour's *American Neutrality, 1914–1917* (1935) is more polemical. Both Walter Millis, *Road to War* (1935), a beguiling popular account, and Charles Tansill, *America Goes to War* (1938), reflect the pacifism of the 1930s, but both volumes have reputations as one-dimensional studies that they do not deserve. Millis' article, "Will We Stay Out of the Next War?: How We Entered the Last One," *New Republic*, LXXXIII (July 31, 1935), is one of the most level-headed pieces written in the 1930s. Although economic interpretations are not fashionable today, no historian can neglect Paul Birdsall, "Neutrality and Economic Pressures, 1914–1917," *Science and Society*, III (1939). Alice Morrissey, *The American Defense of Neutral Rights, 1914–1917* (1939), is a solid monograph. For public opinion, a subject which Seymour largely neglected, see Edwin Costrell, *How Maine Viewed the War, 1914–1917* ("University of Maine Studies," Second Series, No. 49 [1940]), one of a number of state studies; H. Schuyler Foster, Jr., "How America Became Belligerent," *American Journal of Sociology*, XL (1935); and Harold Syrett, "The Business Press and American Neutrality, 1914–1917," *Mississippi Valley Historical Review*, XXXII (1945). Marion Siney, *The Allied Blockade of Germany 1914–1916* (1957), an impressive study based on the archives of several European countries, and Daniel Smith, "Robert Lansing and the Formulation of American Neutrality Policies, 1914–1915," *Mississippi Valley Historical Review,* XLIII (1956), explore the development of neutrality in the early part of the war.

Since World War II, historians have been more concerned with examining American foreign policy from the vantage point of power relations. Robert Osgood, *Ideals and Self-Interest in America's Foreign Relations* (1953), is the best work to come out of this school. Edward Buehrig, *Woodrow Wilson and the Balance of Power* (1955), also concentrates on power considerations. Buehrig has edited *Wilson's Foreign Policy in Perspective* (1957). He presents his viewpoint more briefly in "Wilson's Neutrality Re-Examined," *World Politics,* III (1950). One of the most judicious studies of American entrance into the war is Arthur Link, *Wilson the Diplomatist* (1957); Link follows Seymour, for the most part, but modifies Seymour in the light of later scholarship.

David M. Kennedy, *Over Here* (1980), is the best book on the impact of World War I on American society. For the industrial mobilization, see Paul A. C. Koistinen, "The 'Industrial-Military Complex' in Historical Perspective: World War I," *Business History Review,* 41 (1967); Robert D. Cuff, *The War Industries Board* (1973); Daniel R. Beaver, *Newton D. Baker and the American War Effort, 1917–1919* (1966); Valerie Jean Conner, *The National War Labor Board* (1983); Maurine W. Greenwald, *Women, War, and Work* (1980); James P. Johnson, *The Politics of Soft Coal* (1979); Harold M. Hyman, *Soldiers and Spruce* (1963); William J. Breen, *Uncle Sam at Home* (1984); and Ronald Schaffer, *America in the Great War* (1991). On the head of the War Industries Board, Bernard Baruch, Jordan Schwarz, *The Speculator* (1981), is first-rate. Seward W. Livermore, *Politics is Adjourned* (1966) covers the war Congress. George T. Blakely, *Historians on the Homefront* (1970), is a disturbing account of scholars genuflecting to the State, and John A. Thompson, *American Progressive Publicists and the First World War* (1987), is a penetrating analysis. Especially important for the academic profession is Carol S. Gruber, *Mars and Minerva* (1976). For the growth of "the war welfare state," see the contrasting views in Allen F. Davis, "Welfare Reform and World War I," *American Quarterly,* 19 (1967) and Christopher Lasch, *The New Radicalism in America* (1965). Allan M. Brandt, *No Magic Bullet* (1985), is superb on wartime prostitution. Robert H. Ferrell, *Woodrow Wilson and World War I, 1917–1921* (1985), is the standard overview.

Some earlier studies are still worth consulting. Frederick Paxson, *American Democracy and the World War* (3 vols., 1936–48), was long the standard source, supplemented by Benedict Crowell and R. F. Wilson (eds.), *How America Went to War* (6 vols., 1921); Grosvenor Clarkson, *Industrial America in the World War* (1923), and Bernard Baruch, *American Industry in War* (1941). George Mowry, "The First World War and American Democracy," in Jesse Clarkson and Thomas Cochran (eds.), *War as a Social Institution* (1941), discusses the baleful effect of the war; in a commentary on Mowry's article, Max Lerner dissents. Sidney Kaplan, "Social Engineers as Saviors: Effects of World War I on Some American Liberals," *Journal of the History of Ideas*, XVII (1956), is suggestive. William Waller (ed.), *War in the Twentieth Century* (1940), assembles a number of essays on World War I and its aftermath.

The most reliable sources for the military and naval phases are Harvey A. DeWeerd, *President Wilson Fights His War* (1968); Edward M. Coffman, *The War to End Wars* (1968); Russell F. Weigley, *The American Way of War* (1973), which includes an analysis of the AEF; and Frank Freidel, *Over There* (1990). John Whiteclay Chambers II, *To Raise an Army* (1987), goes well beyond his subject of the draft to illuminate the relationship between progressivism and nationalism. For the experience of black troops, see Arthur E. Barbeau and Florette Henri, *The Unknown Soldiers* (1974). Earlier works that are still of value include Elting Morison, *Admiral Sims and the Modern American Navy* (1942); J. G. Harbord, *The American Army in France, 1917–1918* (1936); John J. Pershing, *Final Report* (1919); Leonard Ayres, *The War with Germany* (1919); and George Davis, *A Navy Second to None* (1940). George Sylvester Viereck (ed.), *As They Saw Us* (1929), is a fascinating volume in which Foch, Ludendorff, and others give their impressions of American troops in France; Ludendorff's essay is a pre-Hitlerian sample of his bizarre political views.

For suppression of civil liberties, see Harry N. Scheiber, *The Wilson Administration and Civil Liberties, 1917–1921* (1960); Donald Johnson, *The Challenge to American Freedoms* (1963); H. C. Peterson and Gilbert Fite, *Opponents of War* (1957); Joan M. Jensen, *The Price of Vigilance* (1968); Frederick C. Luebke, *Bonds of Loyalty* (1974); and Charles Stewart, "Prussianizing Wisconsin," *Atlantic Monthly*, CXXIII (1919). Stephen L. Vaughn, *Holding Fast to Inner Lines* (1980), takes a new look at the Creel Committee. Carl Resek, *War and the Intellectuals* (1964), is the best source for the provocative essayist, Randolph Bourne. Richard Polenberg, *Fighting Faiths* (1987), is outstanding on the *Abrams* case.

Over the past third of a century a talented group of historians has given us a new understanding of what was at stake at Versailles and in the fight over whether the United States should participate in the League of Nations. See especially David F. Trask, *The United States in the Supreme War Council* (1961); Lawrence E. Gelfand, *The Inquiry* (1963); N. Gordon Levin, Jr., *Woodrow Wilson and World Politics* (1968); Ralph A. Stone, *The Irreconcilables* (1970); Arthur Walworth, *Wilson and His Peacemakers* (1986); Lloyd Ambrosius, *Woodrow Wilson and the American Diplomatic Tradition* (1988); and two books by Arno J. Mayer: *Wilson vs. Lenin* (1959) and *Politics and Diplomacy of Peacemaking* (1967). Christopher Lasch, *The American Liberals and the Russian Revolution* (1962), is a well-written account.

The best introductions to the earlier literature on Versailles are R. C. Binkley, "Ten Years of Peace Conference History," *Journal of Modern History*, I (1929), and Paul Birdsall, "The Second Decade of Peace Conference History," *Journal of Modern History*, XI (1939). H. W. V. Temperley *et al.,A History of the Peace Conference of Paris* (6 vols., 1920–24), is a standard source, but Thomas Bailey, *Woodrow Wilson and the Lost Peace* (1944), is more rewarding. For Wilson's role, see R. S. Baker, *Woodrow Wilson and World Settlement* (3 vols., 1922).

John Maynard Keynes, *The Economic Consequences of the Peace* (1920), had an enormous impact on thinking about the conference; Keynes's sparkling wit concealed the weakness of his thought. Étienne Mantoux, *The Carthaginian Peace, or The Economic Consequences of Mr. Keynes* (1946), makes an eloquent reply. Paul Birdsall, *Versailles Twenty Years After* (1941), is an important reappraisal. Thomas Bailey, *Woodrow Wilson and the Great Betrayal* (1945), is the best book on the League fight, although Bailey is too critical of Wilson. John Garraty, *Henry Cabot Lodge* (1953), is friendlier to his subject than earlier accounts, but Lodge's obnoxiousness manages to overcome Garraty's generosity. Dexter Perkins, "Woodrow Wilson's Tour," in Daniel Aaron (ed.), *America in Crisis* (1952), is admirable on that tragic episode.

Robert Murray, *Red Scare* (1955), is the standard work on the postwar hysteria, but students should also consult Stanley Coben, *A. Mitchell Palmer* (1963); William Preston, Jr., *Aliens and Dissenters* (1963); and Paul L. Murphy, *The Meaning of Freedom of Speech* (1972). John Blum, "Nativism, Anti-Radicalism, and the Foreign Scare, 1917–1920," *Midwest Journal*, III (1950–51), is penetrating, and Stanley Coben's "A Study in Nativism: The American Red Scare of 1919–1920," *Political Science Quarterly*, LXXIX (1964) is brilliant. The flavor of the Red Scare is preserved in Calvin Coolidge, "Enemies of the Republic: Are the 'Reds' Stalking Our College Women?" *Delineator,* XCVIII (1921). R. L. Friedheim, *The Seattle General Strike* (1965); Kate Holladay Claghorn, *The Immigrant's Day in Court* (1923), which contains a good chapter on the deportations; and Nelson Van Valen, "The Bolsheviki and the Orange Growers," *Pacific Historical Review,* XXII (1953), are special studies. Francis Russell, "Coolidge and the Boston Police Strike," *Antioch Review,* XVI (1956), provides a pleasant reminiscence. See, too, his *A City in Terror* (1975). Zechariah Chafee, *Free Speech in the United States* (rev. ed., 1941), is the classic account of violations of civil liberties in this period.

Theodore Draper, *The Roots of American Communism* (1957), makes a superb start on his history of the Communist Party. Joseph Freeman, *An American Testament* (1936), is perhaps the best book produced by an American Marxist. The basic sources for studying American socialism are David Shannon, *The Socialist Party of America* (1955); Daniel Bell, "Marxian Socialism in the United States," in Donald Egbert and Stow Persons, *Socialism and American Life* (1952), Vol. I; Ray Ginger, *The Bending Cross* (1949), a biography of Debs; and James Weinstein, *The Decline of Socialism in America, 1912–1925* (1967). William L. O'Neill, *A Better World* (1982), is critical of the infatuation of intellectuals with Stalinism. Granville Hicks, *John Reed* (1936), written when Hicks was a Marxist, is important. G. L. Joughin and E. M. Morgan, *The Legacy of Sacco and Vanzetti* (1948), is indispensable, but also see David Felix, *Protest* (1965). Francis Russell, in *Tragedy in Dedham* (1962) and *Sacco and Vanzetti* (1986), raises doubts about the innocence of Sacco.

Arthur Schlesinger, Jr., *The Crisis of the Old Order, 1919–1933* (1957) is a well-written introduction to the political history of the period by a liberal partisan. For the end of the Wilson era, see Gene Smith, *When the Cheering Stopped* (1964); Melvin I. Urofsky, *Big Steel and the Wilson Administration* (1969); and Burl Noggle, *Into the Twenties* (1974). Much of the best political writing on the period is by newspapermen. William Allen White, *Autobiography* (1946); his *Masks in a Pageant* (1930); Walter Johnson (ed.), *Selected Letters of William Allen White, 1899–1943* (1947); and Johnson, *William Allen White's America* (1947), all place the historian in the debt of the Sage of Emporia. Clinton Gilbert wrote *The Mirrors of Washington* (1921) anonymously and *"You Takes Your Choice"* (1924) under his signature. Among the more important sources on Republican political figures are Henry Pringle, *The Life and Times of William Howard Taft* (1939), Vol. II; William Hutchinson, *Lowden of Illinois* (2 vols., 1957); and Joel Paschal, *Mr. Justice Sutherland* (1951).

Robert K. Murray, *The Harding Era* (1969) is the most substantial source on that subject, but see, too, Andrew Sinclair, *The Available Man* (1965); Eugene P. Trani and David L. Wilson, *The Presidency of Warren G. Harding* (1977); and, for the 1920 election, Wesley Bagby, *The Road to Normalcy* (1962). For the programs of the Harding era and later, consult Ellis W. Hawley, ed., *Herbert Hoover as Secretary of Commerce* (1981); Craig Lloyd, *Aggressive Introvert* (1972); Donald L. Winters, *Henry Cantwell Wallace as Secretary of Agriculture, 1921–1924* (1970); and Donald C. Swain, *Federal Conservation Policy, 1921–1933* (1963). The most reliable sources on the major scandal of the period are J. Leonard Bates, *The Origins of Teapot Dome* (1963), and Burl Noggle, *Teapot Dome* (1962). Harry Daugherty and Thomas Dixon, *The Inside Story of the Harding Tragedy* (1932), should be read *cum grano salis.*

Donald R. McCoy, *Calvin Coolidge* (1967), offers a not uncritical appraisal of "the quiet president," but no one should ignore William Allen White, *A Puritan in Babylon: The Story of Calvin Coolidge* (1938), one of the finest political biographies in our literature. Claude Fuess, *Calvin Coolidge* (1940), is more orthodox. Gamaliel Bradford, "The Genius of the Average: Calvin Coolidge," *Atlantic Monthly,* CXLV (1930), is perceptive. William H. Harbaugh, *Lawyer's Lawyer* (1973), a biography of John W. Davis, is one of the best studies ever written of an "also ran," and Robert K. Murray, *The 103rd Ballot* (1976), is a pleasure to read.

L. Ethan Ellis, *Republican Foreign Policy, 1921–1933* (1968), is a standard introduction, but it should be supplemented by later works, including Melvyn P. Leffler, *The Elusive Quest* (1979), and Warren Cohen, *Empire without Tears* (1987). Jon Jacobson, "Is There a New International History of the 1920s?" *American Historical Review,* 88 (1983) is a valuable review essay. Frank Simonds, *American Foreign Policy in the Post-War Years* (1935), is a provocative analysis by a foe of collective security; although his central thesis is dubious, he makes a number of shrewd observations, particularly with respect to economic policy. Dexter Perkins, "The Department of State and American Public Opinion," in Gordon Craig and Felix Gilbert (eds.), *The Diplomats 1919–1939* (1953), is excellent. George Kennan, *American Diplomacy, 1900–1950* (1952), argues the now familiar thesis that American foreign policy in the twentieth century was founded on unreasonable assumptions about morality and power.

Selig Adler, "The War-Guilt Question and American Disillusionment, 1919–1928," *Journal of Modern History,* XXIII (1951), and "Isolationism Since 1914," *American Scholar,* XXI (1952), both trace the process of America's retreat from world affairs. Special interpretations which should be noted are William Appleman Williams, "The Legend of Isolationism in the 1920s," *Science and Society,* XVIII (1954); Daniel Boorstin, "America and the Image of Europe," *Perspectives USA,* XIV (1956); and Charles Beard, "The American Invasion of Europe," *Harper's,* CLVIII (1929). Akira Iriye, *After Imperialism* (1965), develops Far Eastern affairs and Joseph Tulchin, *The Aftermath of War* (1971), U.S. policies in Latin America, also the subject of Robert F. Smith, *The United States and Revolutionary Nationalism in Mexico, 1916–32* (1972).

Historians have given increasing attention to the persistence of American imperialism in these years. Frank Costigliola, *Awkward Dominion* (1984), and Emily S. Rosenberg, *Spreading the American Dream* (1982), both show that in this "isolationist" era the United States continued to pursue interests abroad. Other works with an economic emphasis include Herbert Feis, *The Diplomacy of the Dollar* (1950); Joseph Brandes, *Herbert Hoover and Economic Diplomacy* (1962); Joan Hoff Wilson, *American Business and Foreign Policy* (1971); and Michael J. Hogan, *Informal Entente* (1977). Simon Kuznets, *Economic Change* (1953), has an important chapter on foreign economic relations. F. W. Taussig, *The Tariff History of the United States* (1923), contains a chapter on the 1922 act by the chief scholarly critic of protectionism. Abraham Berglund, "The Tariff Act of 1922," *American Economic Review,* XIII (1923), presents another valuable review of Fordney-McCumber. The best of the early works on economic foreign policy are James Angell, *Financial Foreign Policy of the United States* (1933); M. F. Jolliffe, *The United States as a Financial Centre 1919–1933* (1935); Benjamin Williams, *Economic Foreign Policy of the United States* (1929); and John Madden, Marcus Nadler, and Harry Sauvain, *America's Experience as a Creditor Nation* (1937).

Merlo Pusey, *Charles Evans Hughes* (1951), Vol. II, is the standard, and uncritical, biography of the most important Secretary of State of the era. It should be read in conjunction with the brief volume by Dexter Perkins, *Charles Evans Hughes and American Democratic Statesmanship* (1956). Thomas H. Buckley, *The United States and the Washington Confer-*

ence (1970), is the most recent work on that topic, but one should also consult John Chalmers Vinson, *The Parchment Peace* (1955); A. Whitney Griswold, *The Far Eastern Policy of the United States* (1943); and H. H. and Margaret Sprout, *Toward a New Order of Sea Power* (1940). Robert Ferrell, *Peace in Their Time* (1952), is good on the Kellogg-Briand pact; see, too, Waldo Chamberlin, "Origins of the Kellogg-Briand Pact," *Historian*, XV (1952).

W. S. Myers, *The Foreign Policies of Herbert Hoover, 1929–1933* (1940), is the standard work. E. E. Schattschneider, *Politics, Pressures, and the Tariff* (1935), and J. M. Jones, *Tariff Retaliation* (1934), discuss the adoption and impact of Smoot-Hawley. Henry Stimson and M. Bundy, *On Active Service in Peace and War* (1948), is Stimson's personal account, while Richard Current, *Secretary Stimson* (1954), hauls Hoover's Secretary of State over the coals. Elting E. Morison, *Turmoil and Tradition* (1960), is friendlier. On Stimson in the Far East, see Robert Langer, *Seizure of Territory* (1947), and Sara Smith, *The Manchurian Crisis, 1931–1932* (1948). Robert Ferrell, *American Diplomacy in the Great Depression* (1957), is the most systematic analysis of Hoover's foreign policy.

The fate of progressivism in the 1920s is discussed in Richard Hofstadter, *The Age of Reform* (1955); Eric Goldman, *Rendezvous with Destiny* (1952); Arthur Ekirch, *The Decline of American Liberalism* (1955); and Peter Filene, "An Obituary for the Progressive Movement," *American Quarterly*, XXII (1968). Important regional studies of the disintegration of progressivism include C. Vann Woodward, *Tom Watson* (1938), a first-rate biography of the Georgia Populist; George Mowry, *The California Progressives* (1951); and Albert Kirwan, *Revolt of the Rednecks* (1951). The most seductive of the memoirs of the period is *The Autobiography of Lincoln Steffens* (1931), but Robert Morss Lovett, *All Our Years* (1948), should not be neglected. Edgar Kemler, *The Deflation of American Ideals* (1941), is iconoclastic. Claude Bowers, *Beveridge and the Progressive Era* (1932), emphasizes the role of nationalism in the progressive movement. Informative biographies of major progressives include Howard Zinn, *La Guardia in Congress* (1958); Arthur Mann, *La Guardia* (1959); and Richard M. Lowitt, *George Norris* (1963). Preston Hubbard, Jr. has contributed *Origins of the T.V.A.* (1961).

Charles Forcey, *The Crossroads of Liberalism* (1961), analyzes thoughtfully the ideas of Herbert Croly, Walter Weyl, and Walter Lippmann from 1900 to 1925. Ronald Steel, *Walter Lippmann and the American Century* (1980), is a *tour de force*. David Noble, "The *New Republic* and the Idea of Progress, 1914–1920," *Mississippi Valley Historical Review,* XXXVIII (1951), traces the loss of confidence of the intellectual wing of the progressives. For contemporary analyses of progressivism, see Walter Weyl, *Tired Radicals and Other Essays* (1919); Herbert Croly, "The Eclipse of Progressivism," *New Republic,* XXIV (October 27, 1920), and "The Outlook for Progressivism in Politics," *New Republic,* XLI (December 10, 1924); and Charles Merz, "Progressivism, Old and New," *Atlantic Monthly,* CXXXII (1923).

Kenneth MacKay, *The Progressive Movement of 1924* (1947), is the standard monograph. The background of the 1924 revolt is developed in F. E. Haynes, *Social Politics in the United States* (1924), and Robert Morlan, *Political Prairie Fire: The Nonpartisan League, 1915–1922* (1955). Alexander Harvey, "The Advantage of Senator La Follette," *American Mercury,* III (1924), is a shrewd analysis of Battle Bob. The major biography is Belle Case and Fola La Follette, *Robert M. La Follette* (2 vols., 1953), unabashedly hero-worshipping but nonetheless important. The results of the election are canvassed in Hugh Keenleyside, "The American Political Revolution of 1924," *Current History,* XXI (1925), and James Shideler, "The Disintegration of the Progressive Party Movement of 1924," *Historian* (1951). Paul Carter, *The Decline and Revival of the Social Gospel* (1956), is an excellent study of American Protestantism from 1920 to 1940. In *Seedtime of Reform* (1963), Clarke Chambers argues for the persistence of progressivism in the 1920s, a theme first advanced in Arthur S. Link, "What Happened to the Progressive Movement?" *American Historical Review,* LXIV (1959). Among the important studies of intellectuals pertinent to progressivism are Richard Hofstadter, *The Progressive Historians* (1968); David W. Levy, *Herbert Croly of The New Republic* (1985); John P. Diggins, *The Bard of Savagery* (1978), on Thorstein Veblen; and Steven C. Rockefeller, *John Dewey* (1991), which emphasizes the philosopher's religious outlook.

Gilbert Fite, *George Peek and the Fight for Farm Parity* (1954), is the best treatment of farm politics in the 1920s. Other major sources are Theodore Saloutos and John Hicks, *Agricultural Discontent in the Middle West, 1900–1939* (1951); Grant McConnell, *Decline of Agrarian Democracy* (1953); Harold Barger and Hans Landsberg, *American Agriculture, 1899–1939* (1942); Russell Lord, *The Wallaces of Iowa* (1947); and James H. Shideler, *Farm Crisis, 1919–1923* (1957). Two of the more revealing articles are Malcolm Sillars, "Henry A. Wallace's Editorials on Agricultural Discontent, 1921–1928," *Agricultural History,* XXVI

(1952), and Alice Christensen, "Agricultural Pressure and Governmental Response, 1919–1929," *Agricultural History,* XI (1937).

For the history of labor in this period, Irving Bernstein, *The Lean Years* (1960), is indispensable. Other useful sources include David Brody, *The Steel Strike of 1919* (1965); Robert Zieger, *Republicans and Labor, 1919–1929* (1969); Selig Perlman and Philip Taft, *History of Labor in the United States, 1896–1932,* the final volume of John Commons' monumental "History of Labour in the United States" (4 vols., 1918–35); and Leo Wolman, *Growth of American Trade Unions, 1880–1923* (1924). For the Industrial Workers of the World, Melvin Dubofsky, *We Shall Be All* (1969), supplants Paul Brissenden, *The I.W.W.* (1919); J. S. Gambs, *The Decline of the I.W.W.* (1932); and Ralph Chaplin, *Wobbly* (1948). Philip Taft, *The A.F. of L. in the Time of Gompers* (1957), is sympathetic to the American Federation of Labor. J. B. S. Hardman (ed.), *American Labor Dynamics* (1928), performs an autopsy on the labor movement from 1918 to 1928. The more important articles include Sumner Slichter, "The Current Labor Policies of American Industries," *Quarterly Journal of Economics,* XLIII (1929); David Saposs, "The American Labor Movement Since the War," *Quarterly Journal of Economics,* XLIX (1935); and Lyle Cooper, "The American Labor Movement in Prosperity and Depression," *American Economic Review,* XXII (1932). Matthew Josephson, *Sidney Hillman* (1952), is essential for the clothing workers.

There is a rich literature on the intellectual and cultural history of the era. The best guides are Henry F. May, *The End of American Innocence* (1959); Loren Baritz, *The Culture of the Twenties* (1969); Alfred Kazin, *On Native Grounds* (1942); Frederick Hoffman, *The Twenties* (1955), and *The Modern Novel in America, 1900–1950* (1951); Maxwell Geismar, *Last of the Provincials* (1947); J. W. Beach, *American Fiction, 1920–1940* (1941); Malcolm Cowley (ed.), *After the Genteel Tradition* (1937); Oscar Cargill, *Intellectual America* (1941); and Stanley Cooperman, *World War I and the American Novel* (1967). John Hutchens, *The American Twenties* (1952), is an anthology of the literature of the era. Edmund Wilson collected two volumes of essays and occasional pieces which he wrote during these years: *The Shores of Light* (1952) and *The American Earthquake* (1958). Van Wyck Brooks, *The Confident Years 1885–1915* (1952), a wearily impressionistic account of the years before the war, is the fifth and final volume of his "Makers and Finders." His *Days of the Phoenix* (1957) is autobiographical.

SUGGESTED READING

Malcolm Cowley, *Exile's Return* (1934; new ed., 1951), is an evocative survey of the "lost generation." Among the more discerning articles on the period are Henry May, "The Rebellion of the Intellectuals, 1912–1917," *American Quarterly,* VIII (1956); W. H. Auden, "Henry James and the Artist in America," *Harper's,* CXCVII (1948); John Aldridge, "The Predicament of Today's Writer," *Sarah Lawrence Alumnae Magazine,* XXII (1957); T. R. Fyvel, "Martin Arrowsmith and His Habitat," *New Republic,* CXXXIII (July 18, 1955); and Arthur Mizener, "The Novel in America: 1920–1940," *Perspectives USA,* XV (1956). George Snyderman and William Josephs, "Bohemia: The Underworld of Art," *Social Forces,* XVIII (1939), is an unpretentious social analysis.

The bleak intellectual mood of the period is caught in Joseph Wood Krutch, *The Modern Temper* (1929), and Walter Lippmann, *A Preface to Morals* (1929). Henry Harrison, "Last Days of the Devastators," *Yale Review,* XVIII (1928), is a shrewd commentary on the cult of self-flagellation. Harold Stearns's *America and the Young Intellectual* (1921) and *Civilization in the United States* (1922) are landmarks. Mabel Dodge Luhan, *Intimate Memories* (4 vols., 1933–37), is fascinating. For H. L. Mencken, see Edgar Kemler, *The Irreverent Mr. Mencken* (1950); William Manchester, *Disturber of the Peace* (1951); Charles Angoff, *H. L. Mencken* (1956); and Fred C. Hobson, *Serpent in Eden* (1974).

Morton White, *Social Thought in America* (1949), is a searching study of the "revolt against formalism." Howard Mumford Jones, *The Bright Medusa* (1952), argues unconvincingly that the revolt of youth in the name of art in the 1920s was merely the culmination of a long tradition. Bernard De Voto, *Forays and Rebuttals* (1936), includes an essay, "The Well-Informed, 1920–1930," and a hostile review of Cowley's *Exile's Return.* DeVoto's *The Literary Fallacy* (1944), a searing indictment of the writers of the 1920s, is a curious mixture of sense and nonsense. Stanley Edgar Hyman, *The Armed Vision* (1948), contains a murderous essay on Van Wyck Brooks. Lionel Trilling, *The Liberal Imagination* (1953), is a brilliant collection of essays, some of which, such as the piece on Sherwood Anderson, deal directly with the 1920s, all of which provide fresh insights on the period.

Some of the more important studies of individual writers are Mark Schorer, *Sinclair Lewis* (1961); Carlos Baker, *Ernest Hemingway* (1969); and Hendy D. Piper, *F. Scott Fitzgerald* (1972). Cleanth Brooks, *William Faulkner* (1963), examines the creator of Yoknapatawpha, and Townsend Ludington is discerning on *John Dos Passos* (1980). Elizabeth Drew, *T. S.*

Eliot, The Design of His Poetry (1949), is lucid. In the huge Eliot litera-ture, F. O. Matthiessen, *The Achievement of T. S. Eliot* (2d ed., 1947), and the chapters in David Daiches, *Poetry and the Modern World* (1940), Stephen Spender, *The Destructive Element* (1935), and John Crowe Ran-som, *The New Criticism* (1941), are noteworthy. Hart Crane has been the subject of studies by Philip Horton in 1937 and Brom Weber in 1948. Irving Howe, *Sherwood Anderson* (1951), is a good brief reckoning.

For the art of the period, see Barbara Rose, *American Art Since 1900* (1967); Sam Hunter, *American Painting and Sculpture* (1959); Milton W. Brown, *American Painting from the Armory Show to the Depression* (1955); Oliver Larkin, *Art and Life in America* (1949); James Fitch, *American Building* (1948); John Baur, *Revolution and Tradition in Modern American Art* (1951); and Townsend Ludington, *Marsden Hartley* (1992). Meyer Schapiro, "Rebellion in Art," in Daniel Aaron (ed.), *America in Crisis* (1952), is excellent on the Armory Show.

For the revolution in morals, Paula S. Fass, *The Damned and the Beau-tiful* (1977), is insightful on youth in the 1920's. David M. Kennedy, *Birth Control in America* (1970), explores the meaning of the career of Margaret Sanger. A more recent account is Ellen Chesler, *Woman of Valor* (1992). For contemporary commentary, see Freda Kirchwey (ed.), *Our Changing Morality: A Symposium* (1924); the May, 1929, issue of *The An-nals of the American Academy of Political and Social Science* and the Decem-ber 1, 1926, issue of the *Survey*, both devoted to women; Katharine Fullerton Gerould, "Reflections of a Grundy Cousin," *Atlantic Monthly*, CXXVI (1920); John Carter, Jr., " 'These Wild Young People': By One of Them," *Atlantic Monthly*, CXXVI (1920); Viola Paradise, "Sex Sim-plex," *Forum*, LXXIV (1925); Mary Agnes Hamilton, " 'Nothing Shocks Me,' " *Harper's*, CLV (1927); Dorothy Dunbar Bromley, "Feminist, New Style," *Harper's*, CLV (1927); Eleanor Rowland Wembridge, "Petting and the Campus," *Survey*, LIV (July 1, 1925); William Bolitho, "The New Skirt Length," *Harper's*, CLX (1930); and G. Stanley Hall, "Flap-per Americana Novissima," *Atlantic Monthly*, CXXIX (1922).

Nathan G. Hale, Jr., *Freud and the Americans* (1971), examines the history of psychoanalysis in the United States up to 1917. Ernest Jones, *The Life and Work of Sigmund Freud* (3 vols., 1953–57), is the definitive biography. Walter Lippmann, "Freud and the Layman," *New Republic*, II (April 17, 1915), is one of the earliest appreciations. George Santayana, "A Long Way Round to Nirvana: or, Much Ado About Dying," *Dial*, LXXV (1923), comments on Freud's *Beyond the Pleasure Principle*. Joseph

Jastrow, "The Freudian Temper: And Its Menace to the Lay Mind," *Century*, CXIX (1929), is critical. For the reception of Freud in America, see A. A. Brill, "The Introduction and Development of Freud's Work in the United States," *American Journal of Sociology*, XLV (1939); Celia Stendler, "New Ideas for Old: How Freudism Was Received in the United States from 1900 to 1925," *Journal of Educational Psychology*, XXXVIII (1947); Havelock Ellis, "Freud's Influence on the Changed Attitude Toward Sex," *American Journal of Sociology*, XLV (1939); Karl Menninger, "Pseudoanalysis: Perils of Freudian Verbalisms," *Outlook*, CLV (July 9, 1930); and Grace Adams, "The Rise and Fall of Psychology," *Atlantic Monthly*, CLIII (1934). Frederick Hoffman, *Freudianism and the Literary Mind* (1945), is the best source for that subject. Maxwell Bodenheim, "Psychoanalysis and American Fiction," *The Nation*, CXIV (June 7, 1922), takes a dim view of the "phallic exaggerations" in American literature, especially of stories "in which young men lie upon their backs in cornfields and feel depressed by their bodies." Lucille Birnbaum, "Behaviorism in the 1920's," *American Quarterly*, VII (1955), is admirable.

Dorothy M. Brown, *Setting a Course* (1987), surveys American women in the 1920s. William H. Chafe, *The American Woman* (1972), is a pathbreaking study. William L. O'Neill, *Everyone Was Brave* (1969), explores "the rise and fall of feminism," while J. Stanley Lemon, *The Woman Citizen* (1973), is more positive. Other important works include Aileen S. Kraditor, *The Ideas of the Woman Suffrage Movement* (1965); Winifred Wandersee, *Women's Work and Family Values, 1920–1940* (1981); Nancy Cott, *The Grounding of Modern Feminism* (1987); and Estelle B. Freedman, "The New Woman: Changing Views of Women in the 1920s," *Journal of American History*, LXI (1974).

The history of blacks in this era begins with the awful stories of race war: Arthur Waskow, *From Race Riot to Sit-in* (1966); Elliot Rudwick, *The Race Riot in East St. Louis, 1919* (1967); and William Tuttle, Jr., *Race Riot* (1970), on Chicago. Elliot Rudwick, *W. E. B. Du Bois* (1960), deals with arguably the most significant black figure of the period, and Nancy Weiss, *The National Urban League* (1974), with an important organization. E. David Cronon, *Black Moses* (1955), Theodore G. Vincent, *Black Power and the Garvey Movement* (1971), Randall Burkett, *Garveyism as a Religious Movement* (1978), and Judith Stein, *The World of Marcus Garvey* (1986), offer different perspectives. For the growth of inner cities, see Allan H. Spear, *Black Chicago* (1967); Gilbert Osofsky, *Harlem: The Making of a Ghetto* (1965); Jervis Anderson, *This Was Harlem*

SUGGESTED READING

(1981); and David Levering Lewis, *When Harlem Was in Vogue* (1981). Nathan Huggins, *Harlem Renaissance* (1971), is a sensitive study.

A wide range of writings considers popular culture and the response to the heroes of the period. Kathy J. Ogren, *The Jazz Revolution* (1989), is the most recent work on that large subject. Robert W. Creamer, *Babe* (1974), portrays the Sultan of the Swat, George Herman Ruth. Kenneth S. Davis, *The Hero* (1959), is a portrait of Charles A. Lindbergh, who is also the subject of John W. Ward, "The Meaning of Lindbergh's Flight," *American Quarterly,* 10 (1958), a remarkable essay that is imaginative and discerning.

The economy of this era has been studied to a fare-thee-well. Thanks largely to the initiative of the Brookings Institution and the National Bureau of Economic Research, the student is faced chiefly with a problem of selection. The following lists only a few of the more important early monographs: Frederick Mills, *Economic Tendencies in the United States* (1932); Arthur F. Burns, *Production Trends in the United States since 1870* (1934); Arthur R. Burns, *The Decline of Competition* (1936); Solomon Fabricant, *The Output of Manufacturing Industries, 1899–1937* (1940); Jacob Gould, *Output and Productivity in the Electric and Gas Utilities, 1899–1942* (1946); Ralph Epstein, *Industrial Profits in the United States* (1934); Charles Bliss, *The Structure of Manufacturing Production* (1946); Harold Barger, *Outlay and Income in the United States, 1921–1938* (1942); Robert Gordon, *Business Fluctuations* (1952); Joseph Schumpeter, *Business Cycles* (1939); Edwin Nourse et al., *America's Capacity to Produce* (1934); Maurice Leven et al., *America's Capacity to Consume* (1934); George Stigler, *Trends in Output and Employment* (1947); Thomas Wilson, *Fluctuations in Income and Employment* (1948); Paul Douglas, *Real Wages in the United States, 1890–1926* (1930); and George Edwards, *The Evolution of Finance Capitalism* (1938). Simon Kuznets, one of the great innovators of the period, is the author of *National Income and Its Composition, 1919–1938* (1941) and *National Products since 1869* (1946). President's Conference on Unemployment, *Recent Economic Changes in the United States* (2 vols., 1929), is an invaluable compendium.

Over the last few decades, scholars have both amplified this impressive literature and taken new approaches. Alfred D. Chandler, Jr., *Strategy and Structure* (1962), was an important departure, and Louis Galambos, *Competition and Cooperation* (1966), pointed the way toward an organizational emphasis. Other significant monographs include Loren Baritz, *The Servants of Power* (1960); Elmus R. Wicker, *Federal Reserve*

Monetary Policy, 1917–1933 (1966); Morrell Heald, *The Social Responsibilities of Business* (1970); Robert F. Himmelberg, *The Origins of the National Recovery Administration* (1976); Stuart D. Brandes, *American Welfare Capitalism, 1880–1940* (1976); Roland Marchand, *Advertising the American Dream* (1985); and Gary Alchon, *The Invisible Hand of Planning* (1985).

George Soule, *Prosperity Decade* (1947), is the best economic history of the times. James Prothro, *The Dollar Decade* (1954), is a droll recital of business thought. Charles Chapman, *The Development of American Business and Banking Thought, 1913–1936* (1936), is less useful. For contemporary appraisals, see Thomas Nixon Carver, *The Present Economic Revolution in the United States* (1925); W. Z. Ripley, *Main Street and Wall Street* (1927); J. T. Adams, *Our Business Civilization* (1929); Adolf Berle and Gardiner Means, *The Modern Corporation and Private Property* (1932); and Stuart Chase, *Prosperity—Fact or Myth* (1930). Frederick Lewis Allen, *The Lords of Creation* (1935), offers a sound secondary account. Sidney Ratner, *American Taxation* (1942), is the best treatment of that subject.

The main sources on technology are U.S. National Resources Committee, *Technological Trends and National Policy* (1937); Harry Jerome, *Mechanization in Industry* (1934); Roger Burlingame, *Engines of Democracy* (1940); Siegfried Giedion, *Mechanization Takes Command* (1948); Walter Polakov, *The Power Age* (1933); and Stuart Chase, *Men and Machines* (1929). For automobiles, see J. B. Rae's *The Road and the Car in American Life* (1971) and James J. Flink, *The Car Culture* (1975). Allan Nevins and Frank Ernest Hill, *Ford: Expansion and Challenge: 1915–1933* (1957), is the definitive biography, but Keith Sward, *The Legend of Henry Ford* (1948), a highly critical study, is a corrective.

For analyses of these years in journals, see Joseph Schumpeter, "The American Economy in the Interwar Period: The Decade of the Twenties," *American Economic Review,* XXXVI (1946), with a commentary by Garfield Cox, and Sumner Slichter, "The Period 1919–1936 in the United States: Its Significance for Business-Cycle Theory," *Review of Economic Statistics,* XIX (1937). Other useful articles are Norman Buchanan, "The Origin and Development of the Public Utility Holding Company," *Journal of Political Economy,* XLIV (1936); Sumner Slichter, "The Secret of High Wages," *New Republic,* LIV (March 28, 1928); "Swiss Family Dreyfus," *Fortune,* VIII (September, 1933); "A & P and the Hartfords," *Fortune,* VII (1933); "Woolworth," *Fortune,* VIII (November, 1933); N. R. Danielian, "From Insull to Injury," *Atlantic Monthly,* CLI (1933); and "Fifty Years: 1888–1938," *Printers' Ink,* CLXXXIV (July 28, 1938).

John Higham, *Strangers in the Land* (1955), is a magnificent study of nativism. The best brief history of the movement for immigration restriction is contained in Charles Howland (ed.), *Survey of American Foreign Relations, 1929* (1929). Kenneth Roberts, *Why Europe Leaves Home* (1922), is a vicious polemic. Robert DeC. Ward, "Our New Immigration Policy," *Foreign Affairs,* III (September 15, 1924), is the most reasoned defense of the National Origins Act. Arthur Mann, "Gompers and the Irony of Racism," *Antioch Review,* XIII (1953), and William Bagley, "The Army Tests and the Pro-Nordic Propaganda," *Educational Review,* LXVII (1924), are pertinent articles.

Don S. Kirschner, *City and Country* (1970), is highly illuminating on urban-rural tensions in the Midwest, and Charles W. Eagles, "Urban-Rural Conflict in the 1920's: A Historiographic Assessment," *Historian,* 49 (1986), is a useful review. Eagles, *Democracy Delayed* (1990), places the controversies over legislative reapportionment in the context of urban-rural conflict. Norman Furniss, *The Fundamentalist Controversy, 1918–1931* (1954), is excellent on that subject. It should be supplemented by Ernest Sandeen, *The Roots of Fundamentalism* (1970); George M. Marsden, *Fundamentalism and American Culture* (1980); and H. Richard Niebuhr's succinct article on "Fundamentalism" in the *Encyclopedia of the Social Sciences.* Gail Kennedy (ed.), *Evolution and Religion* (1957), and E. C. Vanderlaan (ed.), *Fundamentalism versus Modernism* (1925), are handy compilations. William T. Doherty, "The Impact of Business on Protestantism, 1900–29," *Business History Review,* XXVIII (1954), is a whimsical account. Lawrence W. Levine, *William Jennings Bryan* (1965), and the third volume of Paolo E. Coletta, *William Jennings Bryan* (1969), cover the Peerless Leader's final decade. For the Scopes trial, see Ray Ginger, *Six Days or Forever?* (1958). Russell Owen, "The Significance of the Scopes Trial," *Current History,* XXII (1925), is the best contemporary report.

Andrew Sinclair, *Prohibition: The Era of Excess* (1962), is informative and also highly entertaining. Joseph R. Gusfield, *Symbolic Crusade* (1963), goes well beyond its subject—the temperance movement—in demonstrating the significance of "expressive politics." Norman H. Clark, *Deliver Us from Evil* (1976), and David E. Kyvig, *Repealing National Prohibition* (1979), are both important. For earlier appraisals, see

Charles Merz, *The Dry Decade* (1931); Herbert Asbury, *The Great Illusion* (1950); and the April, 1928, issue of *Current History*. Virginius Dabney, *Dry Messiah: The Life of Bishop Cannon* (1949), is an acid portrait which is also useful for studying the 1928 campaign.

David M. Chalmers, *Hooded Americanism* (1965), is a lucid, far-ranging history of the KKK. Kenneth T. Jackson, *The Ku Klux Klan in the City* (1967), has caused those of us who thought of the KKK as very largely a rural and small town phenomenon to modify our views. Charles C. Alexander, *The Ku Klux Klan in the Southwest* (1965), shows how necessary it is to study the KKK region by region. Other regional studies include Robert A. Goldberg, *Hooded Empire* (1981), and Leonard Moore, *Citizen Klansmen* (1991), both of which see the KKK as a populist manifestation, and the much earlier Emerson Loucks, *The Ku Klux Klan in Pennsylvania* (1936). Frank Tannenbaum, *Darker Phases of the South* (1924), has a perceptive chapter on the origins of the Klan spirit. Among the best contemporary articles on the subject are Morton Harrison, "Gentlemen from Indiana," *Atlantic Monthly,* CXLI (1928); R. A. Patton, "A Ku Klux Klan Reign of Terror," *Current History,* XXVIII (1928); and Frank Bohn, "The Ku Klux Klan Interpreted," *American Journal of Sociology,* XXX (1925). Robert Moats Miller, "A Note on the Relationship between the Protestant Churches and the Revived Ku Klux Klan," *Journal of Social History,* XXII (1956) is helpful.

David Burner, *The Politics of Provincialism* (1968), is an important study of "the Democratic Party in transition," and J. Joseph Huthmacher, *Massachusetts People and Politics, 1919–1933* (1959), is excellent on the impact of ethnicity on voting. Oscar Handlin, *Al Smith and His America* (1958), treats the Democratic contender, and Allan Lichtman, *Prejudice and the Old Politics* (1978), stresses the influence of religious bias in 1928. Elisabeth Israels Perry, *Belle Moskowitz* (1987), is enlightening on Smith's most important adviser.

Samuel Lubell, *The Future of American Politics* (1952), argues, in a lively fashion, the salience of the "revolt of the city" for the 1928 campaign, but he carries the argument too far. Lubell relies heavily on Samuel Eldersveld, "Influence of Metropolitan Party Pluralities in Presidential Elections since 1920," *American Political Science Review,* XLIII (1949), which is effectively challenged in Jerome Clubb and Howard Allen, "The Cities and the Election of 1928," *American Historical Review,* LXXIV (1969). Roy Peel and Thomas Donnelly, *The 1928 Campaign: An Analysis* (1931), is a sound, brief account. Edmund Moore, *A Cath-*

olic Runs for President (1956), is excellent on the religious issue. V. O. Key, Jr., *Southern Politics* (1949), contains an important chapter comparing the Hoovercrats of 1928 with the Dixiecrats of 1948. Frank Freidel, *Franklin D. Roosevelt: The Ordeal* (1954), is an invaluable source of Democratic party history in the 1920s. For statements by Smith's most redoubtable foe, see James Cannon, Jr., "Al Smith—Catholic, Tammany, Wet," *Nation*, CXXVII (July 4, 1928), and "Causes of Governor Smith's Defeat," *Current History*, XXIX (1928). Washington Pezet, "The Temporal Power of Evangelism," *Forum*, LXXVI (1926), and Robert Moats Miller, "A Footnote to the Role of the Protestant Churches in the Election of 1928," *Church History*, XXV (1956), differ on the political impact of Protestantism.

Most of the books listed on the economy are applicable to the crash and the depression. Robert Sobel, *The Great Bull Market* (1968), covers Wall Street in its heyday. John Brooks, *Once in Golconda* (1969), is gracefully written. Milton Friedman and Anna Schwartz, *The Great Contraction, 1929–1933* (1965), should be read with Peter Temin, *Did Monetary Forces Cause the Great Depression?* (1976). Special studies include Lionel Robbins, *The Great Depression* (1934), and Francis Hirst, *Wall Street and Lombard Street* (1931). Charles Merz, "Bull Market," *Harper's*, CLVII (1929), presents a lively account of the speculative fervor. Joe Alex Morris, *What a Year!* (1956), gives a once-over-lightly view of 1929. John Kenneth Galbraith, *The Great Crash* (1955), is written with a marvellously dry wit. Broadus Mitchell, *Depression Decade* (1947), is the best economic history. E. Jay Howenstine, Jr., "World War I Production Dislocations as a Causal Factor of the Great Depression in the United States," *American Journal of Economics and Sociology*, XIII (1954), minimizes the importance of World War I. Gilbert Seldes, *Years of the Locust* (1933), Mauritz Hallgren, *Seeds of Revolt* (1933), and Jonathan Leonard, *Three Years Down* (1939), are early social histories of the depression.

The most recent studies of Herbert Hoover are Martin L. Fausold and George T. Mazuzan, eds., *The Hoover Presidency* (1974); Joan Hoff Wilson, *Herbert Hoover* (1975); David Burner, *Herbert Hoover* (1978); George Nash, *The Life of Herbert Hoover* (1983), the first volume of a projected multi-volume biography; and Martin L. Fausold, *The Presidency of Herbert Hoover* (1985). Albert U. Romasco, *The Poverty of Abundance* (1965), and Jordan A. Schwarz, *The Interregnum of Despair* (1970), are particularly illuminating on the deficiencies of Hoover's policies. Other important monographs are James S. Olson, *Herbert Hoover and the Reconstruction Finance Corporation, 1931–1933* (1977); William J. Barber, *From New Era to New Deal* (1985); and David E. Hamilton, *From New Day to New Deal* (1991). The case for Hoover is stated in his *Memoirs* (3 vols., 1951–52), W. S. Myers and W. H. Newton, *The Hoover Administration* (1936), and Ray Lyman Wilbur and Arthur Hyde, *The Hoover Policies* (1937). Hoover emphasizes his rural origins in "Boyhood in Iowa," *Palimpsest,* IX (1928), and "In Praise of Izaak Walton," *Atlantic Monthly,* CXXXIX (1927). T. G. Joslin, *Hoover—Off the Record* (1934), is a warm defense; R. G. Tugwell, *Mr. Hoover's Economic Policy* (1932), is critical. Walter Lippmann, "The Peculiar Weakness of Mr. Hoover," *Harper's,* CLXI (1930); Allan Nevins, "President Hoover's Record," *Current History,* XXXVI (1932); William Allen White, "Herbert Hoover—the Last of the Old Presidents or the First of the New," *Saturday Evening Post,* CCV (March 4, 1933); and Mark Sullivan, "The Case for the Administration," *Fortune,* VI (1932), offer contrasting views. For the most dramatic episode of Hoover's final year, see Roger Daniels, *The Bonus March* (1971), and Donald Lisio, *The President and Protest* (1974).

Two of the best accounts of the suffering caused by the depression are "'No One Has Starved,'" *Fortune,* VI (1932), and "New York in Third Winter," *Fortune,* V (1932). John Maynard Keynes, "The World's Economic Outlook," *Atlantic Monthly,* CXLIX (1932); Elmer Davis, "Confidence in Whom?" *Forum,* LXXXIX (1933); Paul Sifton, "Going, Going, Gone!" *Forum,* LXXXIX (1933); J. Russell Smith, "The End of an Epoch," *Survey,* LXVI (July 1, 1931); James Truslow Adams, "Shadow of the Man on Horseback," *Atlantic Monthly,* CXLIX (1932); and Reinhold Niebuhr, "Catastrophe or Social Control?" *Harper's,* CLXV (1932), all view with alarm. David Salmon, *Confessions of a Former Customers' Man* (1932), is typical of the *mea culpa* literature produced by the crash. The book opens: "For almost fifteen years I was a financial parasite and procurer. . . ." R. V. Peel and T. C. Donnelly, *The 1932 Campaign* (1935), Rexford Tugwell, *The Democratic Roosevelt* (1957), and, especially, Frank Freidel, *Franklin D. Roosevelt: The Triumph* (1956), present good descriptions of the 1932 presidential contest.

Acknowledgments

At the end of the original edition of this book, I expressed my gratitude to Daniel Aaron, Richard Hofstadter, Jean McIntire Leuchtenburg, and Arthur Link, who read the manuscript in its entirety and made invaluable suggestions; to the staff of the Columbia University Library; and to Ermine Stone and the staff of the Sarah Lawrence College Library, who went far beyond the hospitality due a neighbor. Much of the volume, I noted, was first threshed out with students in my graduate seminars at Columbia.

For this revised edition, my greatest debt by far is to Jean Anne Leuchtenburg, who spent countless days at the word processor, gave an intelligent reading to the new manuscript, and did it all with characteristic grace and good cheer.

Index

INDEX

INDEX

Terrorism: Ku Klux Klan, 209–10; radical, 70–72, 76–77, 79–80
Terry, Bill, 248
Texas, 209, 219–20
Thayer, Webster, 81–82
Third International, 66–67
This Side of Paradise (Fitzgerald), 148, 172
Thomas, George, 1
Thoreau, Henry David, 168
Three Contributions to a Theory of Sex (Freud), 164, 165
Tilden, Bill, 195
Tilton, Elizabeth, 239
Time, attitude toward, 176
Tinkham, George, 213
Toomer, Jean, 155
"To the White Fiend" (McKay), 38
Townley, A. C., 126
Trade, international: Far East, 114, 116, 118; and U.S. interventionism, 106–11; Wilson policy effects on, 129; in World War I, 14–15, 22, 24
Trilling, Lionel, 148
Trotsky, Leon, 67, 75
Trusts. *See* Monopoly
Tugwell, Rexford, 139
Tumulty, Joseph, 88, 127, 231
Tunney, Gene, 195, 266
Twain, Mark, 4, 146
Twenty-one Demands, 112, 114

U-boats. *See* Submarine warfare
Unconscious, 165–66
Unemployment: in "golden twenties," 193; Great Depression, 247–53, 258–60; mentioned, 85
Union Light and Power Company, 190
Union of Russian Workers, 77
Union of Soviet Socialist Republics. *See* Russia
Unions, labor. *See* Labor unions
United Hospital Fund, 248
United Mine Workers, 74, 99, 131
United States Steel, 91, 178, 252
Universal Negro Improvement Association, 38
Unknown Soldier, 104, 113
Urbanization, 5–6, 132, 225–27. *See also* Cities
Utilities, 190, 255

Valentino, Rudolph, 197
Vallee, Rudy, 196
Van Buren, Martin, 1
Van Doren, Carl, 226
Van Hise, Charles R., 121
Vanzetti, Bartolomeo, 81–83
Vassar College, 159
Vaudeville, 266
Veblen, Thorstein, 125, 126, 142, 177
Verdun, 53
Versailles, Treaty of, 54–63; mentioned, 88, 104, 123, 204–5
Veterans' Bureau, 92, 93, 95, 146
Victorianism, 35, 145, 170–72, 177
Villa, Pancho, 177